ONE MAN'S PILGRIMAGE

*Unorthodox views of a 14th Army veteran,
agricultural graduate, tattie roguer, potato inspector,
farm and estate manager, garden consultant, parish
minister, newsagent – Christ's freeman, global and
cosmic citizen, child of God, human being, two
hundred weight of good humoured loving-kindness.*

JAMES BLYTH

Note for Librarians: A cataloguing record for this book is available from Library
and Archives Canada at www.collectionscanada.ca/amicus/index-e.html

Printed in Victoria, BC, Canada.

ISBN: 978-1-4251-7029-5 (Soft)
ISBN: 978-1-4251-8910-5 (e-book)

*We at Trafford believe that it is the responsibility of us all, as both individuals and corporations,
to make choices that are environmentally and socially sound. You, in turn, are supporting this
responsible conduct each time you purchase a Trafford book, or make use of our publishing services.
To find out how you are helping, please visit www.trafford.com/responsiblepublishing.html*

*Our mission is to efficiently provide the world's finest, most comprehensive book publishing
service, enabling every author to experience success. To find out how to publish your book, your
way, and have it available worldwide, visit us online at www.trafford.com*

Trafford rev: 9/30/2009

 www.trafford.com

North America & international
toll-free: 1 888 232 4444 (USA & Canada)
phone: 250 383 6864 ♦ fax: 812 355 4082 ♦ email: info@trafford.com

Preface

A GOOD DEAL of heart-searching went on before deciding to put my photograph on the front cover of this book. My plea is that before reading look me square in the face for more than a glance, because what you see is what you get.

Boswell and Johnson while at Auchinleck House said to one another "Thank God we do not speak from books." Likewise the many quotations in my book and appendices have passed through the crucible of my mind and heart and are thoughts and beliefs of my own.

This is not a crude "blowing-my-trumpet" invitation to look at a guy who is puffed up by his own importance, but the likeness is of a "scandalous worthy" whose life was set free and transformed by friendship with Jesus of Nazareth.

Late nineteenth century session records for Glenmuick Church, Ballater, describe the parish as being full of "scandalous worthies", most of whom would have been poor hard-working souls whose life styles fell short of the genteel respectability of the "moral wardens" of the kirk.

I align myself with them to endorse the fact that God's love is not discriminatory.

To all who have encouraged and helped me on life's journey I express deep gratitude – parents, teachers, ministers, colleagues and friends. It would take a small volume to list them by name.

As for this book Leslie, my wife, has typed it from the manuscript on to the computer and a good friend Dr. David Lewis, a Christian gentleman and a computer buff, has designed the cover and prepared the photographs and the text for submission to Trafford Publishing who have been helpfully encouraging since our paths first met.

To one and all a thousand thanks.

A Basic Theology for the Self-crowned Kings and Queens of the Global Family

God is love – a cosmic power - not far from any one for in Him we live and move and have our being.

If we love one another God dwelleth in us and we in Him.

A cosmic power dispensing mercy and forgiveness – calling us to abdicate from the thrones of our self-wills to join the global family.

One of the great stumbling blocks to belief in a God who is love is the presence of so much evil in the world.

Question:- What is evil?

Answer:- Man without God.

The most demonic example of man without God is the Holocaust – the murder of six million Jews in Nazi-occupied Europe.

Since this blasphemous outrage the question has been on the lips of Jewish scholars and in the minds of members of every race – <u>Where was God in the Holocaust?</u>

God was there at the heart of the terror weeping billions, trillions of tears. He was there in the persons of the few courageous saintly souls who laid down their lives in the hope of saving another – they were like the fluttering of a candle flame in the demonic darkness.

Many claim that religion is the main source of the mayhem and bloodshed which has plagued the global family through the years and centuries.

<u>Sadly and tragically they are right.</u>

But then faith and belief are the very antithesis of all religion.

Instead of bondage to a judgemental old wizard in the heavens and the daily torments of the fundamentalists and the "true believers" it is a liberation to a new life of peace and joy which passeth all understanding.

The depths of evil to which human beings, singly and collectively, can sink when "unplugged" from God, the cosmic source of compassion and simple loving kindness, are incredible beyond words to record.

<u>What is evil? Man without God.</u>

CONTENTS

1

Earliest Days

For a quarter of a century I was privileged to be a Church of Scotland parish minister, ordained in my fortieth year, and so, before taking up residence in the old manse at the Bow of Fife west of Cupar, my mind was filled with memories of the first two score years. This week, in 2007, I will be eighty-four on All Saints Day and would like to share the memories which led to me "shaking my head in a pulpit".

To my tale. I was born on 1st November, 1923 at 1 Glengyle Terrace, Edinburgh, the flat of my maternal grandmother, and baptised on 1st December, 1923 in St. Cuthbert's Church by Dr. Fisher. The following year, accompanied by my elder brother David, our family of four moved to Huddersfield in Yorkshire.

My mother's maiden name was Stephen. Branches of the family were engaged in the hotel trade in Scotland. Photographs of Princes Street looking east, taken around 1900, show the gable end of a four storey building with "Stephen's Bridge Hotel" emblazoned in large letters. Today the site is occupied by the North British Station Hotel, now called the Balmoral. Other family adventures in the Scottish hotel trade were the Royal George in Perth (Uncle Dickson) and the Tontine in Greenock (Mrs. Service).

My mother was one of seven children, two boys and five girls. The boys, Bob and George, were the eldest, who used the flat roof of the old Waverley Market as their playground. Bob and George were pupils at George Heriot's who trained as accountants and worked in the offices of the North British Railway. Their railway employment must explain how their mother, my grandmother, made the adventurous trip to the top of the newly constructed cantilevers of the Forth Bridge. Both Bob and George emigrated to the U.S.A. before the First World War.

Family visits to Granny Stephen (her husband George had died in 1913) at 1 Glengyle Terrace from Huddersfield were frequent, travelling north on the magnificent rail route from Leeds, through Hellifield, Appleby, Carlisle, Newcastleton, Hawick, Melrose, Galashiels to the Waverley Station.

My mother was a great expert in the field of domestic science and homemaking. Trained at Atholl Crescent she managed the County Hotel on Lothian Road whose proprietors Uncle Brown and his wife were elderly. The County was a favourite haunt of ministers at General Assembly time.

During the First World War German Zeppelins made numerous bombing attacks on Edinburgh. A main target was the Haymarket railway tunnel. One night, probably in 1916, a bomb hit the County Hotel, plunged through the large attic water tank but did not explode. However it caused a good deal of structural damage including the dislodging of a huge lintel from Uncle Brown's bedroom window which, on my mother's entering, was leaning across the end of the bed with her old uncle in shock and covered with stour.

My mother's talents were not confined to domestic affairs. Hanging in our hall is an oil painting of a moonlit scene with fishing boats in a West Highland loch. When the light shines on it it really is a work of art. This was a talent which sadly my mother did not pursue after her marriage.

My father was the third child of a family of four, two older sisters and a younger brother. Their home was at Kinnettles near Forfar where my grandfather was head gardener and farm manager.

Education began at Douglastown on the Glamis-Forfar road. During his early years at Douglastown a new head teacher was appointed who, the story goes, had very long arms and a rather stooping gait. As it was not long after publication of Charles Darwin's *Origin of Species* and other volumes on his theory of evolution one old wag in the village was overheard commenting to a neighbour "We are being told that man is descended frae the monkey – by the look of that new dominie of ours he is just ascending tae the monkey."

My father, as a shy teenager of fifteen dressed in his best knickerbocker suit, accompanied his parents to a party at Glamis Castle. The Queen Mother was lying in a cot and I wonder whether the party was not just a celebration of her birth but a golden wedding party for her grandparents. My father, standing demurely on the verge of the festivities, was approached by a butler who said "Laddie you havenie got a glass" – whereupon he was handed a large bumper of champagne.

Leaving the village school at Douglastown my father became a pupil at Forfar Academy which involved a daily walk of nearly ten miles. Among his fellow pupils was George S. Duncan, who became Principal of St. Mary's College at St. Andrews University and Moderator of the General Assembly. My father was a strong youth who enjoyed most country pursuits, fishing the burns, cycling on the rather rough unsurfaced roads, poaching an odd hare or pheasant. He was at the same time a gifted lad of parts who, after apprenticeship in a lawyer's office in Forfar, moved to Edinburgh before his twentieth birthday. Again he worked in a lawyer's office although he was training to be an accountant. Black jacket, striped breeks, stiff white collar, polished boots and bowler hat were mandatory, even for juniors on around a pound a week.

Mention of polished boots reminds me of my father's prowess as a shiner of footwear. Every year at Forfar Show there was a prize for the best polished pair of, in those days invariably, boots. The prize was five shillings, a considerable sum around 1900. My father lifted the prize for several years in a row. Indeed forty or fifty years later after a busy day at the office my father would gather the family shoes after tea and spend an hour or so as recreation putting a wonderful shine on our footwear.

From around 1904 until the outbreak of the First World War he attended evening classes at Edinburgh University and the Heriot Watt. Fellow pupils at these evening classes were Bob and George Stephen and it would be through them that my father met my mother.

Accountancy was his main bent but in addition he applied himself diligently to language study – principally French and German, but also Spanish and Russian. Although my father never visited the Continent he became very fluent in written and spoken French and German. An indication of this fluency is borne out by a family anecdote that he used to worship in St. George's West under the ministry of Dr. Alexander Whyte and take down his sermons in French shorthand.

In 1938 several pupils arrived at Dollar Academy as refugees from Hitler's rampages. One was Ernst Ludwig Humburger whose parents had had a timber business near Vienna. Travelling on the train from Edinburgh to Carlisle my father joined us at Hawick. Ernst's command of English was remarkably good but after a spell my father broke into German and Ernst would not believe that my father had never been in Germany.

One of my special pals at Dollar Academy was Peter Brush whose parents had befriended Ernst – they left the train at Carlisle for Silloth on the Solway coast, Peter's home town. Peter left Dollar when he would have been around fifteen to finish his schooling on the Conway, the training ship for merchant navy officers, anchored in the Mersey. At one time he was first officer on one of the Queens. He died some years ago.

At the outbreak of the First World War my father was nearly thirty years of age. He became a financial comptroller with the Royal Navy on Clydeside. Despite his youth his rank was such that he used to join the directors for lunch in the boardrooms of many of the world-famous Clyde shipbuilding yards and attended all of the launchings.

One of the last launches he attended, accompanied by his fiancée, was *H.M.S. Hood* in 1918 – too late to be fitted out for service in the First War but tragically sunk in the Atlantic with the loss of nearly all hands in 1941.

Despite Murdo Ewen MacDonald's wise comment that it is possible to be a good parish minister without owning a pair of striped breeks, in some way I had no option. I inherited my father's beautifully tailored striped breeks worn by him at the launch of the *Hood*, and wore them for weddings and funerals during my years in the parish ministry. As a passing tribute to the skills of the old bespoke tailors the breeks are still in my wardrobe as good as new minus only one button.

Murdo Ewen MacDonald was of course the gifted Highland lad who was the famous preacher in St. George's West for many years after the Second World War before becoming a Professor at Trinity College, Glasgow. Murdo was a parachute padre during the war and a prisoner in the famous camp of the wooden horse. One day, accompanied by a guard, he travelled by train for a special dental appointment. Murdo had been teaching this guard English with a New Testament as their sole textbook. While waiting on the station platform Murdo hid behind a pillar. The Guard called out "Murdo where art thou?" and Murdo jumping out replied "Lo, I am here."

While minister of St. George's Murdo had a colleague D.W.D. Shaw, a lawyer and ordained minister who later became a professor at St. Andrew's University. Murdo and Bill were skilled rock climbers and on one occasion at a very difficult pitch they became stuck. Murdo was leading, unable to retreat. After a long anxious period they eventually escaped from a perilous spot. Later on someone had asked Murdo what he had been thinking about during the nightmare pause and his answer was "the Vacancy Committee".

Despite all his gifts my father, like so many Scottish lads of parts, did not have the magic entrée of education (schooling) at, for instance, Merchiston, or Edinburgh Academy, or the mantle of established families networking through membership of clubs such as the New Club or Muirfield, and so he found it difficult to secure employment when the war ended to match his abilities.

To be fair my father would have been considered a civilian in the job hunt lottery swarming with demobilised service personnel. A quarter of a century later my younger sister Elizabeth, a pupil at a grammar school in Halifax, wanted to study medicine. On the promise of a place at Edinburgh University she began studies at Surgeons' Hall. The waves of older demobilised members of the forces in 1945/1946 drowned that promise and she trained to be an almoner.

Like his future brothers-in-law George and Bob Stephen, my father emigrated to the U.S.A. However the bonds of affection for his fiancée, Elizabeth Grace Gibson Stephen (EGGS) were too strong and he returned to Scotland where they were married in the Caledonian Station Hotel, Edinburgh in June 1921. Both my parents were lifelong kirk folks, but chose to be married at the Caledonian.

After their honeymoon at the Fife Arms Hotel, Braemar, my parents moved to Birmingham, making their home on Yew Tree Road, Edgbaston. Brother David was born in Edinburgh on 1st May, 1922, probably in the flat of my grandmother at 1 Glengyle Terrace.

During his employment as an accountant with a leather firm my father was inveigled into joining the Masons. Now I have no desire to be rude to brothers of the craft but later on David and I must have been among the youngest to don the regalia. Despite his Scottish reserve my father was a man of independent mind whose psyche did not meld easily with the secret handshake and so after two or three attendances at the Lodge his regalia was abandoned in a large cardboard box in the back of a Victorian wardrobe where David and I used to come across it from time to time and prance around our Huddersfield home attired with suede apron, gloves, sashes, etc., etc., to the torment of our dear mother.

My father joined a firm of Chartered Accountants in Huddersfield called Armitage and Norton with whom he was to remain for the next thirty-eight years dying in harness in his seventy-seventh year. He was no "two and two make four" accountant but one of the early pioneers of looking ahead and helping firms visualise future market trends in a large range of industries.

My parents had often talked of returning to Scotland which they eventually did in 1949. They had not wanted to move from the family home in Yorkshire while my brother and I were far overseas in the Army. A ground and basement flat was purchased at 20 Belgrave Crescent in the west end of Edinburgh for £6,000, and a fine suite of offices was opened at 22 Walker Street. My father was in his 64th year, an age when many are retired or thinking about it.

I know I am my father's son but it is impossible to blow a trumpet hard enough to begin to record the quality and range of his self-sacrificing service to hundreds of businesses, not only the length and breadth of Great Britain but in India, Canada and the United States of America. During the Second World War he worked closely with several Ministries on plans for, and the implementation of, the amalgamation of British industry, enabling factories to switch to war production while maintaining in many cases capacity for civilian production. A C.B.E. or knighthood would have been a just recognition.

Another blast on the trumpet and I promise to move on with my tale. On one occasion the world-famous firm of Reid and Taylor in Langholm, manufacturers of the most expensive twist Cheviot cloth in the world, had a huge fire in the mill. My father received a telegram "Mill on fire. Come at once."

Involvement with the very early days of amalgamations which later became United Biscuits was part of his portfolio. I remember his returning home to 20 Belgrave Crescent from, I think, McVitie's factory, Robertson Avenue, with a small paper bag with a sample of prototype Jaffa Cakes.

The first Chairman of the infant United Biscuits was Sir Peter Macdonald, partner in W. & J. Burness, a law firm in Edinburgh. Sir Peter and my father were keen salmon fishers. United Biscuits had a large stretch of the River Tweed from above the bridge at Mertoun near St. Boswells downstream – a stretch which involved walking from pool to pool but also on occasion driving to a lower reach.

Salmon fishing has always had a certain social cachet and today beats on the Tweed, Dee and Spey change hands for very large sums, with the result that many of them have shrunk to one or two pools.

The pool above the cauld at Mertoun with a slap in it was fished from a boat and I have a happy memory of catching two salmon around 10 lbs each from the boat skilfully oared by the ghillie whose name has passed from memory – he lived in the cottages on the bank adjacent to Mertoun Bridge.

In case you think this might be angler's imaginative licence a photograph in the back garden at 20 Belgrave Crescent displaying five fine salmon bears witness to the fruits of a very happy day's privilege to fish the Tweed. Cross my heart these salmon did not come from Campbell's, the fish and poultry dealer on the corner.

There is no doubt in my mind that if my father had been personal investment portfolio-minded to the smallest degree he would have been a millionaire. Instead my mother came across him in tears because he had received a communication from the Inland Revenue hinting that he had been fiddling his tax returns. This was the era of surtax when those with large incomes kept only six pence in the pound. His returns would have been submitted by the firm's salary and pay department and may not have been correctly filled in but he would rather have died than fiddle taxes.

Days before my father died he and my mother were guests at a Norton family wedding. At one point my father was introduced to a small group as Mr. Blyth of Armitage and Norton. This took place in the presence of Mary Norton, a good soul in her sixties, who immediately broke in "Mr. Blyth is not of Armitage and Norton, he is Armitage and Norton."

2

HUDDERSFIELD

NOW FOR A word about my beloved mother. She was a talented person in her own right. The painting in our hall is one of many executed by her before her twenty-first birthday. In those far-off days when a couple married there was no thought of the wife, and soon-to-be mother, taking paid employment if the husband's income provided a home with a live-in maid and lots of comforts.

My mother was a superb home-maker, doing much of the cooking herself. Marie Corps was a great wee Yorkshire lass who, after a few years as maid, married her sweetheart Alfred Leadbetter. In 1926 my sister Elizabeth was born and perhaps for as long as a year a nurse was part of our household. The team was completed by a marvellous character, Louisa Brennan, whose husband Jack worked at the I.C.I. Dye Works in Huddersfield. Jack was a strange purple colour, with a not unpleasant odour from his dye works labours. Jack was a Roman Catholic who helped my father with our large garden. Louisa was a Protestant who hailed from around Dumfries. One of her sisters, a stewardess, was lost when the Titanic sank in 1912. Jack, Louisa and an adult son of Louisa's, whose name I do not remember, lived in the coach house of the large home next door to Claremont of a family Welsh. On one occasion Louisa told us she had been dusting and knocked over her husband's bowl of HOLY WATER – with a twinkle in her eye she whispered "I just filled it from the tap."

In the early 1920s washing machines were as scarce as hen's teeth but our house had a Beatty washing machine made in Fergus, Ontario. Fergus is a couthy town with, in those days, a preponderance of inhabitants of Scottish birth or ancestry. To this day Fergus Highland Games are well known in the global gatherings where the caber is tossed.

The Beatty was a sturdy affair – a large copper-coloured tub about a yard in diameter, standing on castored legs with the electric motor underneath. In the tub there was a three-bladed oscillator which whirled the clothes back and forth. There was a small wringer which could be operated above the tub or swung out to the side where the washed clothes could be passed back and forward through the wringer as a final rinse, using two large rectangular galvanised tubs seated on a trolley about five feet long.

That is rather a long-winded introduction to a washing machine trolley, but there is a reason. Years later, by which time we had moved to Ebor Mount, a four-storey terraced house up New North Road, David and I used to don white lab coats, take the trolley round to the front door, ring the bell and announce that we were the nurses from Storth's Hall calling to take Louisa to that mental hospital. Louisa used to enter into the ploy with great gusto as we hurled her on the trolley down the garden path.

Please do not think that this light-hearted tale mocks the "nut-houses" when the very opposite is the case. While minister of Monimail in Fife from 1963 to 1973 Dr. Ross, the Superintendent of Stratheden Hospital, Cupar, was a member. By coincidence the Superintendent of the hospital at Lochgilphead was also a Dr. Ross whose family were educated at Dollar Academy, and Alisdair Ross, the youngest son, was a pal of mine at Edinburgh University when he was studying medicine. While on the subject of hospitals for the treatment of the mentally ill I would mention my own attendance at the Royal Edinburgh Hospital, travelling down from Ballater for sessions with Dr. Weeks who was struggling to get me back on the parish tracks after parish "burn-out". This sounds piously self-righteous to the hundredth degree but I felt it an honour to be seated waiting for my appointment among the resident good souls who were "away with the fairies".

Sadly the stigma of mental illness is still rife in the herd mind which is doubly sad since Christian believers are supposed to be liberated from the shackles of "what will the neighbours think".

The amusing irony of my visits to the Royal Edinburgh Hospital was the fact that my predecessor in the manse of Glenmuick Ballater was Melville King whose retirement flat at that time overlooked the entrance and car park of the hospital. As ministers go Melville King was at the other end of the spectrum from myself but I am sure there were no phone calls from Morningside to some of his special flock on Deeside to report "Who do you think we saw going into the patients' entrance of the Royal Edinburgh Hospital?"

In the 1920s the testing of dairy herds for tuberculosis began in Scotland before England. One of the early pioneers in this certified milk scheme was the Chalmers Watson family of Fenton Barns near Drem in East Lothian. For many months a covered carrier with four bottles of T.T. milk came by train from Drem to Claremont seven days a week. This is perhaps an extreme one but an example of our mother's diligent and loving concern for the welfare of her children – and of course her husband.

My mother was completely devoid of side, and, as an illustration of the fact, one of my earliest recollections was of our coalman arriving with a bag of coal on his back having walked over a mile to make sure that there would be warm water for the new baby's bath. Don't forget this was in the days of the General Strike when the whole country was at a complete standstill – no papers, no milk, no post, no nothing.

My brother David is now four and a half, I am three and my sister Elizabeth is a tiny infant. Life in our large house and garden was very peaceful and comfortable with abundance of delicious home-made soups and meals cooked by my mother. From memory there were no food tantrums – we cleaned our plates or dishes before the second offering. One game that I used to play with lentil soup was to clear a path through when my plate was about half empty and see how long it took for the two separate portions to merge.

Among all the memories buzzing about in my head many are of our years in Huddersfield and so before embarking on details of starting school I must pause to sing the praises of Yorkshire. It is a large county and so are the Yorkshire folk, big in heart, humour, spontaneous friendship and loving kindness.

Even in these days when some conservationists (and I am one of them) would have us believe that Britain is only a few years away from being submerged under concrete and tarmac there are tens of thousands of acres of varied beautiful countryside.

My father was always a keen angler and in the 1930s he was a friend and cost consultant to a family garment factory in Leeds. The business was owned and run by two brothers Frank and Arthur Ibbotson. From memory the basis of their business was the manufacture of school uniforms. Arthur was also a keen angler and once or twice a year my father, David and myself would catch an early train from Huddersfield to Leeds to be met there by Arthur Ibbotson with his large Morris car, the one with leather upholstery and cushions hanging in the corners of the back seat. Our destination was Gouthwaite reservoir near Pateley Bridge. En route we always paused in Harrogate to purchase a box or perhaps two of home-made chocolates sold in a shop across from the Majestic Hotel. David and I were too young to wonder if these chocolates were a sort of peace offering to my mother, and probably Arthur's wife, because return home was always on the day after we set out.

From memory the weather was usually kind to us. Perhaps there were boats on Gouthwaite but my father and Arthur fished from the shore and usually came home with several trout over a pound in weight.

Anglers always feel that the next cast is the one which will hook a larger fish than the ones (if any) already in the bag or basket and so it was always dark before we left Gouthwaite. Any of you who are familiar with that part of Yorkshire know that the country roads are (or were) quite narrow and twisty. David and I were comfortably installed in the back seats while in the front my father would be talking any sort of nonsense to prevent Arthur from falling asleep at the wheel.

Claremont, our first home in Huddersfield from 1924 till 1934, was a large detached house in over an acre of grounds. It was demolished several years ago. It belonged to the Ramsden estate, a family who were the feuars for much of the town and the owners of Ardverikie on Loch Laggan, the venue for the shooting of the TV series *Monarch of the Glen.*

As we grew older there was plenty of scope in the large garden for hide and seek, kick the can, taking gang hostages. Among the shrubberies we had several gang dens where prisoners and warders alike used to picnic on bread and roast beef dripping sandwiches. Memory plays tricks on we oldies who tend to comment frequently that many foods have lost the wonderful flavours of yesteryear – but I can tell you that no tricks are being played on me when I say that dripping which had been used several times to baste a large sirloin roast seasoned with a little salt and pepper had a flavour far excelling that of the legion of dips and sauces conjured up by our present day gourmet chefs. Part of the secret lay in the fact that all our roasts were cooked in uncovered roasting tins and were basted regularly.

Not surprisingly some of our pals would stay for tea. The names of Teddy and Peter Johnston come readily to mind. When my mother would say "You had better stay for tea boys" Teddy used to nip through to the kitchen like a flash and whisper to our maid "Eggs on toast, Marie – eggs on toast."

Although it was easy to imagine we were living in the country at Claremont at the end of our unsurfaced approach road a residential area was soon reached. Cambridge Road was a fine terrace of houses, one of them occupied by a family of Hopkinsons, manufacturers of heavy duty valves, and of recent years working hand in hand with the world famous Weir Group in Glasgow. Sheila and Tony Hopkinson were also members of our gang. In the 1930s fishing for tuna off Scarborough was a great sport, and the first time I ever saw a tuna steak, almost as red as a beef steak, was in their kitchen.

In the early 1920s there was a large group of allotments opposite the terrace of houses, replaced by Cambridge Road Baths, a superb complex of two large pools, a tea room, Turkish baths and so on. Chatting recently with a Huddersfield lass on the staff of Strathclyde University in Glasgow she told me that the splendid baths are no more and the site is occupied with housing.

Huddersfield had an efficient and extensive tram system in the 1920s and early 1930s. It was interesting to watch the evolution of the trams. The earliest were open-topped for their full length. The next stage was a roof over the middle section of the upper deck. Then the roof was extended the full length with open canopies over the drivers' cabs – cabs because a tram had as it were two fronts with driving gear at each end, and at the termini the conductor unhitched a rope and swung round the poles to the wires, often creating showers of sparks until properly connected. The next stage was to enclose the whole of the upper deck, and finally a slight streamlining of the last batch of trams.

Over a period the trams were replaced by trolley buses, quieter and able to swing in and out to pass any vehicles parked at the kerb.

Since the Mayor of Huddersfield, the councillors, the transport engineers and all involved in the construction of the new service will be dead, there can be no red faces. But here is exactly what happened. There was no Guinness Book of Records in the mid-1930s, but here is an account of the world's shortest trolley trip.

It started from George Square in front of the classical building of Huddersfield Station. The trip was to have gone under the railway viaduct and out towards Birkby and Fartown. Unfortunately either the viaduct was too low or the trolley bus was too high, but after a short journey of 300 yards, zonk, the end of the trip. This almost unbelievable tale is borne out by railings at the edge of the pavement below the viaduct and the road level lowered about four feet.

Although Claremont had electric light many dwellings were still lit by gas. In the winter we used to gather at the corner of the garden looking over a high wall to welcome the lamplighter with his pole to light the last street lamp at the top of the short approach road. The majority of homes did not have telephones. Our number was Huddersfield 220, no dials until later, calls made through an operator at a central switch board.

Our second home was at Ebor Mount, 90 New North Road, under a mile from Claremont. My parents must have had the keys for a week or more before we moved because David and I used to walk with our father up a path between two large plots of allotments and across an open area called Highfields. In the springs and summers of those pre-war days the air above the uncut meadows was filled with the beautiful song of dozens of sky larks.

Around 1935 David and I became junior members of Fixby golf club where we played several rounds a week when on holiday. We walked from home to Fixby, a good two miles, and so after eighteen holes we must have covered nearly ten miles, which called for baths on return home. For a while I was puzzled as to why my perspiring limbs were blacker than David's when it dawned on me that he was a better golfer, keeping his ball on the fairways (an American golfing visitor asked his caddy "What is the secret of playing Muirfield?" and the caddy replied "Keep the ball on the clippit bit.") while a good deal of my time was spent hacking my ball out of the rough. Soot deposits from the hundreds of household fires and the tall mill chimneys meant that the long grasses were more sooty than the fairways, hence my dirtier limbs. In passing we wore long grey flannel trousers while golfing which seems a trite comment to make, but we wore short trousers at Dollar Academy on schooldays until we left, in my case to join the army in 1942 aged 18.

Thoughts on Fixby and golf brings to mind an occasion during the war when David was on leave from the army. He had his clubs and took a trolley bus, and as he was getting off an old Yorkshire matron shouted "You'd be better with a gun than them sticks lad." David had his army identification document in his pocket which he whipped out much to the embarrassment of the old dear. David at that time was a private in the Duke of Wellington's Regiment stationed at Barnard Castle, Durham.

A wee comment on the old dear's outburst – one of the scarcest gifts in our relationships with one another is <u>sympathetic imagination</u> and it is more than possible that the good soul was a mother with sons in the forces, even mourning the loss of one at Dunkirk.

Some of you may purchase from time to time the very small tins of ginger ale, bearing the name Ben Shaw's. With all the amalgamations of businesses in recent years it is difficult to know who owns and produces any given product. In the 1930s Ben Shaw's was the Huddersfield equivalent of Scotland's Barr's Irn Bru, and a Ben Shaw son was among my pals. He will forgive me if after sixty years I cannot remember his first name, but Wednesday afternoons at "Kelly's Kollege" were football time in the winter and cricket in the summer. Occasionally the weather was so awful that games were cancelled and on such afternoons my soft drinks pal and I would repair to the source of production, grab a bottle or two of that special North of England nectar, dandelion and burdock, ensconce ourselves on the huge pile of sugar sacks and while away the afternoon hours with the innocent but idle chat of young 1930s boys. The bottles must have been pints although in Yorkshire quart bottles were common.

Pre-war Yorkshire Cricket Club topped the Counties Championship League on a number of occasions, and David and I were among its keenest supporters. Visits were made to Headingly (Leeds), Old Trafford (Manchester), and also the smaller ground at Fartown, Huddersfield. Those were the days of some of cricket's greats, Herbert Sutcliffe, Len Hutton, Hedley Verity, Don Bradman. Despite Yorkshire's prowess they once suffered an astonishing defeat by Essex on the Fartown ground. Dismissed for under fifty runs Essex began to hit Hedley Verity all over the ground. This seems inconceivable but Kenneth Barnes, an Essex batsman, hit four fours and two sixes in one over, with one of the sixes leaving the ground. Hedley Verity was England's left-hand bowling wizard who sadly lost his life in the Second World War.

One beautiful summer day we were on the benches at Headingly, possibly a Test match. Seated a few rows in front was an overweight old man on an air cushion. The wooden benches had the odd splinter, the guy moved and the cushion burst with a most realistic fart. The back of his neck was momentarily on the red side!

Rugby Union being our game I was only once spectating at a league game. My father took David and me to Fartown to watch a game between Huddersfield and Dewsbury. It was a great match with no holds barred, the enjoyment being enhanced by a wee guy, drunk as a coot, sporting a bowler hat, who was shouting himself hoarse, cheering for Batley.

Mention of the 1930s prompts me to record the price of certain things in those far off days. I know for some it is a monumental bore to hear aged mortals, often aged grandparents, rabbitting on about the good old days of thirty oranges for a shilling, a twentieth of a pound. But for better or worse, here goes. One of the great events of the 1930s, I think 1932, was the arrival of the Mars Bar. This famous bar, with its first cousin the Milky Way, sold for two pence and one pence respectively. In other words Mars Bars were 120 for a pound and Milky ways 240 for £1. Morning rolls were half a pence each, or with the baker's dozen, five hundred for £1.

A wee comment on the bandied about term, the good old days. They were good in the sense that there was a stronger community spirit but bad in the amount of unemployment and meagre provision for the dear souls at the bottom of the social pile. Barefooted kids with ragged jerseys and breeks with holes in their seats were common sights on the cobbled streets of many quarters in Britain's cities and towns.

3

EARLY SCHOOL DAYS

THE TIME CAME for schooling. David began at Waverley, a private school owned and run by a small dynamic friendly soul, Miss Shaw. It was co-educational insofar as boys attended for three or four years until aged eight or nine, girls staying on as far as university entrance.

I followed in David's footsteps as did my sister Elizabeth later. Our next move was to another private school, Huddersfield College School on Mount Joy Road. No doubt the word "school" was part of the name to distinguish it from a much larger local authority school, Huddersfield College, about one hundred yards away on New North Road. Harold Wilson, our future Prime Minister, was a pupil.

Huddersfield College School was owned and run by a Mr. Helliwell and four other teachers. It was a good enough outfit in its own way and our times there could be called happy. It was a kind of staging post for the sons of manufacturers, lawyers, doctors, dentists, etc., who mostly went away to school around eleven or twelve to Sedbergh, Giggleswick, Oundle and so on. One pupil in my brother's year was James Hanson, later Lord Hanson of industrial success and fame. It was the time when the song "Kelly from the Isle of Man" was much in vogue and we urchins used to call our seat of learning K.K.K.K. – Kelly's Kollege for Komical Kids.

My parents being Scottish David and I were enrolled as boarders at Dollar Academy in Clackmannanshire in 1935.

A few more memories before moving north. After ten years at Claremont we moved to Ebor Mount, 90 New North Road, much smaller than Claremont but still a largish end-terraced four storey abode – rental £70 per year.

Now I know that I am not the brightest mortal on the planet but as an illustration of the innocent greenness of kids in those pre-television, almost pre-everything age, here for what it is worth is what happened at Ebor Mount in December 1934 when I was eleven.

One evening my father came home more than damp after heavy showers of rain. "One of you lads please nip upstairs and get me a pair of dry socks." I dashed upstairs to my parents' bedroom and drew out the bottom drawer of a large Victorian dresser where I knew my father kept his socks. Half hidden at the back of the drawer were several gift-wrapped parcels. Down the stairs I went like a flash – "I know now who is Santa Claus."

This sounds like a far-fetched tale when many four year-olds know as much about the human anatomy as many adults, but it is genuinely and innocently true.

In the spring of 1934 my father made a four month business trip to Canada and the U.S.A. sailing from Liverpool on the *Britannic*. A family friend, Percy Hall Lightbody, Chairman of Gledhill Brook, the cash register and time recorder firm, drove us from Huddersfield to Liverpool in his Railton car.

Business for Atlantic liners in 1934 was slack and there was no problem in all six of us having lunch aboard before the liner sailed. It was the day after King George V had opened the Mersey Tunnel. Liverpool was all bedecked in flags and we drove through to Birkenhead and back before returning home.

The lunch menu is gone beyond recall apart from sieved spinach as one of the vegetables which David and I felt bore a strong resemblance to boiled lawn clippings. Among the huge choice of desserts was delicious yellow lemon ice cream which had been taken aboard at New York – not that good ice cream was unobtainable in Britain in the 1930s.

My father was always a great letter writer and frequent were his letters and postcards to my mother and ourselves. My brother and I used to hang about the hall at Ebor Mount to beat my mother to the mail, the reason being that we had been subjected to Latin and indeed French study at K.K.K.K. for three or four years (we were now aged twelve and eleven). My father had with him a copy of our Latin grammar and many of his letters held completed versions of our homework exercises. The intention had been that my mother would hold the completed exercises until we had more than attempted to do them. In hindsight my father's correct copies were a mistaken kindness and our use or rather abuse of them probably accounted for my early nosedive in the Latin classes at Dollar Academy.

Since this journal is to be seasoned with some of my feats of strength perhaps this would be a good point to record some of my father's. Open fires in the rooms of offices were common in the early nineteen hundreds. One feat which my father performed with relative ease was to go down on one leg with the other leg straight out parallel to the floor, hook his foot in the handle of a loaded coal scuttle and rise up to his full height, over six feet. Another feat was lifting office or dining-room chairs by grasping a back leg with the hand and arm resting on the floor. The knack was to visualise a line between the grasped back leg and the opposite front leg, brace the arm at right angles to the flight path as it were and with a quick up-and-away lift the chair from the floor and hold it above head height. I have seen big strong men almost in the class of caber tossers struggling to raise a chair from the floor when knowledge of the knack was missing.

Not so much a feat of strength but more a party trick. Standing on the sitting-room carpet my father would turn his feet outwards through ninety degrees so that they were in a straight line and then fully erect with knees straight he would walk smartly across the carpet.

David and I in our early teenage years accompanied my father and a younger colleague, Jack Turner, on a number of occasions chasing hares on the rough tussocky grass of the moors around Huddersfield. There was a huntsman with a pack of hounds – hounds and hares are much fleeter than the fleetest of humans, but it was great sport to cut across country anticipating the course that the hare would choose to shake off the dogs. The chances are that this sport has faded into the annals of history for a variety of reasons quite apart from the campaigners against cruel sports. It was a winter sport, often with frost in the air, but any discomfort from the cold was soon dispelled by the couthy fug of a moorland inn with its roaring open fire. The adults would enjoy a pint or two while we younger fry quenched our thirsts with the distinctive flavour of large glasses of dandelion and burdock. The early evening drew to a close with a steak pie supper.

Talking of steak pie brings to mind the famous Denby Dale pie – a huge affair which was trundled around Huddersfield and district on a large cart, selling portions to raise money for the local hospitals.

What did the Blyth family do for summer holidays? Writing "the Blyth family" causes me to digress.

In the Border village of Kirk Yetholm there is a quaint wee dwelling called The Gypsy Palace which Leslie and I walked past a few years ago while on the St. Cuthbert's Way from Melrose to Lindisfarne. For some years it has been a private dwelling. Why Gypsy Palace? – because it was the home of the gypsy royal family called Blyth. I have seen several old photographs in magazines, one in particular of a stern old character with a beard and a crown on his head – William Faa Blyth.

In brief outline, without any dates of births of the generations we believe that several generations back, possibly as far as the seventeenth century, a male broke away from the royal household to become a crofter or small farmer. We are descended from that gypsy.

Now a few memories of our family summer holidays. Until 1928, when I was five, holidays in Scotland were spent at 1 Glengyle Terrace (Edinburgh) the home of my maternal grandmother - swings and seesaws, which are still there at the end of the terrace, trips on tram cars to Portobello and Joppa, visits to the ice cream shop on the right hand side of Gilmore Place opposite the Kings Theatre.

While having my hair cut a few days ago in Ayr I was regaling the young barber with some memories of the 1920s and his comment was "it sounds more like the time of Dickens than the present day" and in many ways it was.

We arrived at Waverley Station with all our family luggage, plus a large carriage pram which was conveyed to 1 Glengyle Terrace by horse cab. The pram was precariously perched on the roof. Although only four I have a very clear memory of the horse's shod hooves making a terrific racket on the cobbles trying to pick up motion again after halting for a second to negotiate the sharp bend round the Black Watch monument and turn up the Mound across from the Church of Scotland Assembly building.

In the 1920s, even 1930s, there were several hundred, even thousands, of horses in a city like Edinburgh – some of them cab horses (cuddy taxis) and tourist landaus, but the majority were work horses. Coal merchants with their large flat carts would leave the coal yards loaded with fifty or sixty hundredweight bags. Princes Street and most streets and roads were cobbled and the sound of carts clattering over the cobbles was a symphony in itself. Another symphony was the sound of the coal merchants among the canyons of the four-storied flats in Marchmont bawling out "CO-OALS". They must have been hardy fellows to spend all day humping the heavy bags up two, three or sometimes four stories to dump the <u>hard won coal</u> in the bunkers of the flats. I write <u>hard</u>

<u>won coal</u> deliberately as a small tribute to the miners who risked life and limb to hack out the black gold often from seams less than a yard thick in conditions of dampness, darkness and danger beyond the ability of the most imaginative to comprehend. There is an appendix to the great number of cuddies on the streets of our cities and towns, and that is the droppings deposited on the cobbles. One of the street theatricals of those older days was to see two neighbours with brush and shovel suddenly emerge and rush to be first to uplift the home delivery free mulch for their roses.

Another memory was a visit to Donald's the china shop with my mother and an aunt – they were so engrossed with the choosing of a dinner set wedding present that they were unaware of my departure from their long tweed skirts. I had wandered off into the display window among tiered displays of valuable china. Fortunately I emerged at their beckoning without disaster. Four or five years ago on a short visit to Edinburgh we were walking from the museum on Chambers Street towards the McEwan Hall, passing Donald's. I popped in sentimentally and purchased a beautiful mug as a souvenir. Entry to the display windows was now closed by sliding glass doors.

Between Glengyle Terrace and the Kings Theatre runs Valleyfield Street parallel to Glengyle. This seems impossible to believe but in the 1920s there was an auctioneer's cattle and sheep market. Floats, mostly with solid tyres, were coming into vogue but most of the cattle and sheep were still herded to the market on foot.

Across from Glengyle stands the Barclay Church with its massive spire infested in those days, and probably today, with great flocks of pigeons. One beautiful sunny morning after breakfast, which was porridge and the delectable Scottish morning rolls filled with bacon (intentionally called delectable because the "five hundred baps for £1" eighty years ago were a completely different article from today's), my mother went through to the kitchen, the frying pan was on the cooker by the window, the window was open and a small pigeon egg was laid in the pan.

The months of August in 1928, 1929 and 1930 were spent in rented houses in North Berwick, two of them in a house on Clifford Road and the third in a smaller house near the station. Our days were spent at the famous outdoor pool with Mr. McCracken the superintendent in charge or on the beautiful beaches. One of the years, probably 1929, our older cousins Bob and George from the U.S.A. and their parents spent a good part of the month with us. More than once we were late for tea returning from a climb to the top of Berwick Law. In the spring of 2007 we made a visit to North Berwick driving past the house on Clifford Road. A comment to friends retired in the town that the whalebone arch was missing from the top of the Law produced the reply that plans were afoot for the arch to be replaced with synthetic jawbones.

In the early 1930s August was spent in a large villa in Lauder belonging to a Miss Brodie. These were the days before electricity in villages and rural districts, a fact stamped in our memories by the thump, thump, thump of the generator next door at the red house, the home of a local doctor.

A favourite pastime was building dams in the burn to the west of the village flowing down to join the Leader. Footwear consisted of a pair of gym shoes, cost one shilling and eleven pence ha'penny. These did yeoman service for the month and were probably dropped into the dustbin before returning south to Huddersfield.

Across the road from Miss Brodie's there was a grocer's and general merchant's business owned by a family McLauchlan. Like so many they had a large van and occasionally we would clamber up into the front seat and go with them on their rounds of the farms. One of the halts would have been at St. Leonard's Farm, home of a Mr. and Mrs. Torrie whose son Andrew would be a fellow pupil at Dollar Academy.

Another pastime was to watch the blacksmith whose forge was only yards from the house. Not only did he shoe horses, but he also fixed the hot steel rims to wooden cart wheels shrinking them fast to the wheel by contracting the red hot metal with buckets of water amidst great clouds of steam.

On all these August holidays we had with us an older sister of my mother's during her summer vacations from St. Columba School, Kilmacolm, where she was Matron, and Violet, our mother's help.

About a year after moving to Ebor Mount, New North Road, a bonny lass from the Emerald Isle joined the family as a mother's help. Her name was Violet, a very cheery obliging soul who lived with us and who came with us on the summer holidays to St. Andrews. Violet was called up during the Second World War and served in the Land Army. She married Harold Tetlaw whose family had a dairy farm on the outskirts of Huddersfield where Violet, as well as raising two sons, worked very hard on the farm. While Harold died several years ago Violet, now 90, is still living in her own house not far from where the farm was.

In our family photograph albums there are some very amusing snaps. In the very early days our bathing suits tended to be knitted, which on immersion in the sea extended themselves to conceal our limbs. While many older people, even elderly people, would venture into the rather chilly waters, my mother and aunts in their thirties and forties never took the plunge. In fact there are many snaps of them on the beach with straw hats and summer dresses if it was warm but just as often in tweed costumes.

During all our August holidays my father was too busy with clients to spend a month with us but as many of the clients were the tweed and knitting mills of the Borders he would appear for weekends and sometimes for longer breaks.

4

Dollar Academy

A GOOD PART of the summer holiday of 1935 was spent kitting out brother David and myself for boarding school at Dollar Academy. This was done in the schools' department of R.W. Forsyth, entry being from St. Andrews Square. The very odour of its sanctity still pervades my nostrils. It was the most extraordinary temple of salaams to the parents and offspring of those who were destined for Merchiston, Loretto, Glenalmond, Edinburgh Academy, Fettes. I will get rapped over the knuckles if I wonder how Dollar Academy managed to enter this select company. Dollar Academy was and is a great institution, but in the 1930s it was a much more democratic school. One of my special pals while I was a pupil at Dollar for seven years was the son of the local scaffie.

Off we go as boarders to Dollar Academy in September 1935. My brother and I were billeted in Dewar House, a house with fifteen inmates. It lies to the north-west of the former West Church and has, since our time, had a varied career, being for some years Rathmore House for girls. Quite recently it was advertised for sale as a private dwelling, offers over £250,000.

My brother David, exactly eighteen months older, and I were put into Class 1. This was a mistake in my case. Probably my earlier years of Latin and French accounted for my being put in Class 1, remembering that languages in Dollar began in Class 1, the first class in the senior school.

Seventy years ago both the Academy and the village were very different from today. This year, 2007, there was an advertisement in The Herald for several teaching posts in the Academy with a pupil roll of 1130. Now whether that figure includes the junior school or not the fact is that the school is roughly twice the size it was in the 1930s.

The school is not only twice as large but very different. I have no desire to be offensive but seventy years ago a high proportion of the pupils were local lads and lassies whereas today it is more like an English public school. Nothing wrong with that necessarily, Dollar is a first-class school, and perhaps the thoughts of we old codgers are flavoured a bit with envy of the range of activities recreational and of subjects academic provided today.

It would be no problem to fill one hundred pages with accounts of our exploits and adventures during my seven years at the old grey school below the sheltering hills. In the early 1960s I was parish minister of Monimail in Fife, and at an F.P. dinner in the Moncrieff Arms Hotel, Bridge of Earn, I gave a toast to the school. The Rector was present, Mr. Richardson, who had not been long in the post, anticipating a sermonic review of days gone past. Instead I commenced to regale the company with some of our exploits.

I take no special pride in recording some of our mad ploys – but as Rabbie Burns said "Facts are chiels ye canna ding".

A winter train journey in the old carriages without a corridor – it was cold, the light was dim. A handful of urchins (pupils of Dollar Academy) in the compartment next to ours had been playing cards. Someone commented "kind of cold in here." No problem – in a wink a good-going fire was started with copies of the green *Evening Dispatch*, but not such a good idea after all as the flames began to singe the old upholstery. Again, no problem – open the door and kick the offending embers on to the track. So absorbed in the cards were the culprits that they failed to close the door properly and as a result it flew open, wrenched itself off its hinges, hit the parapet of the bridge and dived into the murky waters of the Forth. Panic stations! Our first awareness of anything untoward was a tap on the window of our compartment door. This sounds an unlikely tale, but remember many of those old carriages had double-tiered running boards with outside handles on each side of each door. By now the train had slowed on its approach to Alloa station. We grabbed the leather strap, lowered the window and hauled in the first of six or seven boys from the charred gambling saloon. Moments later the train stopped at the platform. In a flash the rest of the card players dispersed to other compartments. The missing door was on the platform side. Two elderly ladies attired in the costume, felt hat and fox fur uniforms of the 1930s approached the train. Naturally they were delighted to find an empty compartment in what was a packed train. Seating themselves and seeing no other passengers approaching one rose to close the door. No door!! They toddled over to inform the station staff. Several uniformed gentlemen with shocked looks on their faces arrived to inspect the gaping aperture. Possibly a suicide. They processed along the train asking the nearest compartments whether the occupants had heard anything. With blank innocent faces we chorused – never heard a sound.

I repeat that this mad ploy gives me no real pleasure in the retelling of it.

Another escapade was a trip from Dollar Beg down what was known as the Dunfermline road on a large upright postie's or policeman's bike. I was the driver, with four young passengers around ten, one on my shoulders, one on the handle bars, one on the crossbar and one on the back step, a heavy duty carrier. There was no need to pedal, the gradient of the brae provided all the speed required to propel us down and over the Rackmill bridge across the river Devon. Fortunately the sharp bend at the end of the trip was well cambered in our favour and the impetus without pedalling took us well up the road to Dollar, almost as far as the old metal seat on the east side of the road where the side road from Lower Mains joined.

The bulk of the scholars (correction, boys) at Dollar Academy were addicted to fags and a great range of haunts was devoted to this addiction. The boys' toilet (which in those days was a large stone slated building fifty yards from the main building) and the public toilets on the West Burnside beside the Castle Campbell Hotel were two. A bird-watching sister-in-law was recently regaling us with some of the amazing facts about the habits of our feathered friends. One which struck us as particularly amazing was the discovery of sixty-one wrens still alive in the one nesting box. It would be an exaggeration to say there used to be sixty-one junior smokers in the Dollar public toilets but they were jammed in like sardines in a tin. The thing that used to amuse me, a non-smoker, was that the odd pal would ask if I could detect smoke from his clothing. Of course woollen blazer cloth was like a sponge or filter and would be reeking to high heaven, and it was quite a test of friendship to assure him that there was a faint whiff of tobacco, but as nearly all the masters smoked in those days the chances of detection were small.

Why did I change the title "scholars" to "boys" at the Academy? At any age a scholar is a self-motivated, hungry-for-knowledge, character and while there were a goodly number of gifted pupils, male and female, most of us were sloggers driven and encouraged by the masters. Three fellow-pupils who stand out in memory as scholars, head and shoulders certainly above me, were Ian Pitt-Watson son of the minister of St. Mungo's, Alloa, (the Rev. James Pitt-Watson. Moderator of the General Assembly in 1953), Henry Hutchison (both Ian and Henry were gifted musicians and ministers of the Church of Scotland) and the third was George Rattray, whose father was a valued member of staff with the Misses Christie of Cowden (George used to cycle from Cowden in all weathers on a large upright policeman-style bicycle). Although our paths have never met since schooldays I remember he studied agriculture, probably at Edinburgh University and, as one step up in his career, was at the School of Tropical Agriculture in Trinidad.

Readers must be puzzled as to why a lad with a measure of intelligence should take seven years to complete a five year senior school course. The reasons are complex. At eleven I was a "gey wee loon" – my brother only eighteen months older was nearly a foot taller than me. My parents were kindness itself but perhaps over-protective and the change from the comforts and super catering of my mother to the rough and tumble of boarding school life was a very difficult adjustment. However, regardless of age, all life's experiences are "grist to the mill" and the time came when I really enjoyed my time at Dollar Academy. Before leaving to join the army in the late spring of 1942 I was a prefect, head of McNabb House and a formidable second row player in our 1941-1942 Scottish Champion rugby XV.

For years I harboured the conviction that Dollar 1st XV 1941-1942 was unbeaten. Subsequent enquiries revealed that my memory was playing tricks on me for in fact Glasgow Academy had beaten us 11-3. The truth of the matter is that Dollar and George Watson's were of equal standing in the Scottish Schools rugby league towards the end of the season.

As luck would have it our fixture with Watson's had been cancelled because of bad weather. Dollar Rector, Harry Bell, was reluctant to allow a mid-week game at the beginning of March as the Highers exams in those days took place around that time and he was concerned that someone be injured and not able to sit. In the end Mr. Bell relented and we travelled by bus on a Wednesday for an afternoon match played on the large pitch at Myreside with the stand backing on to the road separating Watson's ground from the University games fields to the west where some years later a few of us sat on the benches feet away from Prince Philip newly engaged to Princess Elizabeth.

The match itself was a terrific struggle – a good game – from which we emerged triumphant, the score being something like 11-8.

Should these memories ever see the light of day there will be from time to time mention of my physical prowess, not in any self-adulatory sense but always with profound gratitude for a sound carcase which has weathered well the ravages of over four-score years. In fact, update here – ten days ago on All Saints Day, 1st November 2007, I celebrated my 84th birthday enshrined in a medication free, pain free old carcase.

I described myself as a formidable second row forward, a fact acknowledged by "Sneep" Henderson, head of maths at Dollar and our most enthusiastic and able rugby coach who said to me "You can go as far as you like in the game of rugby."

In fact my name was set before the Scottish selectors for a possible war time trial but before this idea could bear any fruit I was commissioned in the Black Watch and on overseas service.

One more wee anecdote before ending writing words about the oval-balled game. Over the years with a home in Huddersfield my brother David and I were welcomed as forwards at Waterloo, the Huddersfield Old Boys' ground. In my possession I have a newspaper cutting about an inch in depth, which, unlike the modern reports, has no large close-up photographs of a player diving over the line to score or mind- and heart-stretching reviews of even quite mediocre games. The wee report is headed "Shock for Sale – Sale 3, Huddersfield Old Boys 18". Even in the inch depth report there was room to pay tribute to the Huddersfield pack ably led by Blyth.

My paternal grandparents, Kinnettles Forfar

On the estate rounds

At my parents' wedding, 23rd June, 1921   *My parents at their wedding, Edinburgh, 1921*

My mother, myself, David and Elizabeth, 1927

Ebor Mount, Huddersfield

With Violet, Huddersfield

Waverley School uniform

North Berwick Law, about 1929

My parents in the late 1950s

My father and Elizabeth in the 1950s

Rugby 1st XV 1941-1942

Dollar Academy (by courtesy of the Rector)

Redford Barracks, Edinburgh, July 1942

Commissioned in The Black Watch, 1943

With David in Kenya   *At Jinja, Uganda, now a captain*

Kindrogan

*My jeep when I was
employed by F.K.*

*Mr. and Mrs. Balfour,
middle of the rows*

5

ARMY CALL-UP

NOT LONG AFTER the Highers and our triumph over Watson's three or four of us were summoned to attend a forces' medical at Stirling Castle. A few weeks later a large brown envelope O.H.M.S. was delivered by the janitor to the classroom. Report to Redford Barracks, Edinburgh.

My call up coincided with a holiday which my parents had booked at Rodono Hotel on St. Mary's Loch where I joined them for a few days instead of making the much longer journey to Huddersfield.

Rodono had always been a favourite with my parents. In those days mine hosts were Mr. and Mrs. Lillie and their two daughters, Sheila and Gladys. In his younger days Mr. Lillie had been a butler to the Duke of Buccleugh and certainly our family was always welcomed and treated as ducal guests on our not infrequent visits to that haven of peace and beauty midst the Border hills. Scotland has a great range of country house hotels, many of them of world class, but now after a spell of over sixty years it is difficult to describe the couthy kindness and catering of a place like Rodono.

On the east side of the hotel there was a wee hill burn which provided electric power. The dining tables were graced with white linen cloths, the cutlery, if not solid silver, shone with a brilliance which only a ducal butler could produce. The home-cooked meals were a special delight for all the guests but particularly so for a hungry youngster of eighteen on his way to join the army. Porridge, kippers, bacon and eggs, rolls, toast, home-made marmalade for breakfast. Lunch and evening meals of equal gastronomic delights. Open fires.

Fishing on St. Mary's Loch was not world-class but after a summer's evening spent casting a fly over the waters with the chorus of lambs bleating on the surrounding hills and a return to Rodono in the fading light of evening to be greeted with a cheery welcome to the warmth of the hotel kitchen with its big stove was, for those in the early years of life, a bliss far beyond the promises of paradise. Moments later our ears would hear the crackle of bacon on the stove and before retiring certainly I would consume tea and bacon baps which today would keep me awake all night.

Tired as they must have been after a busy day the Lillie family shared the cheery crack around the dying embers of an open fire before all of us retired for the night.

The cost for a week at this haven of peace including transport from Peebles or Selkirk stations in their magnificent old Rolls Royce was around £4.

The last stage of my journey to join my parents at Rodono had been by leg power on my Rudge Whitworth bicycle. Departure was by the same mode. After breakfast on the day before reporting to Redford Barracks my parents and sister Elizabeth walked to the old humpback bridge over the Megget Water, long since replaced by a modern structure, where on the arch of the bridge we embraced and I pedalled off into the uncertainties of army service in the Second World War.

Life in the army began as a gunner in the 42ⁿᵈ Signal Regiment Royal Artillery, stationed in Redford Barracks, Edinburgh. There were forty of us in the troop, all in one barrack room, each with a full length metal wardrobe for our kit. Sleeping was on straw-filled palliasses on the floor. Not surprisingly we were a mixed bag, social background, age and educationally. Even for the older ones it was their first time away from home. Three or four of us had had army training experience in school corps but I think I was the only one who had been at a boarding school.

Despite our different backgrounds we quickly entered into the spirit of this new adventure and got on well with each other. Lots of physical training and runs in the countryside which surrounded the south side of the barracks in those days. I had an aunt and uncle who lived at 4 Braid Hills Road and frequently after a long busy day I would squeeze through a gap in the metal paling fence in the corner of the east barrack block and walk through the fields which are now covered with houses. My aunt and uncle used to be amazed at the number of cups of tea which I drank. It was early summer with sunny warm days which accounted for my thirst. The food was good and plentiful – freshest in my mind is the aroma of fried bacon as we filed past the buffet-style cook house famished by a five-mile run before the first feed of the day.

Days were passed learning Morse code, field wireless technique, and to drive trucks and motor cycles, and of course there was physical training both on the large square and in the huge gymnasium.

One morning on the square the P.T. sergeant passing me said "Have you ever done any wrestling?" My out of puff "No" was the end of that encounter.

Mention of his question allows me to tell you of some of our work-outs in the gymnasium. The roof was high and a heavy rope was anchored at floor level on both the east and the west wall and sloped up to a fixture on the middle of the roof. The challenge was to monkey up the rope in full kit to the ceiling and then monkey down the rope to the other wall of the gym. We are all endowed with different physiques and I write this as fact rather than any boasting about my prowess. Some of the troop could not even get off the gym floor, laden with about 50 lbs of kit. Boasting is not really one of my sins, but I have to admit getting a certain buzz at being able to hand over hand, without feet or legs on the ropes, nip up to the ceiling and for cheeky devilment execute three or four pull-ups and then hand over hand descend to the floor. I plead the brashness, I was only eighteen.

The motor transport sergeant was a real old (probably around 35) regular soldier (as some used to say, of old-time regular soldiers "born in a kitbag in India"). Recalling this allows me to record my wonder and admiration for the British army officers and other ranks who served in India and other outposts of the empire for long periods of years, not always with the companionship of their wives and families.

To get back to our "old" friend the transport sergeant, who from time to time was missing because he was attending an army medical board at Edinburgh Castle. He was in the early days of laying the grounds of an extra pound or two on his service pension. He had a pronounced limp. He used to speak of the "atmosphetic valve" as he pointed to the small pinhole in the top of a motorcycle's petrol tank.

Motorcycle training consisted of two periods of riding round the football pitches and then a convoy trip through the douce southern suburbs of Edinburgh, and even along Princes Street. If the good pedestrians had known how little experience we had had on our Nortons and B.S.A.s they would have given us a wider berth.

In fact one of the nearest escapes from death during the five years in the army was one beautiful summer morning when on driving instruction in three-ton trucks. With a bombardier instructor four or five of us would venture out taking turns to learn the driving skills needed to handle a lorry with double de-clutching (clutch-neutral-pause-clutch-engage gear, quite a tricky operation until acquiring the knack). With three of us in the back leaning on the roof of the cab, the good lad who was on the controls, despite ample warning from the instructor, missed a change down in gear and the lorry was in free-wheel. He panicked and mounted the pavement above Colinton Dell. We wobbled along for several yards and fortunately bounced back onto the road, instead of crashing through the concrete parapet and plunging fifty feet into the Dell. Our route had been out by Juniper Green and Balerno and the near miss was on our return at the almost right-angled turn on to the bridge at the foot of the brae. Of course there were no dual controls on these army vehicles.

Earlier I mentioned that there were forty of us in the barrack room. Every Saturday morning there was a kit inspection laid out to a given plan – spare socks rolled and tucked in in a special way, spare boot studs polished, even spare bootlaces rolled and placed exactly according to plan. Our troop sergeant Rawlings had the bright idea of running a sweep on the kit lay-out judged to be the best. Forty of us in the barrack room, forty sixpences to the pound – simplicity itself, sixpence each in the kitty and the winner takes the pound. No prizes for guessing who got the £1. After winning three or four weeks in a row the rest of the gang rebelled – end of sweep. A pound today seems like a tiny amount but remember our weekly pay was twenty-one shillings, three shillings a day – of which we received only fifteen shillings at the pay parade, the army keeping six shillings for what was known as the contingency, set against any loss of equipment or barrack room damage, etc. Memory does not record what happened to any balance which one might have had when moving elsewhere. So by winning the sweep my weekly income was more than doubled.

Seventy-five new pence per week (180 old pence) was a modest reward for all the hard physical training but it was still enough to provide for off-duty relaxation. Some pints of beer were four old pennies – a wild night out on four half pints set us back eight pence.

The beer was fine but truth to tell the canteens run by volunteers bore more attraction for us. Edinburgh, like every city, town and village throughout Britain, had forces' canteens staffed by volunteers. (We do not forget the NAAFI canteens but they were invariably in camps and barracks.)

Considering the rationing and shortage of many staple items the canteens had a great display of manna for hungry uniformed lads and lassies. All the canteens were good but inevitably the range of their offerings varied from day to day. However we soon located the ones with, say, egg and bacon on Tuesdays and Fridays and fish and chips probably on Fridays. Lothian Road Church, across from the Usher Hall, was always worth a visit, as was the large canteen on the right hand side of Waterloo Place beyond the general post office at the east end of Princes Street, and the canteen below the Catholic bookshop in the cul-de-sac off Queensferry Road, and many more.

May I record the gratitude of the tens of thousands of service personnel who found not only food but friendship and many kindnesses from the good volunteers who manned these havens.

Baptised in St. Cuthbert's Church, Edinburgh, on 1st December, 1923, the answer to the question RELIGION on my army enrolment form had been C of S. Not surprisingly a good proportion of the inmates in Redford Barracks were also, if only nominally, Church of Scotland. Around one hundred of us paraded on Sunday mornings and marched down to Colinton Parish Church. All to the good! However a few of us had our ears to the ground and learned that in the community hall across the road from the east or cavalry barracks there was a much shorter and less formal (liturgical) service conducted by a Methodist minister or occasionally a layman. Forsaking the church of our fathers a few of us became Methodists, and instead of parading we toddled over under our own steam not only for the shorter period of devotions but also because of the attraction of a well-stocked canteen through a door from the hall sanctuary.

Most humans enjoy good food and without being paranoid about filling the stomach with good things I have had my share of gastronomic delights and now over-weight and over eighty I try to cut down, but whatever the fodder I give genuine thanks in a world where so many fellow passengers on our planet home are slowly starving to death.

On the strength of seven years in Dollar Academy cadet corps, remembering the days when there were four ranks not three in an infantry platoon – form fours, reform two deep - and the holder of a Cert. A, I was called to attend a W.O.S.B. (War Office Selection Board) held in Oswald House in Edinburgh's upmarket Grange district. Oswald House has long since been demolished and the site occupied by a large block of flats. The few days' stay in Oswald House consisted of lectures, interviews, seminars and assault course antics in the field at the corner of the entrance to the Genetic Department at Kings Buildings. This site has also been built over.

Before continuing with service in the army during World War II mention of Dollar Academy cadet force seems to be an appropriate place for a few thoughts on soldiers and soldiering.

As boarders it was mandatory to serve in the corps (or later the Air Cadets or the Naval Cadets). Coming down for breakfast in McNabb House in 1938 my eye fell upon the large print headline on the front page of probably *The Bulletin* - Six Months' Conscription to Start Immediately. I have no desire to be melodramatic but I nearly died.

Playing at soldiers was not my idea of fun. Dollar Corps was affiliated to the Argyll and Sutherland Highlanders with their regimental base at Stirling Castle. Our uniform was a very coarse "tickle the knees" Argyll kilt, khaki tunic, hose tops, flashes and blancoed spats. The longest day in the year for me was the annual inspection day when two or three officers and the same number of senior N.C.O.s arrived from Stirling Castle. We used to march down the Dunfermline road and up on to the Sheardale Braes where there was a large area of undulating heather and scrub land. The platoons took turns at being the "enemy".

It would be infantile to suggest that I was a pacifist in those early years but already the seeds of wondering at the madness of war had been sown in my mind and heart.

In recording these personal thoughts the last thing which I have in mind is to pour scorn on the armed services of the crown and indeed on the uniformed forces of any country. The bravery and sacrifices of servicemen and women and of civilians in unimaginable numbers during the wars and civil strife of last century are past words to record – the only response is humble silence seasoned with compassion and tears.

Our beautiful war memorial in front of Dollar Academy bears the names of over seventy fellow pupils who did not return home from the carnage of the Second World War. An article I wrote in tribute a few years ago is included in the Appendices.

6

OFFICER TRAINING

ALTHOUGH ONLY EIGHTEEN and a half years of age I was judged to be possible officer material and before many more weeks passed I was posted to a pre-OCTU (Officers' Cadet Training Unit) camp at Wrotham in Kent. By now it was around the middle of November, 1942, very cold and wet in what was a kind of hell camp. Everything was done at the double, even going to the messes for meals. The basic object of this incarceration was to break your spirit.

We must have been four or five weeks at Wrotham, not incarcerated all the time. There are happy memories of a few evenings spent in the Cricketers Arms at Meopham Green and the odd half day visiting Maidstone where there was a splendid canteen on a corner above Burton's the tailors.

Day and night the air at the camp and its surroundings was rent with loud assault course explosions. Despite this almost constant bombardment one evening there was a bang louder than the rest. The training officers in the camp had their mess in a larger than usual Nissan hut, larger in the sense that the arch of the roof was twice the height of the standard hut. A party had been in progress and while there were toilets en suite, as it were, the demand on them as the evening wore on became greater than the empty stalls. No problem – it was dark outside, the only snag being that the exit doors had right-angled brick baffle walls to reduce the possibility of infringing the very strict blackout regulations. One particular officer, a little unsteady on his feet, and needing to go, crashed his head into the brick wall and on returning to the party cursed the offending structure. His words were overheard by one of the field works (explosives) officers who indicated that this particular flaw in the enjoyment could be taken care of. Two or three of them went down to the explosives store and returned with several "sticky bombs anti-tank". These were round affairs, with an outer orange-coloured metal case, and a handle, a wee bit like a huge toffee apple. They were intended for disabling tracked vehicles, even larger tanks if the sticky bomb, after the outer casing was removed, could be banged against the tracks. Several of these lethal weapons were clapped against the offending brick wall. It was a miracle that no one was injured or killed. I don't know how effective they were in disabling tracked vehicles but they certainly made a mess of the mess.

This is a true tale. Not only was the wall demolished but a huge swathe fifteen feet wide was cut from front to back of the hut. After breakfast the next day we ran past the wreckage and at the first halt our instructor confirmed the facts of the above.

The dilemma of repair was compounded by the fact that the Brigadier was due a visit in about ten days' time. Recalling this mad prank has taken up more words than I had intended. Suffice it to say that all hands were on deck, Royal Engineers, Pioneer Corps, etc., and a couple of days before the Brigadier drove into the camp the huge mess was if anything better than ever.

After surviving the ordeal at Wrotham a few days' Christmas leave followed, and before New Year's Day I was one of a draft assembled in an awful transit camp in a park in Preston. It was a Sunday and half a dozen of us strolled into the town. I would have been the youngest of the group on "beer patrol". The first surprise was to find pubs open on a Sunday when Scottish pubs were closed and only "bona fide" travellers (those making a journey of over three miles) could get a drink on the Sabbath after signing the book. Hereby hangs a tale, Dollar was exactly three miles from Tillicoultry and in the 1930s a double decker bus ran back and forward between the small towns transporting the Dollar drinkers to Tillycoultry and vice-versa. Strictly speaking this was illegal, a Sunday traveller was supposed to be on a genuine journey of over three miles.

Such is life. Here we were entering the pub at the centre of Preston and confronting us on the wall was a large notice "Draught Bass". In the twinkling of an eye my new friends ordered pints of Bass and of course I had little option but to follow suit. I have no idea what the alcohol content of Bass was pre-war but for me still in the "nappy stage" of imbibing, it sported quite a powerful punch and after two pints, possibly three, we set off to spend the night in the most awful small transit camp, in my case "stepping on feathers" (swaying a little).

The next day, a cold wet windy Monday morning, a short train trip took us from Preston to Fleetwood. I was hungry and the dockside canteen at Fleetwood was devoid of food, even a cup of tea. My intake was so bizarre at mid-morning that I remember it was a bar of Cadbury's Milk Chocolate washed down with a bottle of Guinness.

The Irish Sea can be rough, and it was that day. I have never been sea-sick but if the Isle of Man had been a few miles further from Fleetwood the stout and chocolate and myself would have parted company.

We were destined to spend four months on the Isle of Man billeted in the large five-storey hotels/boarding houses on the promenade next door to the much larger Villiers Hotel (now no longer there) on the corner. Most of the lectures were held in the Villiers public rooms. It was a strange experience to be listening to illustrated lectures on infantry tactics through the wall from the hotel bars, still open for business. And don't forget the licensing hours on the island were very liberal, once open at 9.00 a.m. they remained open until midnight at a time when the pubs in dear old Scotland closed around 9 p.m.

The Isle of Man has an equitable climate and my recollection of our time there was not unlike an army holiday camp after the trials of Wrotham.

Wisely or unwisely large numbers of Italian café proprietors and other Italians were interned in a large block of hotels and boarding houses further north on the promenade. There was a high barbed wire fence around their section but despite that once or twice a week a large contingent of them was marched along the front to the cinema. When I write above "wisely or unwisely" I have in mind the fact that many of the internees were loyal to Britain and well known successful business people in post-war years.

Many incidents from our stay on the island come to mind but I am a wee bit puzzled as to how we were gainfully occupied for four months with a short leave at the halfway stage.

A new entry of cadets each month, a passing-out parade each month – an entry must have consisted of about fifty cadets, not all of whom finished the course to be commissioned. Sadly a few were R.T.U. (returned to unit).

Brother David was commissioned in the Black Watch on 20th February, 1943. His name is listed above mine in *Officers of the Black Watch, Vol. II* compiled by Major-General Neil McMicking. The volume is prefaced by Sir John Moore's opinion of Highland infantry dated 1803, which reads:-

'It was Sir John Moore's opinion that Highlanders, under an officer who understood them, were amongst the best military material in the world.

"Under such an officer, they will conquer or die on the spot, while their action, their hardihood and abstinence enable them to bear up under a severity of fatigue under which larger and apparently stronger men would sink. But it is the principles of integrity and moral correctness that I admire most in Highland soldiers, and this was the trait that first caught my attention. It is this that makes them trustworthy, and makes their courage sure, and not that kind of flash in the pan which would scale a bastion to-day and to-morrow be alarmed at the fire of a picket. You Highland officers may sleep sound at night, and rise in the morning with the assurance that your men, your professional character and honour, are safe".'

I endorse Sir John's opinion when I think of the extraordinary bravery and sacrifices of not only the Black Watch officers and other ranks but of infantry soldiers in general.

It was a great privilege and honour to hold a commission in the Black Watch but when I recall the "luck of the draw" postings which allowed me to escape the worst of the Second World War carnage there is a tinge of guilt at having survived. My Dollar school friend Duncan Gulloch was commissioned in the Black Watch on 20th November, 1943, and presumed killed in action in Burma as a lieutenant on 12th February, 1944, thirteen weeks after he was commissioned. This is an unusual entry in the Black Watch Register. I assume it must mean that Duncan was killed but his body never recovered.

On a lighter vein each passing-out parade was attended by a well-known public figure who took the salute and presented a trophy to the top cadet. In brother David's case it was Lord Nuffield of Austin and Morris car fame. He arrived at the edge of the parade ground in a large limousine and as he stepped out he was seen (at least I saw him) to be smoking a cigarette which he quickly "nipped" and popped the stub into his waistcoat pocket. Lord Nuffield would have been a millionaire and I am sure the nipping of his fag was prompted by a desire not to litter the parade ground rather than with any thought of the economy of lighting it up again.

While the sea-front hotels and boarding houses would have been commandeered I think the owners ran them in the sense of providing meals and clean bed linen.

Possibly the most strenuous day in our four month stay was a long march of over thirty miles in full kit with mock skirmishes from time to time. Leaving Douglas we moved roughly west and then up towards the north of the island, returning in the evening to Douglas by trucks. Many miles of our marches were on sections of the famous T.T. course and we must have passed several times the memorial tribute to the champion motor cyclist James Guthrie from Hawick.

One day we were given a demonstration firing 3-inch mortars across the wide glen running down from Snaefell. The mortars were being fired at a range of 1,000 yards. From memory the weight of the bomb dropped into the barrel fired itself. The bulk of us were seated on a dry stone wall when one bomb instead of blasting off on its flight slowly emerged from the mouth of the barrel like toothpaste coming out of a tube. Before the unexploded bomb dropped onto the grass all of us had done back flip dives behind the protection of the dyke.

On another memorable day we marched south out of Douglas to a country house hotel which sported a large pond or small lake in its grounds. This outing was to practise river crossings with flat-bottomed collapsible boats which carried eight to ten men. These could be paddled, but with a rope attached were pulled back and forwards. The draft of these vessels was rather shallow and as the day progressed the returning boats with their flat sterns were getting lower and lower in the water to the point of being swamped. The eventual sinking of these crafts with instructors and cadets cavorting in the waist deep water can be explained. As we started the picnic lunch break an older cadet informed us that army directives dating back to the Napoleonic wars allowed troops a measure of beer. He gave a section number and paragraph which while possibly based on a grain of truth were certainly fictitious. A few beers were enjoyed, the sinkings became more and more frequent as the afternoon wore on, and instructors and cadets alike must have been a bedraggled gang as we marched back into Douglas, fortunately camouflaged from the eyes of the locals by the fading light of the evening.

Despite the above tomfoolery our four months on the Isle of Man were demanding but happy. It was not Sandhurst with drill sergeants screaming their heads off. The instructors, mostly captains who had had experience of active service in earlier campaigns, were friendly patient encouragers.

During our stay *Gone with the Wind* ran for several weeks in the main cinema. One evening three of us began with three bottles (half-pints) of Manx beer, four pence each, i.e. one shilling, good seats in the cinema, ten pence, ending the evening with a visit to a forces' canteen for eggs and chips, bread and butter and tea, eight pence. Thirty pence in all, or an old half-crown, twelve and a half new pence.

One final anecdote before leaving the island. All during the war an Irish Free State boat with tricolour painted on the sides came into Douglas harbour. The result was that eggs, butter, etc. were plentiful and about every ten days my brother and I would send a box of two dozen eggs to our parents and younger sister in Yorkshire. On the day after graduation as I was boarding to return to the mainland I had amongst all my gear a parcel containing two dozen eggs in the old style heavy duty sectioned box. This parcel was handed to a colleague to hold while I helped with the loading of some heavier baggage. As the friend handed back the parcel a customs officer approached and asked what was in the box. Innocently I replied "Two dozen eggs." "Oh, you cannot take these off the island." "But", says I, "we have been sending regularly boxes of eggs to my parents in England." "Yes, that is quite legal, but you cannot carry them with you." "What will happen to the eggs if you confiscate them?" "Taken to an old people's home." Rightly or wrongly I dropped the box on the quayside, leapt three feet into the air, landed on the box and kicked it into the harbour.

7

THE BLACK WATCH

I WAS COMMISSIONED on 23rd April 1943 and spent a few days' leave at home in Huddersfield before reporting to the 8th Battalion Black Watch stationed in a camp near Winchester. Newly commissioned officers were given a modest grant towards the purchase of uniform – large greatcoat, tunic, tartan trews, kilt, sporran, etc. etc. R.W. Forsyth with shops in Edinburgh, Glasgow and London supplied my kilt which cost £10 and was collected from their shop at Vigo House, Regent Street, London.

Although commissioned in the Black Watch my service with the famous regiment was relatively short. Posted to the 8th Battalion stationed near Winchester I was given command of a platoon. The company commander was Major Robin Thomson from Dundee.

Bearing in mind that it was little over twenty years since the end of the First World War quite a number of the older "jocks" wore medals from that war. The amusing irony of my situation was that before leaving the Isle of Man we were given a small booklet for the guidance of newly commissioned officers. High-lighted among the advice for being a good officer was the instruction to be a father to your men. I was nineteen and a half.

One week our company was duty company and as there were not enough tasks to gainfully employ around a hundred men Major Thomson told me (ordered me) to take the twenty or so left over and give them a lecture on current affairs. On the wall of the barrack room there was a large map of Europe, the Mediterranean and the whole of North Africa. It was the time of the final victorious advance of the Allied armies, the 8th Army under the command of General Montgomery.

After a short time I felt it would be a good idea if one of the jocks in the front row pointed out on the map the route of the advance. After quite a long pause it dawned on me that he had no idea how to read the map. Perhaps I should not be recording this rather embarrassing situation for I would rather have died than embarrass him.

Their complete lack of skill in reading at least a large atlas map taught me a lesson. Privileged to have been educated at Dollar Academy, where my only prize during my seven years was the geography prize, it began to dawn on me how disadvantaged so many children and young adults were, and in many cases still are, when launched out into the tough turmoil of life in Great Britain.

Memories of Winchester are hazy, partly because of the shortness of my time there. However, one event firmly fixed in my mind is our participation in a Wings for Victory parade. Many of these parades were held during the war with the dual purpose of encouraging patriotic fervour while at the same time raising funds for aircraft production. A Spitfire cost £5,000. Many of you must have heard of Lady MacRobert whose mansion house near Tarland in Aberdeenshire is still a convalescent and holiday home for air force personnel. Lady MacRobert lost three sons serving in the Royal Air force and donated at least £15,000 for the purchase of three Spitfires which were named MacRobert's Reply.

The Black Watch contingent for the parade consisted of a captain, two second lieutenants (my brother and myself), and ninety-nine other ranks. There were many early morning practices and on the parade day three ranks of thirty-three were led by the pipe band. At the head of the parade was a very smart contingent from a light infantry regiment, with their band in front. Next a smart contingent of A.T.S. girls, then the Black Watch pipe band. There were also several other contingents behind us, one from the Navy, one from the Royal Air force and so on.

The unfortunate thing was that light infantry march to their band at 180 steps to the minute while a pipe band leads their squad at 120 steps per minute.

Of course the poor A.T.S. lassies could hear both bands and most of their time was spent changing step. We were quite upset and our hearts went out to them.

While the battalion was still at Winchester I was sent on a residential course based upon Avon Tyrell mansion house near Ringwood. We were involved in a few night exercises and on one of these we were marching along in single file passing below the boundary hedge of a large house when we heard the sound of boots running on the gravel driveway. The house turned out to be an army divisional headquarters and the guard thought we might be "commandos" from the other side. This is not as fanciful as it may sound – we were not far from the south coast. In fact at that time brother David was in command of a platoon of Black Watch guarding a military installation at Christchurch and one night two sentries were murdered by a raiding party of Germans who had sneaked ashore in an inflatable boat from a submarine surfaced in the bay.

The duration of our stay at Avon Tyrell was three or four weeks. We were a mixed body of young allied officers, British, French, American, Dutch, Norwegian, and one purpose of our living together was to help us to grasp the fact that despite our differences of language and national psyche we were involved together in a common cause.

We were free at weekends and I was invited by three American officers to spend it at the American Red Cross Club in Bournemouth. Some years ago on a visit to Ian and Margaret Keating who live in Poole, parents of Andy, daughter Helen's husband, we were able to track down the hotel which served as the American Officers Club. In true American style it was run like a first-class hotel.

One Sunday afternoon accompanied by my American companions we were walking around the attractive park area in the centre of downtown Bournemouth when we fancied a beer. The nearest watering hole happened to be the Royal Norfolk Hotel. As we approached the entrance we joined a considerable group of service and civilian people with the same desire as us when a hotel porter appeared to say that the day's allocation of "booze" had been dispensed and the bars were closing. It must have been around 4 p.m.

As we turned to leave a middle-aged gentleman in the black jacket/striped breeks uniform of a hotel manager dashed down the steps and grabbed me by the arm. For many years the manager of the famous hotel was a good soul from Perth, the home town of the Black Watch. My Black Watch kilt was the magic key to our special treatment. With my American pals we were ushered into the cocktail bar. Our indulgence was modest but the congratulatory amazement and gratitude of the "Yanks" was head-swelling and heart-warming.

While absent from Winchester the battalion had moved to a hut and tented camp on the Isle of Wight near to Quarr Abbey where we used to collect fresh vegetables and other produce for the mess. On a day visit to the Isle of Wight in 1999 we called at the Abbey where the Brother on duty in the bookshop was from Clydeside. We made one or two small purchases and presented him with a £20 note. He was profuse in his thanks when I asked him to keep the change as a small "thank-you" for the Abbey's kindnesses to us during the war.

In the early summer of 1943 infantry battalions were issued with an anti-tank weapon PIAT (Projector Infantry Anti-Tank). It was fired from the shoulder, but compared to modern successors it was like a pea shooter.

Near our camp there was on the south side of the main road a small gravel quarry in which there was, probably by chance, one of the famous huge coloured enamel advertising boards common in the 1920s and 1930s. Set up against the edge of the quarry members of my platoon were to take turns at firing the PIAT. This was done from a standing position in a small slit trench. We were not long started when one blank missile hit the advertising board with a loud clatter, ricocheted off to the left and struck the upstairs window of a double decker service bus travelling from Ryde. The window was shattered but fortunately no one was injured. End of the PIAT training for that day.

Since Winchester days either my company commander had been changed or I had changed companies. Instead of Major Robin Thomson my company commander was Major the Lord Douglas Gordon, younger brother of the Marquis of Huntly. Douglas Gordon was a perfect gentleman and an astute shepherd of young raw officers.

Before leaving the Isle of Wight for the 10th Black Watch at Barrow-on-Furness I record the kindness of Walter Smith, a territorial officer. Through his friendships with a few local families some of us were able to have the luxury of an occasional hot bath, the camp washing arrangements being on the primitive side. Walter's kindness to me, a raw second lieutenant of nineteen, extended far beyond his "agency" for hot baths. Twenty years later when I was minister of Monimail I used to visit Walter and his wife Mary at Denhead, their farm near Cupar. Sadly Walter developed spondylitis and had to spend increasingly long periods lying rigid in a sort of coffin. Walter was a big man, not only in body but in heart. He was a keen curler and "made me a curler" with the curling fraternity's "curlers' cuddy" capers in Letham village hall.

8

EMBARKATION

THE 10TH BLACK Watch stationed outside Barrow-in Furness was a holding battalion – a source of reinforcements for battalions, mostly overseas, and also a staging post for officers who were being seconded to other branches of the army. In my case I became one of a draft, code letters R.N.J.S.M., which assembled in London, the final destination unknown to us. My embarkation leave included a detour to Edinburgh to say good-bye to my aunts, uncle and cousin. The train south from Edinburgh was scheduled not to stop before Newcastle. My intention had been to take with me a handful of Scottish soil and here was I in a train passing through Dunbar when I suddenly remembered about this. I could not believe my good fortune when the train stopped at Reston. I flung open the carriage door, leapt on to the platform, grabbed a handful of soil from a flower bed and jumped aboard as the train began to move. My fellow passengers must have thought I was mad. Mad or not I had a boot polish tin ready in my kit. This tin of Scottish soil never left my possession and accompanied me for about 70,000 miles during service in Africa, Ceylon, India and Burma.

A short stay with my parents and sister Elizabeth at home in Huddersfield and I was off to the unknown. After a few days in London the draft left by train – destination unknown. In fact we arrived at the dockside in Liverpool to board a troopship, the *Riena del Pacifico*. On the train journey we had spent some of the time choosing our cabin companions for the voyage. A complete waste of time! Most of a deck of cabins was reserved for King Peter of Yugoslavia and a large mixed bag of retainers. The remaining cabins were occupied by senior officers and a large contingent of Wrens and Nursing Sisters. For junior officers the sleeping accommodation was in bunks constructed in the huge lounge. Pre-war the *Riena del Pacifico* was a luxury liner on the South American run and in these ships the first-class lounge and ballroom was high-ceilinged allowing for three-tier bunks around the edge of the dance floor and five tier-bunks in the large centre area. From memory there were 498 junior officers enclosed in this huge stuffy "cabin". The stuffiness was accentuated by the fact that the exits to the outside promenade decks were draped with huge blankets to prevent even a chink of light betraying our presence to any enemy submarines.

We left Liverpool and sailed round the north of Ireland and far out into the Atlantic before turning east to pass through the Straits of Gibraltar. We were in convoy with a large destroyer escort. It was not long after the end of the fighting in North Africa. We sailed past Cape Bon in Tunisia close enough to see the wrecked tanks and vehicles on the beaches. Two or three times during the voyage which ended at Port Said destroyers sped off and dropped depth charges.

At nineteen or so we were more interested in sun bathing on the upper decks and chatting up the girls than pondering any threat of danger.

Included in the tropical kit we had been issued were the most ridiculous-looking sun helmets. As we sailed on the impression grew that these helmets were really surplus to requirements, and so word was passed round and one fine morning a large bunch of us took part in a formal leave-taking of the surplus headgear. With a "one, two, three" possibly a hundred of them were cast overboard from the stern rail. I retain a vivid memory of them bobbing about in the wake as we steamed on.

To break the monotony of the voyage various games were organised – a tug-of-war competition and also boxing matches at various weights. One day a sergeant-major physical training instructor approached me – he was short of an opponent for an army lieutenant in the heavyweight category. I may have looked the part but I had never been in a boxing ring in my life. With a little persuasion I agreed to enter.

We were the last bout in a programme spread over two days. A ring had been erected on a large open deck. The referee called out our names – then seconds out and we faced one another. My opponent was a few years older than I was and at least as heavy. Although I had never been in a boxing ring before I could look after myself and opened with a fusillade of blows. In forces' boxing a bout was usually three rounds of two minutes, stopped at any stage if a "knock-out" looked about to happen. Halfway through the second round the match was halted in my favour.

Who should present the prizes but King Peter! My prize was a four-shilling voucher to spend in the ship's canteen, enough to buy twenty-four Mars bars. King Peter had a remarkably strong handshake.

After a voyage of nearly three weeks we finally reached Port Said.

Half a day was spent aimlessly on the dockside and in a railway marshalling yard. A meal appeared and we boarded a train for Suez. The congestion on the railways during the war was a huge problem. The journey of 100 miles from Port Said to Suez took ten hours. Although our compartment was several coaches from the engine the Egyptian driver kept drifting along the platform if at a station or along the side of the track. His visits turned into quite a friendly fellowship. Anticipating a journey of under two hours we had little to drink and there was nothing on the train. The "kind" driver, sensing our plight, offered to secure beer for us at Ismalia. About ten of us parted with a pound each. Before Ismalia we received several more visits from our "friend". Eventually we reached Ismalia and two of us went forward to collect the beer. Surprise, surprise! CHANGE OF ENGINE DRIVER. Our friend went off duty with at least a month's pay – our introduction to the foibles of life in the Middle East.

The next stage was spent in a tented transit camp on the bare desert outside the town. We slept in EPIP tents, like small rectangular marquees. We had our bed rolls, black metal trunks and canvas beds. There were six of us in a tent, three down each side with a wide gap at one end. Entering the tent I was in the left-hand corner near the doorway and opposite me was a chap Williamson, I think from Edinburgh. We were woken on our first morning in the desert by Williamson shouting out "It's all gone – it isn't here." Sure enough every bit of his kit was gone, including his black metal trunk.

It was the time of a full moon which seemed to shine brighter in the dry desert air. We were sleeping under mosquito nets. In the middle of the next night I awoke to see a stealthy figure crawling into the tent a few feet away. EPIP tents had stout bamboo rods inserted at intervals to strengthen and make more rigid the walls. I had a spare one lying on the ground alongside my bed. The problem was to extricate myself from under the tucked-in mosquito net. Slower than slow I worked myself free and leapt out with a mighty shriek as I grabbed the bamboo rod. In bare feet I chased the intruder, flung the rod in a sort of skimming sweep which caught him behind the knees, and he went down like a bag of flour. Discretion dictated no pursuit. However he would have had no difficulty in translating my loud verbal outburst into the fact that his after-hour visit was unwelcome.

Our stay near Suez could have been as long as two weeks, much of it spent at a French club swimming in the Red Sea.

This next anecdote sounds too far fetched to be true, but here it is. Outside the camp perimeter (in fact there was no perimeter in the sense of a fence, hence the intruders) – and so a few hundred yards from the camp area there was an open air cinema. The "building" was constructed of large interwoven palm leaf sections attached to upright poles driven into the ground. Admission was through a gap. One evening the "owner" became agitated, and here is what had happened. A wise guy with a couple of helpers had cut a gap through the palm leaf walls on the other side of the cinema and was selling "tickets" at reduced prices. Whether the owner caught the culprit I do not know but there was the most unholy racket before we enjoyed the film seated on rather hard benches.

The time came for us to sail again – this time on a much smaller vessel called the *Salween*, probably a British India boat on the U.K.-Bombay run before the war. It was a neat ship-shape affair with possibly less than five hundred passengers. Most of the cabins had windows as distinct from portholes, windows outside of which there was a narrow open deck. One morning before lunch I was walking along the deck when my eye caught sight of Neptune's trident and other "cross the line" equipment leaning against the window frame. It was the task of a moment to remove these badges of office and transfer them to a large cleaning equipment cupboard.

We assembled in the dining room and found that Neptune and his team were obviously perturbed. (I do not recall whether I had an accomplice in this daft ploy). Natural kindness prevented me (us) from keeping them strung up too long and so I (we) told them where to find their gear. Whether we received an extra large lathering with the barber's brush I do not know – but the ceremony for the crossing of the equator was good clean fun and all of us were quite proud of Neptune's certificate.

Our first port of call had been Aden for half a day to disembark a few naval personnel. By now the veil of secrecy had been lifted and we knew Mombasa was our destination.

At one point on the voyage, probably while still on the Red Sea, another boxing match was staged. A proper ring was erected on the open deck and again it was a two day programme. A repeat invitation to box was extended to me, but not by the same physical training instructor as on the *Riena del Pacifico*. "We are short of an opponent for the 12 stone and over bout. I suggest you come up on the boat deck tomorrow around 10 a.m. and the two of you can spar to see if you are well matched."

After breakfast I went up on the boat deck where forward a good bit was the instructor and a group of five or six. My opponent to be was a stoker in the Royal Navy – he was not quite as tall as I was but he had shoulders like a barn door. On with the gloves we sparred for half a minute and the instructor said "Great – you are made for each other." One of the objects of the exercise was for an officer to get a good "doing" from another rank. I don't mean in any malicious sense.

We were the last bout the next afternoon. Into the ring – "On my right John Wilson, Royal Navy (not his name) and on my left second lieutenant James Blyth, the Black Watch – seconds out."

Bracing myself for the fray I received one jab on the point of the chin which produced four or five punches from me in as many seconds with the result (in fact there wasn't enough time for a result) that my opponent shouted (his words are echoing in my ears as I write) "He's too good for me" and he leapt through the ropes and I was left standing in the middle of the ring like a cloutie dumpling.

We landed at Kilindi, the harbour for Mombasa, where a train was waiting to take us up country. Although it was still warm with bright sunshine when we set off, on the equator darkness falls with surprising speed at about the same time throughout the year, about 6 p.m. Nairobi, our destination, was about 400 miles distant which took, with prolonged stops, around eighteen hours. It was a great thrill to be in Africa with its red soil, distinctive smells and the sighting of zebras, giraffes, gazelle, etc., etc. from the slow moving train.

A few days were spent in Langata camp from where I was posted to the 14th Battalion King's African Rifles at Moshi in Tanganyika. The askaris were from Nyasaland (Malawi) and the bulk of them were home on leave and so the camp was sparsely populated.

Unlike many of the tribes in Kenya and Tanganyika who are tall the askaris from Nyasaland tended to be much shorter, in fact I was given an orderly, Whisky, who barely came up to my shoulder. Stature was irrelevant since he turned out to be a super orderly who constructed a small house for me out of long grasses bound tightly between long split vine stems. Then with half a dozen stout forked poles dug into the ground and two longer ones to hold the cross-pole for the apex of the roof he secured the beautifully made grass panels to the uprights. My abode was completed with a five foot high screen in a semi-circle from the door and in the centre of the area was a large hollow in the ground to hold a groundsheet. Two five gallon drums of hot water provided a remarkably good bath. Ensuite in the bush.

We were in the bush all right. At night there was a steady stream of hyenas possibly hoping for leftovers from the mess kitchen. The summit of Kilimanjaro was clearly visible most mornings. The camp was on the flat plain a few miles west of Moshi. One morning we woke to find a dozen elephants wandering around. We kept quiet and they left without any trouble.

With most of the battalion on leave in Nyasaland there was little training activity which allowed two or three of us to make the odd trip into Moshi for a cool beer at the Lion's Cub hotel. Absent from the camp I would give our cook and mess steward a few shillings to purchase any fruit or vegetables that the local villagers might turn up with.

One day our return from Moshi coincided with a strawberry-purchasing exercise. The villagers had two large enamel bowls each containing about 10 lbs of super strawberries, shaded with banana leaves. The price was 2 shillings per bowl. The cook and mess steward were about to part with 4 shillings for both bowls. As there were only three officers in our company mess and the mess staff of two I suggested 10 lbs of strawberries would probably be sufficient.

Our cook had been a chef at the famous Outspan Hotel at Nyeri, the company who operated the Treetops Hotel which was closed during the war. Many a delicious meal he provided for us. Some months later before embarking for service with the 14th Army in India and Burma two of us had a holiday leave at the Outspan Hotel. Although not in operation there were photographs of the Treetops Hotel which in pre-war days really was tree tops, a large platform in the tree (trees) above the water hole. From brochures and articles the present Treetops is a vastly expanded affair.

While at the Outspan Hotel Leslie Wise and I visited Lord Baden Powell's grave in the cemetery at Nyeri. Leslie was older than I was, a captain in the K.A.R. He belonged to London where his family had a stamp dealer's business, I think near St. Paul's Cathedral.

On two occasions we went fly fishing for trout on the Tana, without success. Fishing on the Tana was stocked and supervised by the Kenya Fly Fishers' Club. The hotel issued permits and supplied a ghillie. This seems a microscopic amount for a day's ghillieing, but there was a notice asking fishers not to pay more than a shilling a day. There were twenty shillings to a Kenyan pound, a shilling being ten cents instead of twelve pence.

We had hired a twelve cylinder Lincoln Zephyr from Tiny Gibbs who ran a garage on Delamere Avenue, Nairobi. From memory he had been a butler to Lord Delamere at one stage in his life. It was a large bright yellow tub, which served us well. On the return journey to Nairobi we were driving up a hill on a dirt road when here was a bus coming flying down the middle making no signs of moving over for us to pass. I was driving and drew over to the left, slipping into quite a deep ditch. A moment's panic. No need to worry, the massive engine with the car in low gear came out of the ditch like a Sherman tank.

The Outspan was a beautiful haven of peace. Among the many trees and shrubs in the policies were grapefruit trees laden with fruit.

On one of the fishing trips up river passing through the small African shambas (farms) we ran into a great cloud of locusts. Every shamba had several youngsters out among the maize stalks rattling heavy sticks in large cans trying to prevent the locusts from settling. I think they had modest success but returning to the hotel in the late afternoon locust damage was visible everywhere.

During the few weeks outside Moshi we spent a good deal of time on the big rifle range marching out the few miles along the edge of large fields of sisal. The sisal fibres were used for rope making and a dozen other products. At one point we passed close to a large sisal factory.

Among the officers and other ranks who returned from leave in Nyasaland was padre David Rose. David Rose was a Church of Scotland minister who had been a missionary in Nyasaland before the war. On a couple of Sundays I was among the worshippers seated on wooden benches in a large grass-roofed shed with open sides. After the war

David Rose was minister of Kirkwall Cathedral and then Marchmont St. Giles on the south side of the Meadows in Edinburgh (a building which was later demolished).

K.A.R. battalions were officered by whites from the U.K. or locally from Kenya, Rhodesia and Nyasaland, also white sergeant-majors and sergeants. After the war I believe some Africans were commissioned, but in my time the senior African rank was Regimental Sergeant-Major. Invariably the senior N.C.O.s were regular soldiers, some of them with twenty years' service and good soldiers they were.

Our next move with reinforcements was to Gilgil, the huge cantonment area between Naivasha and Nakuru. Here there were assault courses where we had to lie face down with Bren guns firing on fixed lines striking the ground a yard in front of our heads. Explosives were also detonated all around and one day there was a casualty, killed by a stray bullet.

In addition to all the training with the askaris I was sent on a three-week battle course for junior officers based on the airfield at Nakuru. Due to start on a Monday morning I arrived in Nakuru on the Friday afternoon and checked into the Stags Head Hotel. After breakfast on Saturday I walked out on to the veranda wearing my Black Watch balmoral with red hackle to be greeted with a loud "Hello there". It was the local bank manager who hailed from Perth living in the hotel while his wife was away from home on a family mission.

Throughout the weekend I was entertained regally. There was a race meeting attended by a great mix bag of characters. We must have been fed and "watered" during the day but my special memory is of around twenty of us in a local farm house enjoying bacon and eggs after midnight.

Brother David was an instructor at the school and he entertained me to dinner one evening in the Nakuru club where he was a member.

It is difficult to record some memories of my months in Kenya before sailing for India and Burma without giving the impression that most of the time was spent in clubs and hotels, but a short leave was spent at the Highlands Hotel, Molo, a superb pub, a little bit of England transported to the Kenya highlands. There was a local hunt with a huntsman often dressed in his scarlet hunting jacket.

Adjacent to the hotel there was a golf course which used to vie with a club in northern India as to which course had the highest tee in the British Empire. (Molo stood at nearly 9,000 ft. where a lot of pyrethrum and wheat were grown). The story goes that after moving the highest tee fifteen feet up the slope the secretary of the Molo Club would write to the secretary of the club in India announcing the new altitude, say 8,730 ft. A few weeks later a reply would come from India – our highest tee is now 8,755 feet. And so it went on. Apocryphal or not it makes a good story.

The time came for me to be one of the junior officers to escort a large draft of askaris overseas from Africa. A few days were spent in a camp north of Mombasa on the beach at Malindi, a beautiful beach washed by the clear warm waters of the Indian Ocean and a reef possibly half a mile offshore. Local Africans would take us out to the reef in their dugout canoes for a small sum.

9

Mombasa-Ceylon-India

OUR NEXT ADVENTURE was aboard a troop ship (whose name I cannot remember) from Mombasa to Colombo, Ceylon. On the way we anchored for half a day among the Seychelle Islands, possibly to take on fresh water, but also to await escorts for the convoy remembering that an earlier convoy was attacked by Japanese submarines which sank several allied ships including one packed with Wrens and Nursing Sisters.

We reached Colombo safely then travelled by train towards the capital Kandy, stopping short at Kurunegala, settling into a camp scattered among the tall coconut palms. These would have been commercial palms harvested for the coconuts. A coconut straight from the palm tree is a very different article from those sold in supermarkets. It is shiny dark green, the size of a rugby ball and the ones at the camp must have weighed at least 2 lbs. There was an element of hazard walking about the camp as occasionally a ripe coconut would crash to the ground. In fact an askari was struck on the back of the head and knocked unconscious. Fortunately for him it was a glancing blow and not a direct hit and he soon recovered.

The nuts were harvested manually by plantation hands with a fibre "halo" band around their ankles, then with a kind of machete they would shin up the forty foot trunks – the speed with which they climbed was wonderful to behold – and hack down the bunches of nuts.

Before leaving Ceylon for Calcutta and eventually Assam and Burma I was one of a small bunch of officers sent on a jungle warfare course in south India, near Shimoga, one hundred and twenty miles north-west of Bangalore. It took nearly three days to reach Shimoga from Kurunegala. Most of a day was spent at Bangalore at the luxurious United Services Club. This may not be the correct name, but it was the club which appears in a famous photograph of Winston Churchill mounted on a white charger standing before the pillared entrance. Fact or fiction but among the anecdotes about the rumbustious old warrior is one that there is an unpaid mess bill pinned to the notice board in the bar bearing his name.

The club was complemented by a fine outdoor swimming pool along one side of which was an outdoor bar. Walking over I bumped into an old classmate at Dollar Academy, Ian Jack. Ian was a major in the Indian army. Sadly Ian died on 27th May,

2007. The December issue of our school magazine has a fine tribute to Ian whose career was in hotel management. In the course of his career he was manager of the Queen's Hotel in Leeds and of Gleneagles Hotel in Perthshire.

Brother David and Ian were golfing pals, David and his wife Sheena living in Ilkley while Ian was in Leeds. This detailed preamble allows me to record the occasion when we were spending a few days in David and Sheena's home in Ilkley when early one evening David returned home with the most amazing confection of meringue, cream, fruits, etc. etc. which must have been well over a foot in diameter. There had been a large wedding reception in the Queen's and David, passing to arrange their next golfing date, fell heir to that magnificent "left-over". Helped by Sheena and Leslie David and I soon made short work of it.

Back to India. River crossings were made with all our kit carefully wrapped in our groundsheet to form a buoyant raft pushed ahead of us. Each of us had a rifle balanced on top clear of the water. Unfortunately one guy's raft turned turtle and his rifle disappeared. Several attempts to retrieve it from seven to eight feet of water were unsuccessful. The chances are that the Lee Enfield is still lying on the river bed.

Mention of Lee Enfield rifles allows me to digress again with a modest blow on my physical prowess tooter. One of my parlour or barrack room tricks was to grasp the extreme muzzle end of two Lee Enfields and scissor them like semaphoring up and down, meeting above my head. Believe me when I say that one hundred times was only a warm up.

The training area around Shimoga was teak forest and tiger country. One night we were taken out by lorries and dropped at quarter mile intervals along a forest ride. Alone with a compass and rifle and a rendezvous point about three miles distant each of us set off through the teak forest. Helped by a half moon and a luminous compass we all reached the rendezvous. I had never seen a tiger in the wild but earlier that day we came across tiger spoor the size of a small plate. The forest was pretty spooky at night to say the least, but at one point, about half way, there was the most almighty racket of a large animal crashing about in the undergrowth. It took a good while for my heartbeat to slow down – I had disturbed a cow which had escaped through the thorn bush hedge surrounding a tiny Indian village.

Another day our detachment was marching in single file along an open break in the forest when we came across a python moving slowly through the grass. It must have been twenty feet long and as thick as a slim man's waist. Snakes have thin skulls and a couple of guys were all for killing it with a rifle butt. We persuaded them that it was not a good idea and the python disappeared into the undergrowth.

From vivid accounts many people get the idea that a country like India is almost carpeted from wall to wall with snakes. Sleeping on the ground in India and Burma in both teak forests and bamboo jungle I have no memory of seeing a snake and so it is hard to believe that we had hardly seen the python disappear when a few yards further on we came across another python at least as big – this one was coiled and stationary forming a "huge heap of snake".

The meeting with the pythons can be verified by contacting John Mull, the older brother of Arthur Mull who features in memories of Uganda days at Jinja after the war. I jest. John, if he is still alive, will be nearly ninety. The fact is that John, a major, and Arthur were fellow pupils at Dollar Academy. By the odd quirks of life when he was on the course at Shimoga John was almost in his family's back yard by Indian scales. Their father worked in India, I think with the railways as an engineer or administrator, based at Hubli, a name I remember seeing on the mandatory weekly letter home for boarders at Dollar. Hubli was only a hundred miles due north of Shimoga. Mention of the mandatory home letters to parents allows me to tell you that many envelopes did not contain long newsy epistles but sometimes "Dear Mum and Dad, I'm fine. Hope you are the same. Love, James."

Back to Ceylon. On the ferry crossing from India to Ceylon customs officers came aboard and I was sorry for one older officer – nothing to do with our group – who had purchased shoes and other gifts for his wife living in Ceylon. I wasn't eavesdropping but just happened to be standing nearby as the demands of the customs officers grew and grew and grew and must have far exceeded the purchase of the gifts. Like me with the box of two dozen eggs when leaving Douglas on the Isle of Man the purchaser of the gifts threw them overboard.

Ceylon is a lush island – the Pearl of the Indian Ocean – and before leaving for the next stage of our travels, a troopship from Colombo to Calcutta – allow me a couple more memories. For a few days in Colombo we were based in the G.O.H., the Grand Oriental Hotel, on the corner across from the landing stage for liners. We were on administration duties, something to do with pay for ourselves and the askaris and regulations dealing with overseas allowances. While it is possible at any age to live without a dram or two the situation we encountered was as follows. The G.O.H. had a bar upstairs open for about an hour in the evening. After a small dram we went down to the large ground floor lounge to await the evening dinner. Seated nearby was a friendly-looking old character, possibly in his sixties. He heard our Scottish voices and got on the chat. He of course was a fellow Scot, a tea planter from Nuwara-Eliya and down in Colombo for a day or two. He was alone but his personal bearer was behind the scenes. A waiter was sent to summons the bearer who was asked to nip upstairs. He returned with an unopened bottle of Dewar's. There were four of us in the company and the envious glances of many other guests added to our enjoyment.

We had a vehicle at our disposal and one afternoon heading south from Colombo three Wrens were walking along the verge. It was a very warm day and simultaneously we three thought it would be a kindness to offer them a lift. The outcome was that they jumped aboard. Administrative duties were put on hold and we went swimming at Mount Lavinia. I had to hire a pair of trunks at the pool and it was only when we were halfway to the Galle Face Hotel that I realized I had left without my deposit being returned, quite a large sum. However the pleasure of being with the girls soon softened my financial loss. We had afternoon tea at the Galle Face Hotel, a luxurious contrast to our rather primitive camp site in the coconut palms. There was an officer's night club in Colombo which I am going to call the White Hart. We spent a happy evening together, driving the lassies back to their quarters around midnight. Duty called. Next day we completed our assignment and drove back to Kurunegala. We never saw the lassies again but I record loving thanks for their cheery company and hope that life was kind to them.

Time to set sail again. Boarding a troop ship at Colombo we sailed for Calcutta, a voyage without incident. Calcutta is on the Hubli and it is difficult even on a large scale atlas to clearly distinguish it from the huge fan of river outlets grouped under "mouths of the Ganges".

Half a day's sail up the Hubli we all assembled on the boat decks wearing life jackets. At first glance this seemed a strange exercise but the reason was explained. The name of that reach of the river is Diamond Harbour with sandbanks changing with every tide and on one occasion a troop ship, many years before, turned turtle with the loss of many lives.

Despite the teeming throngs of residents Calcutta was awash with Allied service personnel. The 11th East African Division fighting in Burma had a transit camp a few miles from the city centre. Our stay lasted only a few days but in that time we managed to pack in quite a lot – a visit to the air-conditioned Lighthouse cinema to escape the heat, a couple of superb curries in Firpos, the famous restaurant upstairs off Chowringhee, and an afternoon and evening as guests of the manager for one of Britain's largest insurance companies. A slightly older officer who had begun his career with the company before joining the army knew of the company's instruction to entertain any employee in the forces who might show face. He showed face and the manager very kindly took us out to the Tollygunge Club for lunch and to his home for dinner in the evening. The manager and his wife were most gracious hosts. One memory of that evening was after dinner. Our host pulled a bell cord beside his armchair which summoned a servant who took a small box from the mantelpiece, took out a pipe and filled it. Our host lit the pipe himself.

We sailed again, possibly on the same troopship which brought us from Colombo. It was a relatively short voyage, Calcutta to Chittagong, on the east side of the Bay of Bengal.

There was time for a quick visit to the Chittagong Club. The degree to which top hotels, e.g. the Taj Mahal in Bombay and the Norfolk in Nairobi, and dozens of others, and private clubs such as the Muthaiga in Nairobi, opened their doors to Allied officers was commendable beyond all praise. After all I was a pretty raw dweller on our planet home despite the two pips on my shoulders.

Off we go again, this time by train from Chittagong to Comilla, one hundred miles, and then flights from Comilla to Imphal, two hundred miles.

In 2005 a scheme was launched by the National Lottery in co-operation with other bodies such as the British Legion – the scheme was called "Heroes Return". Funds were provided for Second World War veterans to visit in the 60th anniversary year countries where they had served on active service between 1939 and 1945.

I applied and received a cheque for £2,100, the amount granted to a veteran who served in the Far East. My wife and I felt that the distance and heat of a trip to India and Burma might be too much for us and so we were allowed to spend fourteen days on the fortress island of Malta.

Prior to going I was interviewed by a reporter from the *Ayr Advertiser* which resulted in an article headed "Two Heroes Return to Recall War Victims". Why I was chosen from among a number of other veterans living in Ayr or nearby I do not know. All I would say is that the article reads as if I almost single-handedly drove the Japanese from Imphal and Kohima and down the Kabaw valley to the river Chindwin.

The fact is that by the time our draft reached Assam and Burma the 11th East African Division was beginning to withdraw while the British 2nd Division with their Cross

Keys emblem passed through. I was down the Kabaw valley towards the Chindwin river and was shot at, but when I recall the nightmare experiences of the East Africans with their Rhino shoulder emblem in the jungle and mud of the monsoon I hand over to George MacDonald Fraser, author of the "Flashman" novels, who served in Burma and wrote one of the great personal memoirs of the Second World War *Quartered Safe Out of Here*. Here is a quotation from p.95:

'Jap was digging in for a last desperate stand on the Rangoon road: if he could hold us at Pyawbwe for just a few weeks, until the monsoon broke, he might stave off defeat indefinitely, for when the rains came they would turn southern Burma into a huge swamp where no armour or truck could operate effectively. "You can't fight through the monsoon" was the received wisdom.'

Received wisdom or not, the 11th East African Division refuted it by fighting and chasing the Japs during the monsoon down the Kabaw valley to the river Chindwin soon to be bridged with one of the longest pontoon Bailey bridges ever constructed. The best account of this staggering achievement is an illustrated book *Monsoon Victory* by Gerald Hanley published by Collins in 1946. Early in the spring of 1945 General Slim, Commander of the 14th Army, made a special visit to the 11th East African Division then stationed north of Dimapur in Assam to thank them for their huge contribution to final victory.

Sixty years later with fighting in Iraq, Afghanistan, and the endless struggles between the Israelis and Palestinians we have to ask what is "victory"? Victory will come only when weapons are turned into ploughshares and the great diversity of peoples and beliefs begin to live together as a global family.

Mention of Dimapur brings to mind the day when Neil Stewart, a fellow Black Watch officer in the 13th King's African Rifles, came bounding into the mess with the shout "I've got a date". This proclamation was greeted with the shout "We've got a date", and so it turned to be. Dimapur was a largish garrison town on the railway down to Calcutta, not by rail all the way. En route there was a ferry crossing of the huge Bramaputra river at Gauhati. Dimapur sported a garrison theatre for ENSA shows and other forms of entertainment. The day of the date arrived and three or four of us piled into a jeep and drove the twenty-five miles into the town. The good lass was a Nursing Sister. We went for a superb meal in a quaint Chinese restaurant and then off to the theatre. I have the most vivid memory of swains jockeying to secure a seat next to our female companion – I was out of luck – but the whole evening was a hilarious relief from camp life and if by a million chances to one that good angel is still alive and reads this, then here is a wee peck on the cheek from one of the gang.

10

Burma and India

IMPHAL WAS ONE of the main supply bases for the battles driving the Japanese from Burma. As part of the divisional withdrawal team several of us were in a transit camp outside the town. Days of frantic activity were interspersed with the odd day or two off duty. Several times when off duty two or three of us, as lieutenants, went down to the aerodrome to cadge flights on low-flying Dakotas dropping supplies to Chindit patrols far beyond the Japanese lines.

A few weeks prior to these flights an order had been issued from S.E.A.C. (South –East Asia Command) "no joyriding in the Dakotas". The reason for the order was that a few weeks earlier, after months of no Japanese Air Force activity, suddenly several Mig fighters appeared and shot down five or six Dakotas. The low-flying supply planes ambling along around 200 m.p.h. were like sitting ducks. Quite a few joyriding officers were killed in each of the planes, hence the order.

Loading and unloading the planes was hard work and we felt that the air force handling crews were quite happy to have a couple of keen helpers aboard.

Mindful of the order, not all pilots would welcome "joyriders" on board. The pilots were British, American, Australian and so on, but I cannot remember which of the pilots observed the order and would not take us.

The flights were two or three hours in duration and so we were well behind the Japanese front line. Flying at around 200 feet a red light came on, a signal to open the side door in the fuselage. Some of the supplies were dropped with small parachutes, others in several layered bags were dropped freefall. Approaching the dropping zone the Chindits and their mules were easily seen. A green light was the signal to begin pushing out supplies. Depending on the size of the patrol most drops called for three or four shut-offs with a circle round and another green signal drop. (A small comment about standing half leaning out of the open door from one who was never at ease with heights – there was no sense of fear which must be due to the speed of the aircraft).

On another off duty day in Imphal two of us repaired to the Imphal Club for a refresh before lunch. We were seated with our John Collins (gin, lime and lemonade) in a small room when the door opened and in walked Lord Louis Mountbatten in his white naval uniform, the glare of the whiteness being relieved by the large colourful "fruit salad" of the medals on his left breast. Close behind him was a young lady, Felicity Wavell.

Before Mountbatten had time to say "Good morning, gentlemen" we were on our feet, gin glasses drained and we hot-footed out of the club.

Walking along the verge of the dusty road back to our camp a very large staff car with small flags flying approached. Although we were officers in the King's African Rifles we were free to sport the distinctive headgear of the regiments in which we had been commissioned. Wearing my balmoral with red hackle we saluted the car, to be greeted with a very friendly wave from the passenger who was none other than Lord Wavell the Viceroy, a Black Watch officer.

The reason for the Viceroy's visit was to knight four generals on the airfield at Imphal, General Slim, General Stopford, General Leese and General Christison. Lord Mountbatten, the last Viceroy, succeeded Lord Wavell. A fine memory to have seen two Viceroys in the space of half and hour.

By early January 1945 the whole division was camped about twenty miles north of Dimapur, a rail junction and considerable town in Assam. From memory we had Christmas dinner about the 11th of January.

The monotony of camp life was relieved from time to time by stars from ENSA, among them George Formby with his ukulele, and a character billed as Blackpool's own comedian. Crude would be a diluted description of his jokes.

My stay in the camp near Dimapur was short lived as two of us were sent on a staff course to the Indian Army equivalent of Sandhurst at Dehra Dun north of Delhi. About fifty majors, captains and lieutenants were on the three week course – much of the time seated on tiered benches around a huge sand table about the size of four billiard tables. The creation of the sand table was a masterpiece with hills, roads, rivers, railways, small towns, woods, and isolated farms on which the instructors took us with much questioning through field tactics.

The course over, my lieutenant colleague from the 13th K.A.R. and I were destined for leave – we had chosen to spend it in Bombay. Bus from Dehra Dun to Saharanpor and an evening meal in Spencer's Restaurant, Spencer's being in those days a famous chain of hotels (such as the Connemara, Madras) and restaurants at main stations throughout India.

Soon after dining the Frontier Mail drew in, a famous train from Rawalpindi to Bombay. We were in possession of army travel warrants but no reserved seats. On the platform was the conductor in a very smart uniform. Showing our warrants we requested seats. "Sorry sahib – no seats available." Abreast of us was a single shiny aluminium coach. "What is that coach?" "It is the air-conditioned coach." "Any possibility of a berth?" "Ah sahib, there is one vacant coupé but it is reserved for Dr. Watson who is joining the train at Delhi." Pause, my right hand slowly moving to my hip pocket - "What about popping into the station office to telephone Delhi to confirm Dr. Watson's reservation." The conductor disappeared for about five minutes. Emerging from the office he said "Ah sahib, you are in luck, Dr. Watson has cancelled his reservation." A five or ten rupee note changed hands as the conductor opened the door of a splendid coupé – two berths, with ensuite facilities, a squat toilet, wash basin, and possibly a shower (I do not remember all the details), but the air conditioning alone after the oppressive heat of the evening was a blessing in itself.

From memory we arrived in the magnificent Victorian station in Bombay and engaged a taxi to take us to the famous Taj Mahal Hotel. Officers in the Allied forces were given special rates – and they were special compared with the full scale of charges. Apart from our sleeping accommodation which was an attic dormitory with six metal hospital style beds, we had the full run of the public rooms, the huge dining room with lots of wealthy Indians, their ladies bejewelled and dressed in beautiful saris. There was the famous harbour bar, where incidentally three of us assembled for a pre-lunch John Collins (gin, lemonade and lime) – I was on the bell and hardly had the words "three John Collins please" escaped my mouth when one companion blurted out "Oh there is Jimmy Wilson." Jimmy was accompanied by two pals who joined us. I was still on the bell when one of Jimmy's pals blurted out "Oh there's Sandy and Bill" who joined us too. Not to prolong the description of this pre-lunch "snifter" these were all fellow service officers, not all in the army, but I paid for a round of seventeen John Collins.

The Taj was a super base for a few days' leave. The iron hospital beds had their legs in small tin lids with water to prevent ants from crawling up. Although our initial arrival from the magnificent Victorian Bombay rail terminal was by taxi I have a memory of a bunch of us arriving back from a party on a bullock cart. Our tip probably exceeded the driver's weekly income and the majordomo in his field marshal's uniform was not unduly upset by our rather unorthodox arrival. Not surprisingly, since we probably tipped him as well.

Most days we went swimming at Breach Candy, a magnificent open-air pool near the Towers of Silence, the burial columns for the numerous Parsee communities in that, even in 1945, teeming city. This fact evades me, but from either reading or watching travel programmes on television, the beautiful pool is tiled and shaped like a miniature model of the Indian sub-continent.

Shortly after returning to Dimapur from leave in Bombay the division received orders to move to Ranchi in Bihar in India, by which time I had been appointed A.T.O., Animal Transport Officer. This move would have taken place in May 1945 only days after the end of the war in Europe.

Unfortunately the mules and riding ponies of the division were initially denied access to the camps at Ranchi because of concern about the spread of epizootic lymphangytis, a disease of mules and horses. For several weeks until the Indian veterinary services gave us the all-clear the animal transport lines were down in the plain near Chas. While there the temperature reached 124 degrees Fahrenheit, over 50 degrees Centigrade.

Providing analytical details of the ingredients in every possible edible item in our supermarkets gives loads of ammunition for endless articles in the press and on TV seeking to guide us in healthy eating. One of the taboo substances is salt with dire warnings about taking too much. But then what is too much when the body cannot live without salt?

Dressed in our light-weight jungle green battledress, with the upper half like an aertex blouse, it was not necessary to expend a great deal of energy on a hot day before the armpits, indeed well down the sleeves and lumbar areas became encrusted with a white deposit – salt. Swallowing a small salt tablet daily was mandatory.

Salt not only for humans but animals also. One day after a long march in great heat one of our mules, Jenny by name, one of the oldest, collapsed. Without consulting our divisional veterinary officers we got a pail of cool water with a small handful of salt thrown in and askaris took turns in lapping the cool dilute salt water onto Jenny's drooping tongue. It was a long patient process but eventually she began to stir and before night she was back to her sedate elderly friskiness.

In the battalion we had fifty mules, each with its own muleteer and two riding ponies. The job with its large measure of independence suited me down to the ground. One day the colonel said to me "Blyth, I have not seen you at pre-breakfast P.T. (physical training)." "Oh, colonel, please give me a break, we are on the go early feeding and watering the mules." The colonel was a great wee guy, possibly a regular soldier. One day on route march exercises, which of course continued after the end of hostilities, I was riding up and down the battalion from company to company, and from platoon to platoon, it was hot and everyone, including the colonel, was in full order, big pack, small pack, pouches, water bottle, Tommy gun or rifle, whereas I was mounted on a magnificent chestnut gelding called Richard. Two leather satchels were attached to the saddle and apart from a web belt and crossed braces I was unencumbered by packs, pouches or anything heavier than a holster with a revolver.

One morning we were on battalion exercise with a detachment of mules allocated to each company. I was riding up and down to see that all was well with the mules and their drivers. It needed a big mule to carry a 3-inch mortar though whatever the weight of the load it was important to have the surcingles (the belly bands) not too loose or too tight. A mule with saddle sores, of which we had very few, was out of commission. Riding past the colonel whose green jungle battledress was drenched with perspiration I accorded him the courtesy of "Good morning, colonel." His looks would not have killed me, but with the faintest smile on his face I was aware of him thinking "Blyth, you are a lucky b... ."

Another bonus available to the transport officers in the battalion – and I use the plural deliberately – was the question of batmen and orderlies. (The motor transport officer was a young Irishman, Paddy Bamford, whose address was 17 Cypress Gardens, Belfast. We have not seen one another for over 60 years, but this is one memory the details of which I would bet my shirt on being correct.) A word about the bonus. A battalion order came out that only the colonel and the majors were to have a personal batman and the rest of us, captains, lieutenants (we were lieutenants) were to share a batman. In both the animal transport and motor transport platoons there were several good askaris surplus to establishment numbers. The story is told. Both of us had two batmen each. Here I go again plugging into the old memory box, but my two were Saidi Ali, older than me, who had been a steward in the Zomba Club in Nyasaland (Malawi) and Aliseni Wasili, a cheery lad about my own age who hailed from the tea growing area in the south of the country near Mount Mlanje.

The three of us got on like a house on fire and one of my regrets is that I did not keep in contact with them after our soldiering days were over. One small compensation, and I hope it is a compensation, is that some years ago my cassock and gown were taken out to Malawi by a British missionary doctor as a gift to a Malawian Presbyterian minister.

In August 1945 the 11th East African Division was still stationed in camps outside Ranchi, the capital of Bihar State in India. August in India can be hot. Ranchi, several thousand feet above the plains is marginally cooler. The division was undergoing training for a planned invasion of northern Malaya. While I was strolling over to the mess one afternoon in August a jeep came flying into the compound with a brigadier, precariously perched on the bonnet clutching a bottle of booze, shouting out "It's all over." The second atomic bomb had been dropped on Nagasaki and the Japanese had surrendered.

After the division's heroic battles down the Kabaw valley in pursuit of the retreating Japanese in 1944, the whole operation hampered by deep mud caused by the relentless monsoon rains, August 1945 was no time to moralize about the blasphemous outrage of the atomic annihilations – quite simply we were all overcome by tearful joy.

After the cessation of hostilities in the East the repatriation of allied forces was a huge logistical task. All British service members had a demob number depending upon when service in the Navy, Army or Air Force commenced.

Some dates become not just hazy but lost after sixty years. Our turn for repatriation to Africa duly arrived starting with a train journey from Ranchi to Deolali Camp outside Bombay. India's railways are one of the great transport systems on the planet. The father of fellow pupils at Dollar Academy, John and Arthur Mull, was part of the great team of engineers and administrators of different races who ran this huge transport service. John and Arthur's parents were based at Hubli, south of Bombay.

A journey on India's railways would easily supply material for a book, the tea wallah caterers at halts, the endless appeals for "buckshees", the passengers, on some trips on the roofs of the carriages or hanging on to the door handles exceeding those seated in the coaches, coaches with a big range of comfort or discomfort from the hard benches with open slatted windows to the plush comfort of the air-conditioned coaches and coupés.

11

India-Africa

THE DAY ARRIVED when what was left of the battalion joined other units and we travelled by train from Ranchi to Deolali transit camp, a few miles out of Bombay.

Our troop ship from Bombay to Mombasa was to be the *Strathnaver*. Cooling our heels in the camp we made a couple of final trips into Bombay and managed a swim in the beautiful open pool at Breach Candy.

Returning to the camp one afternoon around 5 p.m. we were met by the most extraordinary sight on entering the very large mess anteroom – a vast sea of empty Whitbread screwtop bottles. While Indian beer had been available during the war – and very good it was – the Whitbread empties were the Deolali allotment of the first shipment of British beer to arrive in India since the end of the war. Before the mess stewards could launch the rationing of the English nectar to "two bottles each" the officers in camp had got their hands on them and drunk the lot.

As battalion mules officer I had always been a "hands on guy" but quite out of the blue I was appointed messing officer on the *Strathnaver* for 3,500 Africans. This new job called for boarding ahead of the rest.

By this time I was a captain and approached the Indian government officials granting exit permits. At one point there was an Indian doctor seated behind a small table. On presenting my officer's service book he blurted out "you are not having yellow fever inoculation?" Oh ho, said I to myself in a flash, no yellow fever inoculations if I am to be messing officer for 3,500 askaris. Retreating round the corner of the large godown (warehouse in parts of East Asia, especially India) I paused for about an hour during which time I became a medical doctor. My blue officer's service book is somewhere in our attic with the large YF and illegible signature ending in MD scribbled on it. What a great blessing it was that most doctors' signatures are like a hen strutting across a page!

At the end of the hour I approached the Indian doctors' table again, possibly a different doctor on duty, but that was me free to step up the gang plank.

At some stage in this saga a lieutenant had been appointed as my catering assistant. Once on board we were taken by a *Strathnaver* officer to the boat deck where he showed us an office with two or three telephones. Not to be the smart guy but it took me ten seconds to realize that providing food for 3,500 askaris was not a task to be done by making telephone calls. Sensing that my lieutenant assistant was less "hands on" than myself I have to record that I never saw him again.

The following morning we set sail. Breakfast for the askaris consisted of tea with as much sugar as possible and a few hard ships biscuits. The main meals were midday and early evening. Nourishing, but very monotonous. The basic ingredients were rice and "posho" meal, with ladles of a liquid meat vegetable mix poured over.

The voyage lasted about eight days. The routine was to supervise breakfast tea and biscuits, self down to the cabin to don my army shirt with three cloth pips on each shoulder, quick breakfast in the table-clothed dining room, back to the cabin, off with the shirt, and up to meet with that day's ration fatigue party (possibly two lots of twenty askaris with an African sergeant or corporal). The cold storage and ration stores were almost in the bowels of the ship at the prow - sugar, rice and posho meal in 224 lbs(2 cwt.) sacks and meat, vegetables, etc. All these had to be humped up five or six decks and carried the length of the ship to the stern deck where there were open fires which were mounted on heavy steel plates and with hoods to shield the whole affair from the worst of the sea breezes.

While most of the askaris were quite fit muscular guys they chose to carry the 224 lb. sacks of sugar, rice, etc. four to a sack, one at each corner where there were quite large "lugs". Once or twice for devilment, and showing off, I would say "come on – here is the way to carry these sacks." The sacks were all well stacked up making it easy to get underneath one and grasp two of the lugs hoisting the heavy load well up on the shoulders, then up the five or six decks and through the length of the large ship and dump them down at the stern. The askaris used to kill themselves laughing at this daft show-off feat of mine.

On board we must have had around 100 mess decks, each with about 35 askaris. The food was served in the traditional army camp kettles. Each mess deck was issued with two kettles, one with rice or posho meal and the other vegetable stew. Dishing out the food was the trickiest part of the whole exercise. With the help of African sergeants I supervised the distribution of every meal.

One evening I was up on the boat deck relaxing over the rail when a major approached me. "You struck one of my sergeants today." I smiled and said "I may have held up my arm and given your sergeant a slight push to control the noisy mêlée of hungry mess deck fatigue parties, but strike anyone – no, and incidentally if you would like the job it is yours now. Goodnight."

To relieve the rather monotonous routine of the voyage one day about halfway to Mombasa trouble broke out in one of the mess decks. An African sergeant had told an askari to get his hair cut. Only a few of the askaris were regular soldiers, most of them were conscripts in high excitement at getting home after two to three years' absence from their homes. The askari's response was "God gave me my hair to grow." Things got heated and began to get out of hand. Don't ask me why I should have been present at that moment but two majors appeared with two or three senior African sergeant majors. The appeal for calm was met by the steely clatter of a panga against the bulkhead. An armed guard was formed under the command of Gordon Hay (a former pupil at Dollar Academy and then Edinburgh Academy when his father, Rev. Sutcliffe Hay, moved from St. James the Great Episcopal Church in Dollar to the large Episcopal

Church at Holy Corner in Edinburgh). Calm was restored but I think that two or three of the ring leaders were given time in jail by a court martial in Kenya.

During the voyage I must have covered a lot of miles at the double trot as, dressed in an old pair of shorts and gym shoes, I carried out my "hands on" duties as messing officer.

By chance our unit of several hundred askaris was first to disembark. It was a beautiful morning at Kilindini harbour, Mombasa – and as I came down the gangplank a colonel who was standing there said to me "Christ you can work!"

Long before lunch we were off on the long haul to Nairobi and beyond. The troop train must have had twenty coaches hauled by two of the huge double-tendered wood burning engines. Nairobi is 4,500 feet above sea level and some of the gradients posed quite a challenge. At one spot the train backed, got up extra steam, and, with grit coming from boxes above the driving wheels, we were on our way.

During the war Gilgil, between Naivasha and Nakuru, was one huge transit camp – a pause there for a couple of days and we were off on the next legs of the long journey to Nyasaland (Malawi).

Gilgil to Kisumu on Lake Victoria, a sail across the lake to Mwanza in Tanganyika (Tanzania), train from Mwanza to Tebora, Tebora to Lake Tanganyika near Ujiji where Stanley met Dr. Livingstone, sail across the lake to Albertville in the Belgian Congo, train to Lulaba an upper reach of the Congo which although over 1,000 miles from the sea still had a vast volume of water.

On via Kamina, Kabolo to Kabongo, meeting up with the great north-south railway which stretched through Northern Rhodesia (Zambia), Southern Rhodesia (Zimbabwe) to Cape Town in South Africa. One of the stages, I think Kamina to Kabala, was by road in those days – in our case it was a night drive and a nightmare. We set off at dusk. I was in the cab of the leading truck, the drivers were civilians, and my chauffeur was a cheery wee guy with bare feet who had his rations with him in the form of dried fish in a small wicker basket. Apart from the danger of the basket rolling under the brake or the clutch pedal the stench in the cabin would have killed all the bees in creation.

There was sufficient light for us to edge over the lip of an escarpment and see hundreds of feet below a small wooden trestle bridge without parapets. Apart from the natural acceleration of the down gradient I am almost certain my wee pal had his bare foot on the accelerator. I closed my eyes and by a miracle we flew across the bridge. Mercifully we completed the rest of the two hundred mile trip in the dark. It was known in army transit circles as "the death ride".

While I had been with African askaris for about three years, sometimes stationed with a detachment of mules in the jungle with a colleague Sergeant Price, the only white men for miles, I never felt a moment's unease. (Sgt. Price's home was in Nyasaland and he hoped to become a veterinary surgeon after the war.) Travelling through the Congo by train to Lusaka in Zambia with one or two prolonged halts – on one occasion for the most of a day in the then capital Elisabethville – the air was pregnant with the foretaste of some of the bloodshed soon to come. It was sinister to say the least and we were all relieved when we crossed the border at Sakania into Northern Rhodesia (Zambia).

After a couple of days in a transit camp at Lusaka we set off on the long road trip to Nyasaland, spending a bivouac night en route. At one point the road near Lilongwe passed through Portuguese East Africa (Mozambique). Our destination was a transit camp near Blantyre and Zomba where others carried out the demobilisation, or in some cases the issue of long leave passes for those who were regular soldiers.

There are two anecdotes of the period before making the long journey north to Jinja in Uganda which took place much sooner than planned. Two of us were due leave and we had decided to spend three weeks in Durban when an order out of the blue arrived "Captain Blyth and one other to escort two hundred askaris of 2ⁿᵈ K.A.R., many of them with their wives, to Jinja, Uganda". So much for our leave.

The second anecdote is about my father who worked as an accountant in Birmingham immediately after the First World War before I was born. The joke goes like this – two working engineers who had not seen one another for a long time bumped into each other in the centre of the city. The natural question was "Where are you working these days?" One chap replied "I am at Wholedays and Onions" whereupon his old pal blurted out "How strange, I am at Halfdays and Tomatoes." My father, bless his soul, thought it to be a great joke. Joke or not, one day on a foot path through the bush from our transit camp on the way to the Zomba Club hidden in the scrub just off the track was an old traction engine with the name boldly emblazoned on its side "Wholedays and Onions, Birmingham".

The return trip north had its own "hiccups" in the up and down adventure of life. The main problem was with the askaris and their wives. Orders were "One wife only". A few askaris managed to smuggle an extra wife on to the convoy. Not all of the women could speak Chinyanja, the official language of the K.A.R., or at least claimed not to understand, speaking in their tribal tongue. A few extra wives got as far as Jinja, Uganda and they were duly escorted back to Malawi.

The trip north was the south trip in reverse with the exception that it ended at Jinja instead of Kisumu. Arriving at Mwanza at the southern end of Lake Victoria we had to wait half a day for the lake steamer. Many everyday articles had been in short supply during the war and I was surprised to see new Parker pens on display in an Indian douka – I bought one for £2 and still have it in good working order.

From memory we spent the night on board in a small cabin arriving at Jinja after breakfast. As we tied up at the jetty I glanced over the side and there was a giant hippo with its huge mouth wide open. I could have dropped a peppermint into it.

The camp at Jinja was a full-flight K.A.R. base with permanent buildings. The officers' mess at the top of the hill had parquet flooring. A few of the white officers and N.C.O.s were regular soldiers but the bulk of us were marking time for the signal to sail back to the UK from Mombasa.

Rehearsals for a ceremonial parade inspected by the Major General in command of the forces in East Africa who was returning to the UK were arranged. Officers in the K.A.R. did not possess swords but we borrowed about half a dozen from the Ugandan Police Force.

In the evening the General and his aides were entertained to dinner, quite a squash seating fifty round a table designed for forty. The setting was in the shape of a "T" with an additional round table placed at the base of the "T". At the end of the meal the tradition is for the port to be passed round clockwise for the Royal Toast. I was among the five seated round the round table, and after the company had retired to the ante room for coffee etc. we five sat on, passing the port round and round. I have no desire to exaggerate but the port decanter must have been filled at least twice.

Next morning I was summoned to the CO's office. I was a captain, Second-in-command of Headquarter Company. Puzzled I entered his office. "Blyth you had your hands in your pockets during the Royal Toast." This of course was utter nonsense. My reply was "We were all very close together standing for the toast and it may have appeared that my arms were by my side but I can assure you that was not the case and I drank the Royal Toast with all the rest."

Although I say it myself I was a good officer, but I have always been my own man, and not for the first time an officer senior in rank felt his authority being challenged – a feeling which was totally unjustified.

Among the officers was Arthur Mull, a fellow pupil at Dollar Academy, who after service in France and Germany had been posted to Africa. We shared a room. Duties were not very burdensome and most Saturdays we were free to leave the camp. The Jinja Hotel was a splendid old colonial hostelry where on the Saturday the speciality was a curry prepared by the Goanese cooks. There are curries and curries, but the one in Jinja was a total masterpiece. Egon Ronay would not have had enough stars in his possession to recognise its merit.

One Saturday afternoon Arthur and I were relaxing with coffee seated outside on the large veranda when all of a sudden two large American shooting brakes drew up. Out stepped a very smartly dressed chauffeur who mounted the steps and asked politely whether it would be possible to obtain boiling water. A waiter appeared and left to bring the water. By now a rather stout elderly gentleman with thick glasses had emerged from one of the cars. It was the Aga Khan en route to Kampala to board his plane home to the south of France returning from having been weighed against diamonds at Dar-es-Salaam.

Of an evening two or three of us in a jeep would drive down to the edge of the golf course, switch on the headlights and frighten the hippos grazing. There was little danger so long as we did not get between the hippos and the waters of Lake Victoria.

Today there is a huge hydroelectric dam at Jinja but in 1946 the waters of the Nile rushed out of the lake in two main floods created by a large island in the middle of the cataract. On a flat stone there was a plaque bearing the words "Henry Speke" and the date (which I think was around 1860). The slack water below the rock was like a gigantic pool in which literally hundreds of Nile perch were swimming. Africans with long fibre plaited "fishing lines" with sort of grappling hooks used to swing the heavy hooks round and round and cast them over the backs of the perch and then with a sudden tug yank them. Very few casts failed to hook a fish, some of which must have been 8 to 10 pounds in weight.

A few weeks more and word came through – sailing from Mombasa on the *Nea Hellas* on such and such a date. The voyage home was quite an experience but we eventually sailed up the Clyde estuary on a beautiful autumn day right into the heart of Glasgow.

12

A Few Thoughts

SUPPOSE AT THIS point we put on hold these anecdotal ramblings and turn to more in-depth thoughts generated in the mind by three years' study for the ministry at Knox College, University of Toronto and a quarter of a century as a church of Scotland parish minister.

It was a dear privilege and honour to be a minister in the Church of Scotland, ordained and inducted to the parish of Monimail in my fortieth year. The service was conducted in the former Free Church (with its small red tiled spire) at the Bow of Fife, four miles west of Cupar. This building is no longer a place of worship. Monimail parish church lies to the west of Letham village close to the hamlet of Monimail. With the linkage and union of churches since my induction in 1963, like so many parishes, the name has been changed and is now called Creich, Flisk and Kilmany linked with Monimail.

In 1963 I was unmarried and lived a bachelor life rattling about in the large manse at Bow of Fife. I was married in St. Leonard's Church, Ayr on 5th December, 1964 to Leslie, the eldest daughter of Dr. and Mrs. James Smith. My father-in-law was Director of the Hannah Dairy Research Institute for around twenty years and died only last year, 2006, a month short of his 100th birthday.

This year, 2007, we will celebrate our 43rd wedding anniversary and for all these years Leslie has been a very dear wife, mother, grandmother and friend. James, our eldest, was born less than a year after we were married. He is married and lives in France. Nathalie, his wife, is a primary teacher and they have three beautiful children – Chloé, eight, Emma, six, and Louis, three. James is a professional mountain guide with his own business.

We have two daughters, Helen and Anne. Helen is married to Andy, and both of them are officers in Strathclyde Police. They have four beautiful children under eight who live nearby. The children are Erin, seven, Eilidh, six, Ryan, three, and Niamh, nearly two.

Anne lives in Glasgow. She is a very intelligent dear soul who, seated in the plane aged ten for a family holiday in Canada in 1981, solved the Rubick cube in mid-air. She was a physiotherapist in Glasgow, but realising that she was a square peg in a round hole she is now establishing herself as a skilled craftswoman bookbinder.

After ten years at the Bow of Fife the family moved to an even bigger manse in Ballater on Deeside where we lived for thirteen years before retiring to Ayr in 1986.

In September, 2007, Leslie and I drove to Oban for a four day break, Ayr to Greenock, a short visit with my cousin Betty Henderson in her 92nd year, a resident in Balclutha Court, then on over the Erskine Bridge. However on this drive north instead of driving up the west shore of Loch Lomond we continued on to Helensburgh, Rhu, and around the rather eerie perimeter of Faslane to Garelochhead, then a U-turn and down the road to Rosneath. This detour was in the form of a pilgrimage to find the grave of John McLeod Campbell (1800-1872).

In 1825 McLeod Campbell, who had been brought up in an Argyllshire manse, was presented by the then Duke of Argyll to the beautiful parish of Rhu on the shores of the Gareloch. Gradually during his ministry he became dissatisfied with God's gift in Christ being reserved for communicant members of the kirk, and began to extend the embrace of God's love in Christ to all. Evangelicals were offended, being strict Calvinists. McLeod Campbell was increasingly thought to be a heretic and in 1831 he was charged with heresy. The General Assembly of 1831, despite a petition in his favour signed by nearly all his parishioners and a moving appeal from his minister father, re-solved by 119 votes to 6 to depose him from the ministry.

Removed from his parish McLeod Campbell ministered to a body of enlightened souls in Glasgow until his health began to fail and he retired to Rosneath where he died and was buried in 1872.

My quarter of a century as a parish minister in the Church of Scotland was a dear and precious privilege, but the kirk's preoccupation with the peccadilloes of life began to cause me more than disquiet such as a neighbouring colleague seated outside the village hall taking the names of members going in for a flutter at the bingo, an earnest elder from lower down Deeside harassing Glenmuick Session for holding a raffle at our annual kirk sale in Ballater.

Dear Lord Jesus, we are but specks of dust on our planet home orbiting through space at 66,600 m.p.h., and as the wee crippled saintly Dane Soren Kierkegaard was wont to say, after listening to another of his bishop's moralizing sermons, "Dear Father in heaven, must this go on for ever?"

I too have become a universalist – why else would we have driven twelve miles down the narrow "no through road" to Rosneath? Sadly we did not find the grave in the old overgrown cemetery but I lent on one stone and offered up a wee word for one who had been a preacher of the global and cosmic embrace of God in the gift of Christ.

There was one bonus – the graveyard was entwined with bramble bushes bearing huge easily pickable fruit – so much so, visiting Fort William one day from Oban we bought two plastic food boxes in the supermarket and on the way home via Rest and Be Thankful we drove down to Rosneath and picked our winter harvest of brambles in less than half an hour.

Among the books reviewed in a recent issue of *Life and Work* is *Children of the Manse – Growing up in Victorian Aberdeenshire*.

Eleven children were born in the Manse of Keig, one of the sons was baptised William Robertson Smith. William was a gifted Hebrew scholar who as a young man became Professor of Old Testament in Aberdeen University. Professor Smith wrote an article which was published in the *Encyclopedia Britannica* raising questions about the literal interpretation of the Bible. The "true believer" hounds detected a whiff of heresy which led to a trial for heresy and the termination of Professor Smith's tenure of the Old Testament Chair.

We are not in the business of mocking the Victorian biblical literalists and their present day followers but the world was not created in October 4004 BC. I used to have a bible with that date, 4004BC, at the head of the middle column of the first chapter of Genesis.

The Bible is a miracle, a collection of sixty-six books, thirty-nine in the Old Testament and twenty-seven in the New Testament, a collection which contains much demonic nonsense. The words of George MacLeod, founder of the Iona Community, come to mind, who on entering a Church of Scotland bookshop where an assistant was busy setting up a special display of Bibles said with a twinkle in his eye "There's a lot of rubbish in the Bible that should be cut out, don't you think?" It is a miracle, a priceless gift from God to mankind, written by a bunch of authors, most of whom never met, over a period of many centuries and yet there is a golden thread running from the first verse of Genesis to the last of Revelation proclaiming His love for the global family in the sacrificial gift of Jesus Christ "the light and hope of the world".

Before venturing any further on this pilgrimage, all of which has been hand written by me and then typed by my dear wife Leslie, please may I digress for a few minutes to record what prompts me to make the effort.

From time to time our son James will say to me "Ah, but there are not many who think like you."

Even a casual reading of the "Global and Cosmic Embrace of Jesus Christ" (see The Appendices) sets me apart as unorthodox, even a heretic to many believers.

What I have in mind is to write and say things which will encourage people to think beyond the prison house of self, beyond family and loved ones, beyond community, beyond country and begin to think globally and cosmically.

This may sound piously self-righteous but every night I have a glass of water at my bedside from which I take in waking moments three sips offering thanks for this taken-for-granted blessing when so many fellow passengers on our planet home have no access to clean water.

Recently I was chatting to a couple of friends over a pint (or two) who found it difficult to understand the sense of guilt which assaults me from time to time when I treat myself to a good bottle of malt whisky. Our discussion was beyond the simple black and white issue, twenty pounds for whisky versus twenty pounds for Oxfam or Christian Aid.

With no desire to spoil anyone's Christmas the vast displays of gifts and the huge range of foodstuffs and confectionery in the supermarkets make me sad. I would hate to be a sales manager for many of these products. Sales managers have homes, wives and families to provide for – how are they going to do this in our cut throat rat race world? – we cannot all be living rough in the trouble spots of the world as agents for works of charity and mercy.

This journal is seasoned with blasts on my trumpet and accounts of my physical strength which might lead you to believe that I have a high opinion of myself – in fact you are right. Not in any bigheaded bombastic sense but as the harvest of belief that we are all subjects of a divine power.

St. Paul tells us "to stand fast in the liberty wherewith Christ hath set us free and become not entangled again with the yoke of bondage" – the bondage of religion.

<u>I live as Christ's freeman</u> – free from the shackles of the institutional church, free from all the pettifogging moralizing Victorian humbug of "what will the neighbours think", "nice people don't do that", free from the conventions of our class-ridden society – and yet a disciplined mortal under the loving constraint of God's embrace in Jesus Christ, a lifestyle which caused the late Professor Holmes, Director of the Wye Research Station in Kent, a colleague of my late father-in-law at whose bedside we met two years ago to remark moments after my wife and I had left the nursing home "What a nice man Leslie's husband is", and Andy, daughter Helen's husband and father of their four children under eight (Andy hails from Poole in Dorset), one day over a pint (or two) looked me in the eye and said "You are one of the nicest men I have ever met."

13

Africa to Britain and Demob

AROUND THE END of August 1946 I left Jinja on the first stage of the long journey to the UK, boarding an old liner doing service as a troopship – it was the *Nea Hellas*. Pre-war it had been part of the British Merchant Fleet, sold to a Greek line before 1939, and commandeered during the war.

I was one of a party of two, the other a K.A.R. captain who had been commissioned in a Scottish regiment. The passengers were a very mixed bag of service personnel. A day after sailing from Mombasa a news flash buzz spread on board. "The propeller is missing a blade – perhaps a detour to a dry dock in Bombay is on the cards". Fortunately, like lots of "news flashes" this (the detour) was untrue and we sailed up the east coast of Africa, round the Horn and into the Red Sea, which in early September was like an oven. Many of us, nearly naked, lay panting under awnings where we were joined by the ship's engineers, the engine room being too hot for steady duty. The engineers would pop down to check the various dials etc. of the ancient tub and hasten back up the companionway. On one quick shift two of us went down, and without exaggeration the metal rails etc. were almost too hot to touch – the temperature was 150 degrees F. Most of us on board felt that the old liner was well named "*Nea Hellas*", as near hell as we ever wanted to be. We eventually reached Suez and passed slowly through the canal to an anchorage in Port Said where we remained for about ten days.

The propeller, not cast in one huge piece, had three or four blades bolted to the shaft. French divers in the murky waters replaced the new blade which, about six feet long, lay on the open deck before being lowered. Like so many tasks for divers it must have been a minor nightmare.

We were free to go ashore. We swam in the Mediterranean or browsed around Port Said. Long before the ten days were up most of us were running short of cash. One morning about a dozen of us, a mixed bag of captains and lieutenants, entered the local army paymaster's office where a captain was seated behind a sort of bank screen. On the screen was a large notice, "NO CASHING OF CHEQUES FOR OFFICERS IN TRANSIT". Pleading started to turn to argument which I felt sure was not going to lead to any cheques being cashed. I retreated, went round the corner for a coffee, keeping a close eye on my watch, wallet and any other valuables. "Gully, Gully, Mr. McGregor, shoe-shine Mr. McGregor" – while the gully gully merchant, a young Egyptian boy with several large "egg" cups detracted your attention by trying to make you guess under which cup the chicken lay, the shoeshine merchant, whether employed to remove desert stour from footwear or not, would have been on wallet reconnaissance. Another favourite trick was if a breast pocket held a fountain pen with the clip fastened a newsvendor would approach "newspaper, newspaper, Mr. McGregor" and with a quick upward sweep of a rolled paper whip the pen out of the pocket.

Back to the paymaster's office. A friendly chat between captains and the good soul cashed a cheque for £10 which was a lot of money in 1946.

Elsewhere I have mentioned that brother David was also in East Africa with the K.A.R. His return to the UK was after mine but we had met in Nairobi where for reasons best known to himself he entrusted me with a few things to take home, among them a bottle of 5-star Martell Brandy. Not surprisingly the temptation was too great, a couple of us had emptied the bottle en route to Suez. My mother, when a widow in her seventies, always had a tiny flask of brandy in her handbag, in case of emergencies. Her younger son was not waiting for advancing years before resorting to the medicinal qualities of good brandy. After all one is not subjected every day to the trials of a sea voyage with a missing propeller blade.

Before leaving Port Said suppose we pause for a moment to record the story of the old country doctor visiting patients on foot, on horseback, or in pony and trap conveyances, in the cold days of winter who would resort to a brandy or two to keep out the cold (the fact that alcohol gives a fake sense of body warmth is a matter for medical research and not a topic for the ups and downs of the adventure of life).

It is difficult to smell one's own breath, as even those with advanced halitosis need to know as they puff into a cupped hand and feel that all is well. The common wisdom is that a whisky breath can be rather unpleasant whereas a brandy breath has a rather pleasant aroma. One cannot but wonder what an embrace from Winston Churchill would have been like.

Back to the doctor who was visiting the old soul lying dying on her bed, who, as the doctor lent over to comfort her, heard her whisper "Speak again doctor, your breath is refreshing."

Mention of Port Said brings to mind an action joke – really for rugby club dinners rather than the gentilities of the Woman's Guild. However, here it is. A battalion of the Highland Light Infantry had been posted to the Middle East and understandably before leaving the "dear green place" had a few pints in a Glasgow pub. Trains during the Second World War were invariably packed. Jammed into a train from Glasgow to London the lads in the middle of the carriages could not wriggle themselves to the relief of the toilets, particularly when wearing big packs on their backs. Into Euston, behind schedule, quick march on to the train for Southampton – sad bladder control situation – detrain on the dockside – single file up the gangplank – the wee jock out of the side of his mouth gasps to the sailor at the top "Where's the toilets Mack?" – "Port side, port side" – whereupon the wee jock almost in tears pleads "Can we no stop at Gibraltar?"

The ten pounds from my paymaster friend allowed me to replace David's empty brandy bottle from Simon Artz, the Harrods of the Middle East and still have a pound or two for socialising before leaving for Malta.

The Grand Harbour at Malta was our next stop where quite a number of mainly air force personnel, some with new wives, embarked. It is crudely unkind to record the thoughts of some of us that as the suntan faded on the white males their new wives would retain their tan. As we left the Grand Harbour there was a sudden cry of "man overboard", certainly a body was swimming about in the wake but we did not stop to investigate.

On the morning we passed through the Straits of Gibraltar we awoke to a thick mist and when it cleared the sea was seen to be calmer than any millpond. A sixpence dropped from the boat deck would have created quite a ripple.

And so through the Bay of Biscay, past Land's End, up the Irish Sea into the estuary of the Clyde – as I write retired in Ayr it is strange to recall that on a beautiful September morning in 1946 we sailed up between Arran and the Scottish mainland far up the Clyde almost into the heart of Glasgow.

In the autumn of 1946 my parental home was still in Huddersfield where I duly arrived after being driven from Edinburgh in a Standard Nine by Margaret Allan's mother. Margaret is a life-long friend of my sister Elizabeth whose father, an Australian, was a doctor in Halifax.

I have a vivid memory, not all the finer details, but of drawing up at Ebor Mount, 90 New North Road, and my excited mother giving me a warm embrace. After a few happy days at home it was still two or three months before my demobilisation number came up.

What to do? For some the route to demobilisation was via John Watson's School in Edinburgh, (yes John, not George, Watson's) where a Major Callender had the task of finding a short term berth for officers. My first trip was to the Cameron Barracks in Inverness, a beautiful trip by train in the autumn sunshine. An overnight stay was followed by an interview with the colonel after breakfast. Very politely he told me that I was no use to him with only two months still to serve. "Now Blyth, would you not consider signing on for a further eighteen months to help with the training of new recruits?" "Thank you Colonel, but I want to leave the army for the next stage on life's journey – possibly Edinburgh University." We shook hands and parted.

Another beautiful train trip in autumn sunshine back to Edinburgh and Major Callender. The next cast of the dice was a trip to Newbattle Abbey, chauffered by an attractive A.T.S. lass. An overnight stay and a day at Newbattle – even during the day at Dalkeith I was puzzled as to what was the object of this trip and so there are no memories of its purpose. Back to Edinburgh.

During the war Scotland was awash with Polish troops, many of them hoping to be repatriated. One camp was at Stewarton in Ayrshire where I duly arrived one dark wet evening. Another camp was at Auchinleck where I moved after a few days at Stewarton.

The large camp at Auchinleck had been a prisoner of war camp but was then the base for several hundred Poles awaiting repatriation. The large wooden huts with two-tiered bunks were designed for about eighty souls. The camp commandant was a lieutenant-colonel in a Scottish regiment who, with little for all of us to do, thought that a weekly kit inspection would be a good idea.

At that time, months after the end of the war in Europe, Poland, and indeed most of the continent, was in turmoil - political, economic and so on - with the result that staging a camp inspection at Auchinleck was well nigh impossible.

The huts, although large, were not of very robust construction, and there were strict orders "Nothing on the rafters" – to no avail – the lads had bicycles and all sorts of gear stowed aloft with the hope of taking their treasures back to Poland.

The Poles were polite gracious souls, who had a special knack in chatting up the girls, much to the annoyance of many a Scottish lad. They were also a great source of many things in short supply. They seemed to get their hands on nylons when they were unavailable in the local outfitters. Perhaps this is one reason for their success with the lassies.

The Poles belonged to quite distinct rival political views rather than parties, and unless placed with compatriots of like mind they would not share accommodation under any amount of persuasion, which resulted in some huts being nearly empty and the others vastly overcrowded.

My stay at Auchinleck was also short but I did accompany at least two large drafts to Auchinleck station as the first stage to Leith for a ship back to their beloved land. I have never been able to verify the rumour that some of these dear souls, after years of absence from Poland, were strung up at the dockside because of their political allegiances. The reason that my stay was short was because all of the Poles, as a major part of the repatriation plan, were required to be interviewed in the Polish Embassy situated in a large London house not far from the famous B.B.C. headquarters.

Train services that autumn were vastly curtailed because of the shortage of coal and so convoys of rather uncomfortable service buses travelled overnight from Ayrshire to London. One early winter night I escorted three buses from Kilmarnock with about one hundred Poles on the long trip to London. Going over Shap we stopped at the wee road-side café which, like so many of these spots during the war and after, was short of supplies. Not to be beat the lads nipped back to the buses and returned with ham sandwiches. They were welcome but rather tough, in fact they were raw bacon, not ham.

Our London base was the old Marylebone Station Hotel where, after a modest breakfast and a wash-and-brush up, we marched along the front of Madame Tussaud's to the west end. Dressed in my kilt and battledress tunic I led the parade as a captain in the Black Watch. Polish army top coats were excessively long, rather like some of the sketches of Napoleon's hordes retreating from Moscow, and each man was invariably clutching a brief case. After a sleepless night in cold buses the three ranks of around thirty-three were not exactly a bonny sight. Usually I am not easily embarrassed, but marching at the head of this tired, rather dispirited, crew prompted me to enrol a London-based Polish corporal to lead them while I popped along on the subway with the files of documents.

My stay in London must have been three or four weeks during which I was entertained to dinner in his London club by Paul Rodzianko, the famous Russian aristocrat who joined the British Army as a private and at that time was a lieutenant-colonel. He was a famous horseman who I am sure was once director of the Irish Olympic Equestrian Team.

Back to Ayrshire for a few days in December 1946, then off to York for demobilisation – a travel warrant to Huddersfield, a few quid in the hand plus a suit or sports jacket and flannels, a couple of shirts, tie, socks, shoes, all topped off with a pork pie hat.

14

Pre-University Farming Experiences

LIFE AT HOME again during Christmas was a strange experience after five years in the army. The problem was what to do now?

I had applied to Edinburgh University to study for a B.Sc. in Agriculture and had been granted a place to begin studies in the early autumn of 1947. One of the requirements for admission to the course was a year's practical experience.

Where to gain this? Crombie's at Grandholme Mills in Aberdeen had a modest farm around the mill. This was managed by a farmer, William Rennie, from the Mains of Dumbreck, Pitmedden, near Tarves. For years my father had been a financial adviser to John Ross the owner of Crombie's and so one January day my father and I travelled by train to Dinnet on Deeside where we had lunch in Profeits Hotel as guests of John Ross. After lunch we repaired to Melgum, the estate near Tarland, where we discussed arrangements for a meeting with Mr. Rennie.

The outcome was that I got settled into digs on another farm, Alehouse of Dumbreck, farmed by a good couple Johnny and Mrs. Lockhart. I lived with the grieve and his wife, a Mr. and Mrs. Gray.

In those days it was the custom for a "mud student" seeking agricultural experience to work for nothing. I always remember Mr. Rennie with a measure of largesse telling me that I was to receive £1 a week. My digs with Mrs. Gray cost 30 shillings, one pound and a half.

1947 was the winter of the tremendous late snows and it would have been March or April before I moved to Aberdeenshire. Mr. Rennie was retired by that time and his son William was the farmer in the farmhouse at Mains of Dumbreck. My time was spent on that farm interspersed with a period at North Mains of Pitmedden to learn milking. North Mains of Pitmedden belonged to Major James Keith, the donor of Pitmedden House to the National Trust.

At North Mains of Pitmedden there must have been about forty Ayrshire cows in the dairy herd milked by Alfa Laval machines but without a piped milk flow to the cooler. The team consisted of the dairyman Edwards, and an older man to help bring in the cows from the fields, wash the udders etc., and myself. Literally days after my joining them the dairyman was carted off to Aberdeen Royal Infirmary I think for an appendicitis operation.

The older man and I coped well, Being summer by now we began at 4 a.m. out to the fields to bring in the cows. My digs would have been a good mile away and I rode my Rudge Whitworth bicycle. One night it had been misty and my bicycle sitting outside had wet rims. Flying along there was a steep brae with a right-handed bend at the foot. The story is told. The brakes on the wet rims were useless and I hit a dry stone dike and finished up in the field below the road. Thinking back on it now it was a miracle that I was not injured or even killed.

One of my pastimes while milking was to run my hand along the backs of the cows feeling for the swellings in the hide below which would be the large maggots of Hypoderma Bovis, the warble fly of cattle (Hypoderma Lineatum being the warble fly of deer). In former years it used to be a common sight to see cattle with their tails up tearing around the fields attempting to avoid the attentions of the warble flies. The life cycle of these flies was a most involved and interesting one as the various stages of development from eggs to maggots progressed through the body. A certain skill was required in determining the ripeness of the maggots as attempts to force them out could lead to them being burst which could result in a rather bad ulcer. Of course warble fly damage to hides could render them in come cases worthless to the tanners.

A large acreage of potatoes was grown, some as "seed tatties", others as ware for eating. All the planting was done by a squad of women, the wives of the farm staff plus a few extra from the village. In our case the potatoes were planted from flat wooden boxes with a length-wise handle. Elsewhere in Scotland in those years the tatties tended to be planted from a potato sack tied around the waist of the planter.

At the Mains of Dumbreck there was a large indoor reed for the winter feeding of cattle destined for the store ring and the butchers. Released to the fields in late spring the mammoth task was getting hundreds of tons of dung to the land. Although there were two tractors on the farm the dung was forked by hand into the boggies then clawed with a special long tined rake from the tilted boggies as they progressed slowly across the fields. The next herculean task was to spread the heaps by hand. Life not only on the land but in towns and cities sixty years ago was vastly different from today. Only one farm worker in several hundred would have an old car or a van, bicycles were the order of the day, down to the bus stop and a hurl into Aberdeen. These hard-working souls with very modest incomes were for the most part a kind happy contented crowd.

One morning during a break I was seated on the end rig beside an old orraman, who, unmarried, had spent all his days living in farm bothies. He must have been born in the 1880s and as we blethered away he showed me proudly a large shiny pocket watch which had cost him six months' wages, £6.

Harvest came round and while there were a few combines in 1947 the bulk of even large farms were without them. The oats and barley (there was very little wheat in Aberdeenshire at that time) were cut with a large binder throwing out sheaves every few feet or yards depending a bit on the heaviness of the crop. All the sheaves were then hand-stooked usually in groups of eight sheaves.

At the Mains of Dumbreck there was a long narrow field of 36 acres, that's a big field – the crop was barley and the bulk of the 36 acres were stooked by the cattleman and myself with occasional help. Barley has prickly awns and after stooking for eight hours on a very hot day our sides were almost raw with a red rash.

Most weekends I bussed into Aberdeen to spend two days with Mary Stephen, an older sister of my mother's. She was the one who had been matron at St. Columba's, Kilmacolm, in her younger days. She was a bit of a rolling stone and at that time was managing a small temperance hotel on Union Street in Aberdeen. Despite rationing she used to feed me up on steaks, lemon sole and all manner of good things.

Sometimes I wonder what might have happened had I joined the local Young Farmers' Club. Who knows, I might have met a farmer's daughter and lived out my days on the fertile fields of Aberdeenshire!

Young Bill Rennie used to do a bit of contracting work on neighbouring farms and one day he was over "furring up" a field of tatties on Bonnyton, farmed by Charlie Sleigh. In the middle of the afternoon we were working in the steading when the tractor came fleeing into the close with Bill as white as a sheet. What had happened was a small meteorite had ploughed into the field only yards from his tractor and given him a tremendous fright. The truth of this tale was verified a couple of weeks later when by then a circular bare patch about thirty feet across was plainly visible from the fields at Dumbreck.

Mr. and Mrs. Gray were good kind souls with no family. Despite rationing we fed well. Occasionally the evening meal's main course was a gigantic steam pudding. Mrs. Gray was not afraid to put plenty of tea leaves in the huge teapot which were masked before we sat down to the meal, the pot being set on the trig at the side of the open fire. She was a great one to talk and I devised a wee game with myself – taking a note of the time elapsing between the boiling water hitting the tea leaves and the first cup emerging from the spout it was never less than twenty minutes. It was a pretty powerful brew but having been out in the fresh air all day it was most refreshing.

In my bedroom there was a double metal bed with no mattress, only the heavy wire netting of the base. It was a hot summer and I slept on or rather in a huge heavy duty cotton bag filled with chaff from the threshing mill. Whether I was on or in this couch depended upon the degree of my restlessness during the night.

Mr Lockhart had been badly wounded in the First World War with the major part of his upper arm missing (I cannot remember whether right or left) but the hand of the damaged arm could still grip and when he came into the cottage to pay his grieve he would remove his cap and place it on the table. On departure he would grip the cap with the handicapped arm, clasp the wrist with his good hand and arm, and clap his bonnet on his head.

One glorious summer day towards the end of the harvest, the stooked sheaves were driven into the stackyard to be built into huge stacks. Building of stacks was a skilled job and the stackers of neighbouring farmers used to vie with one another in the building of the trimmest stack. A Sunday afternoon pastime for some farmers with their ladies was to drive round and pass opinions on which they thought were the neatest stacks – always after their own at home!!

On this day a volley of shots was heard around the steading. When the grieve and the squad arrived back in the close they enquired of the boss whether he had had any success in killing a few rats. Johnny Lockhart with his gammy arm was not the best shot in the district but he answered their enquiry by telling them "I didna' kill any rats but I gave them one hell of a fright."

Apart from all the hard manual work the revolving seasons of the year provided some fun and recreation. Most harvest fields were cut with the binder going round in a clockwork direction and as the standing crop still left uncut became smaller and smaller the young lads from the farm cottages or the village would appear each armed with a stick. Invariably there would be a few frightened rabbits, even hares slowly crowding into the centre. The time came when they would make a run for it and great was the fun as the lads tried to kill a rabbit or two. This may seem a cruel sport to some but these rabbits provided nourishing meals for often large families where the budget was small.

Over the winter the farms without combines were visited by the travelling threshing machine, a massive affair pulled by a large steam traction engine and often with a sleeping cabin for the crew. Drawn up between the neat rows of stacks the whole stackyard was a hive of industry. A wide leather belt round the fly wheel of the traction engine drove the mill which shuddered back and forward. On the top of the mill would be two souls, rather precariously perched, cutting the bands of the sheaves as they were forked to them from both sides. Not only was the grain shaken from the heads of corn, but the chaff was blown out the side, and the straw came out bundled either for bedding or feed. The oats or barley came out of spouts into jute bags which were sitting on weighing machines. The bags when filled weighed two hundredweight, 224 lbs. Tasks on the mill were rotated. Carrying the filled sacks up the old worn stone steps to the loft granary was one of the heavier jobs in the whole threshing process. Invariably the weighing machine was a simple balance affair, four half hundredweight weights on one platform, the bag of grain on the other.

These farm weights provided training for those strong enough to engage in the heavy events at Highland Games and also recreational challenges. On summer evenings after the bothy supper the men would vie with one another as to who could do the most press-ups with the 56 lb. weights.

Even with a few cats prowling about rats were always a problem on farms. Despite the stacks being clear of the ground on stethels (the stone or metal toadstools) very few stackyards would have been rat free. A roll of wire netting made a quick fence and it was quite a sight to see a terrier, often a Jack Russell, kill a rat with one bite, and toss it up in the air ready for the next one.

All of us have regrets in life and two which from time to time come up on the computer of my mind are as follows.

As stated earlier I was paid £1 per week and my digs with Mrs. Gray were 30 shillings and for some reason or no reason at all I did not pay her on a regular basis. On the day of my departure Mrs. Gray was a bit agitated because I owed her about £10 which I had left on the kitchen table. It is hard to express on paper my real sorrow for the behaviour when the household budget of these good souls did not allow for unpaid guests at the family board.

Now for the second regret (there are possibly a hundred reasons during my long pilgrimage on our planet home for being regretful but suppose I confine them to two).

It happened in the Borders at Gilston, the home of Robert and Tommy Dunn, the great Cheviot sheep farmers. All of us had been boarders at Dollar Academy. Among the gang was the late Walter McAinsh, medical student at Edinburgh University. The identity of the other two or three remains a blank. We had been down at the famous Carfrae Mill Hotel for a few drams before returning to Gilston where we continued to imbibe a few more drams to lubricate the increasingly more ludicrous anecdotes of times at the old grey school beneath the sheltering hills.

Robert and Tommy were still unmarried and their housekeeper had more than once keeked round the doors hinting that it was long past time for bed when lo and behold car lights came up the drive and who should alight but Douglas Elliot, a neighbouring farmer and a great stalwart in many a rugby game for Scotland. Douglas was clutching a bottle of good malt whisky which we began to sample. By this time it must have been long past midnight but we thought it would be a good idea to telephone a few neighbouring farmers feeling it would be a shame if they missed such a good going party. Telephone calls were relayed through a local switchboard and after drawing rather abrupt declinings from our invitations there was a pause and the telephone operator called to ask if there was likely to be any further calls that night (that morning). Sadly we abused him with drunken remarks that we were paying for the services of the telephone, etc., etc.

It is too late now to pen a letter of apology to the leading Border paper but this daft episode "gars me greet".

15

EDINBURGH UNIVERSITY AND TATTIE ROGUING

BEFORE THE END of September 1947 I left Aberdeenshire to start the three year course at Edinburgh University leading to a B.Sc. in Agriculture. Bill Rennie was sorry to see me go. Although agricultural wages were modest my one pound a week did not break the bank. I was quite happy to have spent the glorious summer in the open air in a part of Scotland which I had not visited before and master an understanding of the unique "fit like" dialect.

My first berth in Edinburgh was at 14 Blackford Avenue, a large three-storey terraced house owned and run by an elderly Miss MacLean, daughter of a Free Church minister. There must have been ten incumbents including my sister Elizabeth. We fed in a large dining room seated round a big Victorian table. Blackford Avenue was very convenient for classes at Kings Buildings.

The four subjects in first year were Physics, Chemistry, Zoology and Botany, all held at K.B. apart from Botany down at the Botanic Gardens. These four subjects were common to the first year of agriculture and forestry. About half the class would have been ex-service students who experienced (I was going to write "suffered" but that would have been an exaggeration) a measure of difficulty adjusting to the discipline of attending classes.

Here is one wee anecdote from the practical zoology class. In the exam we were required to dissect a rat and name a list of twenty organs sticking small cardboard flags on "cocktail sticks" into each part identified. One character in the forestry class who had been a pilot in the Royal Air Force during the war soon got frustrated with the microsurgery, and plunged a stick into the middle of the exposed innards bearing the letters R.I.P. and promptly walked out!

Before the end of the first year I was offered a place in Cowan House, the men's residence on the south side of George Square. Good as had been the digs at 14 Blackford Avenue I readily accepted sharing a large top floor room with a delightful older regular naval officer, Lieutenant-Commander John Murray. John was married with a home in the Borders and for reasons best known to himself he had resigned his commission.

Although I did enough studying to pass the exams several nights a week I would be out raking the town with a few pals and a few beers. Without a late pass the front doors of Cowan House were closed every night by 10.30 p.m. Frequently John would have been fast asleep on my return and I remember him congratulating me on my silent return. The nursery lock-up hour (by today's standard) of 10.30 p.m. did not bring an end to entry. Among the characters in Cowan House was Harvey Andrews, a medical student who, despite losing a leg in the war, could scale the high wall at the south side of the Cowan House back garden.

Cowan House in the austere days of continued war time rationing was an amazing haven – breakfast, lunch, supper or dinner, plus evening snacks, spotlessly clean rooms with fresh bed-linen and towels all for £3 per week.

Ex-service folks were given grants for further education, in my case £200 per year which sounds a paltry sum today. But in 1947 it went a long way. Mentioned above is the three pound charge per week for residence in Cowan House. Three ten-week terms, £30 per term, £90 per year, leaving £110 for books, socializing, etc. My grant was upped to £220 later on in the course.

Grants were not the total income for the year. Many students had vacation jobs and one which was quite lucrative was potato roguing and potato inspecting. The East of Scotland College of Agriculture ran a course at East Craigs just north of the Maybury roundabout where there were small plots of around one hundred different varieties of potato. At first acquaintance one plot of potato plants looked much like any other. However after a few days it was amazing how the individual leaf characteristics began to register and at the end of the ten day course most of us passed the test to identify correctly twenty-five varieties out of thirty and also identify potato disease such as leaf roll, blackleg and various types of mosaic.

On passing we were appointed potato inspectors by the Department of Agriculture and given a district. In my case it was north-east Aberdeenshire. Before leaving Edinburgh for Aberdeenshire there was time to do a spot of roguing. I palled up with a good friend from school days, John McGilchrist, who played on the wing in our championship rugby XV 1941-1942. John was studying chemistry at Edinburgh University and was a senior member of staff at the Ardeer explosive factory later in life. Sadly John died a few years ago after a long struggle with a degenerative disease.

John had a motor bike, unfortunately with no padding on its pillion. However we did not travel far. Most of our trips were into the Lothians. One roguing job which we took on I will never forget. It was a twenty acre field of Majestic potatoes at Tranent. We agreed a fixed sum for roguing the whole field and came to regret our bargain with the farmer. The shaws of the Majestic were almost shoulder high, there were quite a few rogues, and we had agreed to carry off the rogues to the end riggs instead of laying the shaws of the rogues across the drills for farm workers to pick up later. However we were young men, out in the fresh air and glad to be alive after the carnage of the Second World War. John had also been in the services.

Off to Aberdeenshire. Inspectors worked in pairs – my partner as senior inspector was George Gill from Bloodymyres farm, Macduff. He provided the transport with his Wolseley Hornet car. Our first digs were at Mintlaw Station, west of Peterhead, with a brother and sister. The sister had a daughter, a senior pupil at Peterhead Academy. It was a very interesting but sad household in which the brother and sister had not spoken to each other for about fifteen years. In outline what had happened, and I have no desire to pen a word which might offend any relative or friend who may read this, was that the brother had advised his sister not to marry her husband, the father of the girl. Very shortly after her wedding the husband departed. The brother said "I told you not to marry him" and so sadly the cloak of silence descended.

The brother was the local postman who apart from his round had the small post office with a petrol pump outside. He was a bit unusual, attributed by many to harrowing experiences in the First World War and I have no desire to make fun at his expense – but Wednesday was half day at the post office and occasionally but not too often one of the local wags would enter the post office two or three minutes before 1 p.m. After the usual pleasantries "fit like the day Jimmy?" postie would enquire the nature of the other's need – "two tuppeny stamps please." Postie would open the heavy desk drawer, withdraw the large stamp ledger, and begin to tear two stamps off the sheet – when the large clock on the back wall would strike one. "Half day" declared the postman, the ledger was slammed and returned to the drawer. The local wags who staged this drama three or four times a year knew that there was no point in trying to persuade the custodian of the postage to part with the stamps requested.

We must have had a list of fifty to sixty farms to visit to inspect the crops that were hopefully for the famous and valuable Scottish seed potato trade, not only to England, but overseas to countries such as Egypt and Cyprus. Each farm called for two inspections or occasionally, if the grade we awarded was borderline, the farmer was allowed to re-rogue his crop with the hope that it would finally receive a good grade.

The Aberdeenshire seed tattie growers knew what they were about – and from memory very few fields failed to pass the necessary grade. Of course hospitality for two growing lads in their middle twenties varied from a full flight farm midday meal to a great range of coffees and assorted eats, and of course the occasional dram.

One morning around 11 a.m. we did our second inspection at a farm just west of Sandhaven, farmed by a middle-aged bachelor. His housekeeper received us with the news that the boss was off to the bank in Fraserburgh but would not be long. We inspected the crop, compared notes from our inspection books and agreed to award top grade, and with that he drove into the close. "Come in for a minute lads" – we sat "newsing" and told him the grade for his field. A short pause, then "You'll tak a dram?" With a modest pause we indicated that a dram would be welcome. The good man produced a bottle about a quarter full, placed two tumblers on the table and emptied the bottle between the two while at the same time announcing that he did not drink whisky himself. Diluted with water the two large measures of gold nectar were soon disposed of and we parted with firm handshakes on our way to the Saltoun Arms in Fraserburgh for lunch.

My memory is that the car was an open car, however in the light of what took place on our drive to Fraserburgh perhaps it would have been better had we been hooded in. Between the farm and Fraserburgh there was a fish manure factory at Sandhaven. Now there are Richter scales for earthquakes, scales for gales and hurricanes, but if there had been a scale for the pong coming off the fish manure processing plant the measuring instrument would have blown a gasket. Unfortified by a good dram I genuinely wonder whether we would ever have reached Fraserburgh for lunch.

As a reader of *The Herald* newspaper I enjoy reading Charlie Allan's couthy column. One of the farms on our tattie inspection round was farmed by Charlie's father, John R. Allan of *Farmer's Diary* fame. This farm was visited by George Gill and myself mid-morning and after inspecting the tatties and awarding a grade we were invited into the farm kitchen. Many Aberdeenshire farms in those days had a cheese press at the back door, a heavy granite cube which squeezed the cheese in the early stages of its life. On the kitchen table was a magnificent home-made cheese weighing possibly five pounds. Shall we say that George and I did full justice to that marvellous home-made kebbock.

These ramblings are turning into a book on tattie inspecting or rather personal anecdotes while in Aberdeenshire as a Department of Agriculture potato inspector. Depending on the number of farms and the quality of the crops we were employed for nearly a month. The daily rate of pay was quite good for the late 1940s, and enabled us to save £50 to £60 which was a handsome bonus for a student on a £200 per annum grant (increased to £220 in my final year).

A couple more capers while working in Aberdeenshire, and before writing them down please believe me when I say that George Gill and I were diligent, conscientious tattie inspectors who could cause quite a large financial loss to a farmer if we downgraded or did not pass his crop as seed.

To a large extent we were our own masters and so one year, maybe each year, we took a day off to attend the two day agricultural show at Turriff. One of the entertainment features at the show was sulky racing – lightweight jogging carts tearing around the track. This was no light-hearted fun imitation of the professional sulky jockeys around the globe, but a serious business with bookies in attendance. Lubricated with a couple of beers George and I were strolling along a raised part of the games field perimeter where the arms of the bookies were flaying about with their own semaphore signals, and spontaneously we thought we would give them a hand. We must have looked like a couple of daft fools as we began to imitate their signalling. Not surprisingly we were quickly advised to depart from the track in language which an old retired minister dare not confine to paper.

Another tale from the agricultural show at Strichen below Mormond Hill, where we went to join the marquee dance in the evening. Among the revellers was a farmer whose tatties were awarded a good grade earlier in the week. To avoid the crush at the marquee bar this rural worthy had a bottle of rum in his pocket and he was delighted to share a good part of its contents with "officials" of the Department of Agriculture.

16

STRATHARDLE

IN THE EARLY summer of 1950 I graduated B.Sc. in Agriculture from Edinburgh University. Wisely or unwisely the University had "lowered the cross-bar" for ex-service graduates. In my case even though I had graduated there was a re-sit in practical chemistry. Instinctively I knew that I would never return to Kings Buildings but I went through the motions by starting work on the Bass Rock Farm, North Berwick, handy for Edinburgh and Kings Buildings.

The Bass Rock was a small farm by East Lothian standards but a very successful intensively farmed one, with dairy and poultry departments. The farm was owned by the Wright brothers, Willie Wright being the dairy expert. Traditionally agriculture graduates or students had formed part of the staff. Jimmy was the dairyman assisted by three of us, myself and Maurice, who was another member of our graduating class, and Ruth Dundas.

I lived in digs with postie Malcolm and his wife, firstly in a pre-fab (the famous post-war solution to the housing shortage), and later in a larger council house. Work would have begun around 5.00 a.m. and my task was the feeding and care of the young stock and the two large Ayrshire bulls.

While I enjoyed my time in North Berwick the possibility of re-sitting a chemistry exam soon crystallized into wishful thinking and I began to wonder where to look for another job. It must have been during my stay in North Berwick that I had an interview with Scottish Agricultural Industries. Not surprisingly I was unsuccessful.

A firm of Chartered Accountants on the north side of St. Andrew Square in Edinburgh had among their clients a Perthshire laird, Francis Keir Balfour of Kindrogan and Dirnanean. Keeping financial records was not his forte – once or twice a year the accountants would receive a box of jumbled invoices, receipts, bank deposits and cheque book stubs. A senior partner, I am going to call him Mr. Lorimer, and my father were part of the team who laid the foundation stones for United Biscuits. In the course of a conversation my name cropped up and it was thought that I might become a right hand man to Francis Balfour.

The outcome was that I travelled to Perth by train early in 1951 to be interviewed and have lunch in the Station Hotel. Mr. Balfour offered me the job and a couple of weeks later I arrived in Enochdhu, the wee hamlet north of Kirkmichael in Strathardle, on the road from Blairgowrie via Bridge of Cally and Kirkmichael to Moulin and Pitlochry.

Unmarried my home was the one to the north end of a row of six or seven. These cottages had been recently rebuilt transforming single storey basic dwellings into very comfortable attractive small houses.

The estate office was in Kindrogan House, a large square room with a huge double desk – double in the sense of occupants facing one another about eight feet apart.

Kindrogan and Dirnanean were the heart of the estate plus tenancies of Balvarran, Balnakilly, Whitefield and some Ashintully Castle ground – in all about 20,000 acres. Between shepherds, keepers, foresters, grieves, tractormen, gardeners, chauffeur, and six staff at Kindrogan, the total staff was around forty. They were paid monthly and one of my duties was to make up cash pay packets and deliver them.

The laird, F.K. as I will call him, was a great gadget man. 1951 being shortly after the end of the Second World War surplus vehicles were on offer from many sources. We had several American vehicles, a couple of jeeps (one of them being my transport), a large Dodge truck with four wheel drive and a range of gears which enabled it to challenge the amazing jeeps on steep and difficult terrain, two tracked vehicles not unlike Bren carriers and, F.K.'s pride and joy, a huge Mack snowplough.

During my three and a half years at Enochdhu I lunched Monday to Friday with the family at Kindrogan. Most of the year there were only three of us for lunch as Mr. and Mrs. Balfour had no family. However F.K. had a younger brother Pat who was a tea planter in India. Along with his wife and two schoolgirl daughters they would be part of the household for short periods. Mrs. Balfour's mother, Lady Dolby, was still alive, and she, with son Reginald and his wife and family of four (Joy, George, William and Mary) were part of the household from time to time, particularly during the grouse shooting season. Lady Dolby's sister Mrs. Shaw would arrive to join the household making a round dozen seated at the large dining room table.

Kindrogan had six indoor staff, Rowe the butler (a superb old retainer who must have been over seventy), a table-maid, a cook and a kitchen maid, a housekeeper and her assistant. These good souls were all resident, either in the house or, in Rowe's case, a cottage attached to the rear which he shared with his wife. In another cottage next to Rowe's was an elderly handyman Crerar (I forget his first name) who milked a couple of cows, providing milk, cream and butter. There were too a gardener at Kindrogan, another at Dirnanean and Arthur Walker the chauffeur who lived at Dirnanean. Arthur was a special pal of mine. Mention of first names and their escape from memory makes me write the fact that Rowe, Crerar and the gardeners, and indeed the whole forty on the estate with possibly a couple of exceptions, were addressed by their surnames.

Mr. and Mrs. Balfour were rarely absent from home but on the odd occasion that they were I would be seated alone in the dining room waited upon by Rowe and Margaret the table-maid.

My cottage was a well furnished wee home, with two open fires. Fortified by five days of lunches, and not infrequently dinner of an evening if I had been working in the office late in the day, my own catering tended to be routine. Not every week but many a week I had bacon and eggs <u>fourteen</u> times. The kitchen living room had an oven cooker, and this was supplemented by a two ring Calor gas cooker on which sat the frying pan ready for action. Very few rural dwellings in those days were free from the odd field mouse guest and most mornings while lighting the gas ring there would be traces of mouse activity in the congealed fat. Provided there was no sign of droppings "gas ignited and off we go".

Time in the office occupied only a small part of the day. Outside tasks were many. The blackface sheep flocks were gathered several times a year for inoculations, dippings, clippings and so on. Particularly at the clippings in July the estate shepherds were joined by ten or more shepherds from neighbouring estates. The squad had to be fed and I would collect the lamb stew etc. from the wife of the shepherd whose flock was being clipped that day. In that part of Perthshire the clipping, dipping area is called the fank, hence fank stew. A couple of days before any get-together I would deliver a lamb or sometimes two from the larders and a couple of wives would do all the preparation and cooking. Even on a warm July day fank stew was a super midday meal. Bread and cheese were also on the menu, washed down with screwtop bottles of Whitbread's beer. Clipping is hard work and the squad were hungry, and I used to be amazed at the quantities consumed and wondered how they coped in the afternoon bent over a heavy struggling ewe.

Apart from delivering the lunch I would be part of the squad. One clipping day at Dirnanean there was quite a heavy shower of rain which delayed the start. The fleeces were dry enough around midday. That afternoon I dragged over five hundred heavy ewes to the clippers flipping them over on to their rears to be grasped by the shepherd. Dragging blackfaced ewes by their horns called for a good measure of strength and skill if horns were not to be broken off. Only one ewe lost a single horn. By evening I was pretty tired.

The fleeces were folded in a special way and packed into huge jute sacks which were suspended from a heavy beam. The young folk on the estate loved to take turns jumping up and down inside the sacks to pack the fleeces.

Forestry on the estate was a major enterprise, felling mature trees, thinning plantations, and planting large areas with young spruce and larch. Before my arrival at Enochdhu F.K. had sold a lot of mature trees to the Coal Board, sufficient for them to install a saw mill at the end of the village.

With a potato sack tied round one's middle, and with perhaps sixty young trees in the "pouch", the trees were planted with a spade making a "T" cut in the ground then inserting the tree, stamping around it and on to the next. On a steep hillside this was not work for the faint-hearted.

At the end of January/beginning of February 1953 central Scotland was struck by a tremendous gale with winds more than 100 m.p.h. A great deal of property was badly damaged and in the course of a couple of days more timber was blown down than would be felled in a year.

One morning during a slight pause in the fierceness of the gale F.K. and I were up the back drive with bushman saws trying to keep the road open to Dirnanean. It was absolute madness but being the younger man by about twenty years I did not want to "call chicken". F.K. did not like to be beaten but after a few more near misses he suggested we retreat. We were standing on the open area at the gateway into Dirnanean when there was one particularly fierce blast and a stand of about a dozen sixty-foot high spruce went down like a bunch of skittles.

The estate had an old-fashioned sawmill with two foresters, Bob Dare and Dan McKenzie. The sawmill was fine for milling fence posts and timber lengths for estate maintenance but would never cope with the huge mass of wind-blown trees. Without delay F.K. purchased a Stenner bandsaw mill from Devon which was soon installed on a new site.

Chainsaws may have been available but all the fallen trees were cut with crosscut saws, the largest being seven or eight feet in length. Bob Dare was not a young man but he and Dan McKenzie, who had served with the Black Watch and been taken prisoner at Dunkirk, worked like a couple of men possessed. Some of the ornamental trees around Dirnanean house had huge trunks with butts five or six feet in diameter. Lorries in those days were not fitted with hydraulic lifts and logs were pushed manually up heavy timber skids on to the lorries. Occasionally the men had help from other workers, but to see the size of some of the trunks manhandled up onto the lorries was an endless source of admiration and amazement.

Some months after the installation of the Stenner bandsaw there was an unfortunate accident. Unlike the old estate mill with the "bed" manually operated this "bed" (the long flat platform of the mill) was power driven, forward carrying the log through the revolving blade and driving back to turn the log for the next cut. On the side of the mill was a tubular metal safety guard. Unfortunately Bob stepped to the forward side of this guard and his legs were caught by the returning heavy platform and badly broken. Bob Dare and his wife had no family. They lived in a detached cottage, Woodend, with a fine garden. Like so many of the old Scottish estate workers they were nature's gentle souls full of loving kindness.

This chapter is turning out to be a book in itself, but forgive me for I would like to recall a few more memories of three happy years in a Perthshire glen.

About one hundred acres of potatoes were grown for seed. They were planted by hand, and harvested by being lifted by hand after being spun out on to the top of the drills by a "tattie digger". The lifting was done by a squad of estate wives, school children and others brought in from Kirkmichael. While it was hard work, on a beautiful calm sunny October day it was great to be alive. I was in charge of the squad, perhaps thirty souls, depending upon the size of the field and the length of the drills. Large bunches of twigs were cut from the hedgerows and stuck in the ground to mark out "a bit" for each picker. It required an eagle eye to keep an eye particularly on some of the youngsters who, when backs were turned, would try to shorten their "bit". Tractors with boggies would drive up and down the field while two men would lift the filled tattie "skulls" and empty them into the slowly moving boggie.

The tatties were then driven off to be pitted – a long ridge of potatoes with a triangular cross-section gradually covered with straw and earth. Come the spring or depending on the weather during the winter the potatoes would be "dressed". (Leslie and I were married in Ayr in December, 1964, and Leslie, a "townie", was transported overnight to the peace of rural Fife. For the first time she came in contact with certain farming terms but was particularly puzzled by the term "dressing tatties" – quite understandably if you pause for a moment to think.) Dressing tatties of course is the process of passing them over an oscillating tray, with various sizes of hole. In the case of seed potatoes the too large potatoes go for ware, the domestic market, the too small ones go for animal feed and the middle-sized were bagged and tagged for the valuable market for the famed Scots seed trade. The seed potatoes were exported not only to England but to Cyprus, Egypt and elsewhere in North Africa.

The estate had two or three hundred out-wintered cows, a few Highland with the large horns, Shorthorn Highland crosses, Galloways crossed, and a few pure bred of each.

One winter's day we tied up in the byres at Dirnanean about one hundred and fifty cattle. Bear in mind that many of them had never been handled before – it was quite a rodeo. That evening long after dark my telephone rang, F.K. on the line "James, are you game to come in the Mack snowplough to 'rescue' the vet from Finegand just south of the Spittal of Glenshee?" The cattle were tied ready for a government test and we certainly did not want to release them to the hill and have the rodeo repeated later in the week.

F.K. arrived in the snowplough with Mrs. Balfour seated beside him. I clambered in and we left Enochdhu on quite a calm winter evening. By the time we reached Glenshee from Kirkmichael there was a howling gale with drifting snow. The first mile to the lodge at Glenkylrie was relatively easygoing but then there is a steep S- bend hill with high banks. The snow must have been five feet deep. We battered our way through a yard at a time, reaching the crest of the brae where still today on the east side of the road there is a large roads department yard. The blizzard was arctic. F.K. was the last guy on the planet to be beat, but he bellowed out above the noise of the engine and the storm "We will never reach Finegand tonight." I jumped out and guided the monster vehicle which after several "cuts" was facing back the way we had come. In the half hour needed for these manoeuvres the S-bend was filled to the brim again with snow. However downhill was a much easier task and we escaped from a freezing night stormbound in Glenshee. It was long after midnight when we reached Enochdhu. Despite the lateness of the hour the three of us had tea and something to eat and F.K. drove me home.

Not to bore you with all the details of our adventures but here is another outing with the plough. F.K. was a leading light in the area branch of the National Farmers' Union and he was scheduled to speak at a meeting in Aberfeldy. The highest stretch of the hill road over to Moulin and Pitlochry was blocked. F.K. led the way on the Mack and I followed driving his Land-rover. It was a pretty wild day with heavy snow showers and at one point the huge vehicle slid into the ditch. It must have taken an hour to get back on the road, F.K. with a cigar stub in his mouth lying on his side under the plough and half under the rear wheels while I passed him large wooden battens and huge metal "door-mats" and did a bit of digging. The Mack was parked beside the cottage at the top of the steep brae down to Moulin. We jumped into the Land-rover and finally reached Aberfeldy where amazingly quite a number of farmers were patiently waiting. F.K. sowed his seeds of wisdom on the whole business of British agriculture with special emphasis on the challenges of hill sheep farming.

Incidentally the estate had, if not a contract, a gentleman's agreement to keep the hill road from Enochdhu to Moulin open in the winter.

One weekend I drove to Dollar for a party returning late on the Sunday evening. Foolishly I had no spare wheel on the jeep. All was well, Yetts of Muckhart, Dunning, over the level crossing on the main Dundee–Aberdeen line, across the River Earn and quietly along below the high wall of Dupplin Castle gardens, when there was the most almighty bang – the retreaded front tyre on the offside had "given up the ghost". What to do? After a minute's pause I started up, progressed a few yards slowly. Apart from a shaking in the steering the driving was not too bad. Off we go! It was around one o'clock in the morning and I reckoned that so long as Perth was driven through without being stopped all would be well. Thirty-five miles even in an American jeep with a flat tyre is not to be recommended. However I reached home safely around 3 a.m. Sleep was slow in coming as I lay shaking in the bed. Believe it or not the heavy duty steel wheel was none the worse.

The grieve at the Davan farm raised a huge pig which he wished to sell at Blairgowrie market. One day several batches of lambs were being sold also. Their sale made a sort of day out for the shepherds. F.K. and I were driving down in a small Ford van people carrier – no problem, we will take the huge pig. For the two miles from the Davan to Enochdhu all was well. Before reaching Kirkmichael the pig was getting restless, then it started to butt itself against the back of the front seats, nearly putting F.K. through the windscreen. We stopped at a joiner's yard near Ballintuim and picked up a large piece of thick chipboard. Long before Bridge of Cally I was lying on the floor in the back of the van jammed between the seats and the board being butted by the agitated pig. Two or three miles short of the sale ring the board split in two and you can imagine I was quite a sight on emerging. Our shepherds were gathered nearby and had a good laugh.

Mrs. Balfour kept household accounts, although I wonder what value they were when I recall an incident one evening. We were seated opposite one another at the large desk when suddenly Mrs. Balfour asked me "James, what does 6s.6d. and 7s.6d. make?" I replied "Fourteen shillings" whereupon Mrs. Balfour with a surprised look said "But 7s. and 7s. make fourteen shillings." "That is right Mrs. Balfour." I am not interested in making any "critical capital" out of recording this incident, after all Mrs. Balfour had been to a finishing school in Switzerland. Mrs. Balfour was a kind gracious woman and I simply write down what happened that evening.

We had two pipers on the estate, Dan McKenzie the forester, and Joe Elliot one of the keepers. They were members of Pitlochry Pipe Band. One Saturday the band was due to play at the opening of the small hydro-electric dam at Bridge of Gaur west of Kinloch Rannoch. We went over to Pitlochry in my jeep and then on by bus. Bridge of Gaur is in Menzies country and Sir Robert Menzies, Dame Pattie and their daughter Heather were the guests of honour. The Australian Prime Minister made an excellent speech and pulled the lever to start the turbines.

It was a beautiful sunny day with a large number of guests from the Hydro Board, the contractors, local councillors etc. Fishers Hotel, Pitlochry, did the catering in a large marquee. The afternoon wore on and the pipe band surpassed themselves with the stirring tunes wafting away across the heather. The guests departed, leaving both eats and drinks unconsumed. Pitlochry was a modest wee tourist town fifty years ago where most residents knew one another. Piping is thirsty work – the tale is told. Large drams courtesy of the Hydro Board were dispensed. The beautiful sunny day had turned into a beautiful sunny evening when we arrived back in Kinloch Rannoch. A quick rush to the public toilets – relieved, one or two of the band thought it would be not only a good idea but a kind tourist promotional exercise to give the numerous visitors hanging about a blow on the pipes. I never got beyond struggling with "The Barren Rocks of Aden" on my chanter (which I still have) but I have always had the greatest admiration for those with piping skills.

The Pitlochry Pipe Band was a tremendous asset to the town and the beautiful county of Perth and the slightly wobbly off-tune performance in the large open space in Kinloch Rannoch is to be looked upon with sympathetic imaginative kindness and not as some sort of Calvinistic drunken spree.

Yards from my back door was the village hall where regular Scottish country dances were held with an accordion and fiddle group or sometimes records. These were jolly occasions with the hall packed to the door with sometimes a hundred souls of all ages. I record this incident with affectionate memories of a great wee character, Charlie Gray, who had alopecia and sported a wig on dress occasions. One evening an eightsome reel was birling to shake slates off the roof when Charlie and his hair-piece parted company, the wig fleeing though the air to land under the benches round the walls – the speed of his recovery was wonderful to behold!

Many a concert was held staged by glen dwellers with quite an amazing range of talents. One special evening was when Mr. and Mrs. Balfour presented long-service medals to four or five of the estate staff. A few days before this special evening Mrs. Balfour chaired a meeting to make sure that the evening with music, recitations and songs would go with a swing. At that point no mention had been made of catering. One of the shepherds, Bob Lipp who belonged to Aberdeenshire, roared out "Fit aboot the purvey?" Mrs. Balfour "What was that Lipp?" Her question caused Bob to repeat in a slightly louder voice "Fit aboot the purvey?" My time in Aberdeenshire allowed me to translate "Bob is concerned that there will be no catering."

Another feature on the village's social calendar was the miniature rifle range yards from the hall where several evenings a week the sound of small rifle fire was heard.

Early in my stay a major recreational project was launched – the creation of a bowling green on the flat field across from our row of cottages. The stage was reached when we needed to raise funds, particularly for a Ransome motor mower. A begging letter was sent around the shooting lodges and a fête was staged in and outside the large implement shed. A pound was a pound in those days, but realistically we hoped for donations of a fiver, and indeed received a few, but the millionaire owners of one shooting lodge sent us down a pair of rabbits. Strathardle was not "hotching" with rabbits but we had a great character, Jock Kettles, an estate trapper who must have caught hundreds of pairs of rabbits in a year, and so you will understand their fund-raising value was nil.

The wife of this rabbit donor the day before returning south at the end of the season told the wee kitchen maid, the daughter of one of our tractor drivers, in her first job, to take the less than a dozen eggs in the larder back to their shepherd's wife and obtain a credit note pending their return next spring.

Apart from Kindrogan House and Dirnanean House there were other large dwellings on the estate. One was Invercroskie where during my time the tenants were Ralph and Margaret Dundas. Ralph, if not a brother, was related to Dundas Robertson of Auchleeks and Margaret was the younger sister of the Hon. Miss MacLean of Ardgour. Ralph was keen to learn the ropes of estate management and in due course bought Airds House on the west coast north of Oban. We became good friends and they were very kind to me as a bachelor. Somewhere in my papers I still have the small invitation to their son Alex's second or third birthday party at Invercroskie. A few years ago my wife and I had a short break near Oban and one day walked along the shore and called at Airds House. There was no one at home and so I left a short note in a bread bin beside the front door. In the light of my friendship with his parents I was a little surprised not to have my note acknowledged. Sadly, not long after, Alex's death appeared in the papers. I am sure that my reading of this situation is correct, but if not and it causes any distress to the Dundas family I apologise.

One week a good film was being screened in Blairgowrie – would I like to join the Dundases? That's a good idea said I. Whereupon Ralph telephoned the Clarke Rattrays at Craighall inviting them to join us at the cinema. Jamie Clarke Rattray thought it was an excellent idea, but why not come to Craighall for an early supper before the film? We duly arrived at Craighall and were greeted by two or three huge deer-hounds. After a dram or two we adjourned for supper, washed down with glasses of excellent champagne. It had been a warm and thirsty day which prompted our host to pop down for another bottle, which soon followed the first one. It was a jolly supper party and as the last drops left the second bottle thoughts of cinema attendance began to fade and so to round off a very pleasant evening a third bottle appeared. Before departing for Enochdhu we went out on to the small balcony through the drawingroom window. The north end of Craighall House literally overhangs a cliff forty, maybe fifty, feet above the Ericht and the champagne bottles were bombed into the river. Quite mad! How daft can one get?

In the 1950s the wee kirk near Straloch school was linked with Moulin. The minister was a good soul, Donald Findlay. One beautiful Sunday afternoon in the summer I donned my suit and set off to walk the mile or more to the kirk, falling in on the way with fellow kirk goers, most of them estate employees and their wives and families. On entering the wee kirk I was momentarily knocked off my stride as the sanctuary was prepared for a communion service with the pew backs draped with white linen. Although baptized in St. Cuthbert's, Edinburgh, I had never joined the church in the approved way. Quite apart from not wanting to let my fellow workers and friends know that I was not a "full member" I knew in my bones that Christ would welcome me and so I celebrated the Lord's Supper for the first time.

Throughout the year, and especially during the "season", parties were held in many of the houses in the district, usually with Scottish country dancing. Many of these extended an invitation to me – Colonel Wilson, Ashmore, near Bridge of Cally, the Constables at Ballintuim House, the Gordons of Lude near Blair Atholl, and one larger gathering, a ball at Blair Castle which "killed two birds with one stone" in so far as it was the month of the future Duke's twenty-first birthday and it was also a fund raiser for the Royal National Lifeboat Institution.

Kirkmichael was on the Highland Games circuit. F.K. was the chieftain. These were held in the park beside the River Ardle with piping, dancing, heavy and light events, a tug of war, all entertained by Blairgowrie Pipe Band. It was always a great day, usually blessed with good weather, drawing to a close around midnight with a dance in the village hall.

During my time in Strathardle Tony Reid of Balnakelly came on the scene having recently completed his service, I think in the Irish Guards. Tony was pally with George Balingal who farmed on the north side of Loch Tay near Fortingall. The three of us had a few adventures together. They were joint owners of a fair-sized outboard motor which they were determined to try out. We hired a boat from the Kenmore Hotel and set off on a wet dark evening. With a fair breeze from the west the infant Tay was in full flood and we had quite a job to work our way under the bridge and out into the loch. We went ashore at Fearnan, had a dram in the hotel, and voyaged back to Kenmore. Without life-jackets it was a mad ploy – even with life-jackets it was a mad outing.

My mind in "recall gear" is beginning to throw up more memories than I can cope with and so I plan to leave Enochdhu after three happy years, closing with a tribute to the memories of the great range of people, young and old, with whom these times were shared, and not least to F.K. himself who was quite a character.

17

EMIGRATION TO CANADA

EARLY IN 1954 I was engaged by a bachelor millionaire coal owner who lived in Lenzie to manage two large arable farms in East Lothian near Haddington. The farms were Coates and Merryhatton.

As it so happened the farms were not for sale. The facts are so bizarre that they beggar belief. A local worthy who drove an ambulance based on Haddington during the Second World War had acted as if they were on the market.

The outcome was that my employment came to an abrupt end and weeks later I decided to emigrate to Canada after two aborted "employments" recorded later in this chapter. Somewhere in a box of papers and letters in our attic there are newspaper cuttings of the trial of the bogus farm estate agent who from memory was jailed for two years. These were sent to me by my mother when I was in Canada but I have no intention of unearthing them to verify any facts.

A wise lesson in life, certainly by the time one is over eighty, is to resist the temptation to be certain of the facts when recalling memories of earlier years. The two employments which I am about to record certainly took place and will come as a surprise to my wife and family.

They were short in duration and must have taken place after the fiasco of being manager of the East Lothian farms and before departure for Canada in September 1954.

The first was a "managerial role" with Keir estates at Dunblane. I was housed in a small semi-detached cottage on the north side of the road to Doune, across the road from the home farm steading, where there was a large dairy herd and a big grass drying shed. The shed had two driers, a tray drier with two huge sections with a canopy and door which alternated back and forth on a heavy duty steel rail, and the other was a metal ten feet wide revolving feed chain. From memory the furnace for the tray drier burned continually whereas the oil fired furnace for the chain drier required to be lit each day.

Work began at 6 a.m. with a squad of four from the estate farms – I must have had breakfast but any memory of eating is far overshadowed by the rather scary lighting of the oil furnace which called for crawling under part of the mechanism and lighting a flame torch which was inserted through a small window to preheat the furnace. When the furnace was judged to be heated to the required temperature a tap was turned to release a spray jet of fuel – nine times out of ten all was well but occasionally the flames spewed out of the window and singed my eyebrows.

So much for the morning shift! The estate squad of four departed at 2 p.m. to be succeeded by four Keir and Cawdor characters from Glasgow who arrived from the fair green place in a small clapped out van.

The grass was very lush in the large fields of the fertile estate farms and we had quite a job to keep up with the delivery of huge high-sided trailers of grass. The afternoon shift was from 2 p.m. until 10 p.m. when the gang from Glasgow departed and I was left to shut down the driers and enter the day's production.

Apart from the odd half-hour snooze in my armchair in the adjacent cottage and a quick trip on my bike to Dunblane for a few groceries I was on duty seven days a week for seventeen hours a day, a total of one hundred and nineteen hours. This lasted for about eight weeks.

One Friday afternoon after all the grass drying I was planning a weekend visit home to Edinburgh when the factor/estate manager – a Mr. Douglas – appeared and asked me if I would help in the dairy over the weekend. He knew that I could milk and assumed that was to be my role.

There were well over two hundred cows being milked and while this was done by machine the milk was not piped to the cooler but carried by hand from each cow and poured from the Alfa Laval buckets into the cooler. Apart from the head dairyman the five or six milkers were German prisoners-of-war (still in Scotland nearly ten years after the end of hostilities in Europe) and I was the guy to run back and forward emptying the large cans. To put it mildly I was not pleased and went to Edinburgh for the weekend.

On the Monday morning Mr. Douglas and I met in the steading yard and I will not embarrass any reader with details of the rather heated exchange which signalled the parting of our ways.

The second employment was little more than a prolonged interview which took place in the drawing-room of Megginch Castle, the home of the Drummonds in the Carse of Gowrie east of Perth. Although I was installed in digs in the village of Erroll the week or so of my incumbency quickly led me to realize that Megginch estate was no place for me and we parted company.

All this was on the friendliest terms. Since my youth I had enjoyed reading the illustrated autobiographical histories of the Drummonds of Megginch.

I have often wondered what my dear parents thought and felt when their younger son, now in his thirty-first year, appeared again to take up residence in our family home at 20 Belgrave Crescent, Edinburgh – their patience and kindness was unsullied with any criticism or rebuke.

And so off to Canada!

On the farm at North Berwick

At Peterborough, Ontario, 1955

Knox College, University of Toronto

The residences, Knox College

The Connaught Medical Research Laboratories

After graduation, May 1961

Elizabeth and my friends, Mrs. Chown's cottage

The manse, Bow of Fife

A Letham School outing, St. Andrews, 1964

My mother on her 74th birthday, 1965

Postcard from Hughie

With Leslie, Anne, James and Helen , 1972

The manse, Ballater

Off to the Highland Games,
August, 1973

Another year for the Games, with James

Glengairn church, 1984

A Ballater wedding

Highland dancing on the village green

Leslie's parents at the manse, 1980

The proprietor, Muthill

Dear Ballater neighbours, Allan and Lorna Forbes

THE PAPER SHOP

MUTHILL

PERTHSHIRE

PROPRIETORS JAMES & LESLIE BLYTH

THE DAY RETURNS AND BRINGS US THE

ROUTINE ROUND OF CONCERNS AND DUTIES.

HELP US TO PERFORM THEM WITH LAUGHTER

AND KIND FACES, LET CHEERFULNESS ABOUND

WITH INDUSTRY. GIVE US TO GO BLITHELY

ON OUR BUSINESS ALL THIS DAY, BRING US

TO OUR RESTING BEDS WEARY AND

CONTENT AND UNDISHONOURED AND GRANT

US IN THE END THE GIFT OF SLEEP.

ROBERT LOUIS STEVENSON 1850 - 1894

Prayer for the shop at Muthill

West Highland Way with the S.Y.H.A., 1989

East of Loch Shiel with James, 1993

Goatfell, Arran with Helen, 1996

David and Sheena, 2001

With David at McNabb House, Dollar, 2002

With Elizabeth and her husband John

James, Nathalie, Louis, Emma, Chloé, 2006

Ryan, Andy, Eilidh, Erin, Helen, Niamh, 2006

Anne

On my 80th birthday

18

EARLY DAYS IN CANADA

I SAILED FROM Greenock on the 11th September, 1954 on the *Empress of Scotland*.

Although it was nearly twenty years since I had left home in Yorkshire for boarding school at Dollar Academy - followed by five years in the army during and after the Second World War, much of it overseas in Africa, India and Burma – we were a close-knit family and my departure as an emigrant must have been a heartbreak. I can still see my beloved mother peering round the edge of a dockside warehouse as the tender with the eerie haunt of the bagpipes left dear old Scotland's shores.

From memory I shared a four-berth cabin with friendly male passengers. It being September a good proportion of those aboard were young Canadian university students returning home from a tour of Europe – the 1950s equivalent to the present "year out".

Autumn gales were beginning to blow which made for a rough crossing. Not surprisingly a good number of passengers were sea-sick to various degrees. Our hearts went out to one young woman in particular who survived on sips of water and was a sallow grey-green colour by the time we reached the calmer waters of the St. Lawrence estuary.

After a particularly rough night when the 30,000 ton liner was tossed about like a cork I went to the sparsely populated dining saloon for breakfast. On file I have a letter to my parents recording details of that morning's repast – half a grapefruit, porridge, a kipper, four eggs and bacon, toast, a roll, all washed down with several cups of tea.

Allow me to explain the four eggs and bacon. Two eggs were standard and what had happened is this – our table was some distance from the exit from the kitchens and between our ordering and the arrival of the steward my neighbour at the table had to depart. Rather than return his bacon and eggs to the kitchen and scrape them into the bin the steward glanced over my shoulder and slid the extra portion on to my plate.

It being late summer/early autumn we sailed north of Newfoundland between that large rather rocky barren island and Labrador, through the Strait of Belle Isle. Soon we were in the Gulf of St. Lawrence and the following morning early, a beautiful autumn day, we slowed down to take on board a pilot abreast of Rimouski on the south shore. It was at that moment that I heard the first sound (of welcome) from Canada – the eerie klaxon bell siren of a large steam locomotive.

During the night we must have sailed north of Anticosti Island, 150 miles long, by Jacques Cartier Passage, Jacques Cartier being one of the early explorers who at one time featured on a rather attractive Canadian stamp.

Later in the day I recognised the large white building with its distinctive red roof – the Tadoussac Hotel. Twenty years before, in 1934, my father and a colleague while on a prolonged business trip to Canada took a few days off work to sail from Quebec down the St. Lawrence and up the huge Saguenay tributary to Chicoutimi. His postcards from that trip had allowed me to identify the picturesque village of Tadoussac dominated by its large hotel.

We tied up at Quebec directly below the huge Chateau Frontenac Hotel, the venue for a meeting at the end of the Second World War to inaugurate the Food and Agriculture Organization at which Lord Boyd Orr was appointed the first Director General. The Chateau Frontenac is one of the great hotels of the world which held an honoured place in my hoped-for pilgrimages one day, others being Raffles in Singapore and Shepherd's in Cairo (despite two stays in Egypt during the Second World War I never made a visit to Cairo or for that matter the pyramids).

Talking of pyramids reminds me of a very dear friend and colleague in the ministry still preaching in Canada in his 89th year, Bill Fairley. Bill, like myself, was born in Edinburgh, and he began his working life as a message boy in R.W. Forsyth's on Princes Street, followed by a five-year apprenticeship at Bruce Peebles. Among the first to be called up in the summer of 1939, weeks before war was declared on 3rd September, Bill joined R.E.M.E., the Royal Electrical and Mechanical Engineers, and his unit was posted to Egypt where the men served with the 8th Army. On a day off a bunch of them made a trip out to see the pyramids and as they dismounted from their transport a big matter-of-fact Yorkshire lad glanced at one of the Wonders of the World and blurted "Ee but it's nowt but a big heap o' stones."

Before leaving Quebec for Montreal there is one more anecdote. During a superb five-week family holiday in Canada in 1981 two nights were spent in Quebec City in a Holiday Inn. One afternoon we made a pilgrimage to the Chateau Frontenac and read the memorial plaque on the outside wall near the front entrance commemorating the meeting which established the Food and Agriculture Organization, and then we entered the majestic foyer to browse in one of the gift shops. Not only to browse but to purchase several of the beautifully carved figures of the devout hard-working elderly Quebec peasantry. Beside me as I write is my souvenir, a ten-inch figure of an old man, complete with walking stick. It is a supreme example of the wood carver's skill. His left leg still has the label which reads "Folklore Sculpture created and carved by Les Sculptures Caron of St. Jean-Port-Joli". It was not cheap but more than justified the dollars. The back of the label has this inscription in French and English "The bitterness of poor quality lingers long after the sweetness of low price is forgotten".

After breakfast on what would have been the sixth or seventh day since leaving the Clyde we cast off to start on the final leg to Montreal. It was a beautiful morning and many of us were up on the boat deck. Minutes after leaving the quay we passed below the Heights of Abraham and I kept a special look-out for the cove in the cliff where General Wolfe and his troops clambered up to surprise the Quebec garrison and defeat them on the flat plateau to the west of the Chateau Frontenac. Prominent in the assault force were soldiers and officers of the Black Watch and I had a particular quiet buzz in the heart and mind as I recalled that it was in that famous highland regiment that I was honoured with a commission in April 1943.

Up ahead of us was the famous Quebec bridge spanning the St. Lawrence opened in 1918. Still on the open boat deck it was hard to believe that the ship would pass underneath without losing not only its masts but the top of the funnels.

Quebec to Montreal is about 150 miles and so we must have docked in the heart of that great city before dark. As the taller buildings appeared on the sky line I happened to comment "Oh, there is the Sun Life of Canada head office in Dominion Square!" – my young Canadian companions expressed surprise until I explained that postcards and hotel letterheads from Canada were among my treasures back home in Scotland.

We disembarked after breakfast when I experienced one of the strangest sensations of my life. Although it was twenty years since I first left home the camaraderie of the voyage changed in what seemed like a twinkling of an eye and as I stood beside my cabin trunk as a new immigrant to Canada I felt very alone in the world.

A small point, I left Scotland as an EMIGRANT and docked in Montreal as an IMMIGRANT.

The sense of abandonment did not last long as a room had been booked in the Queen's Hotel (?) on the left-hand side of the dock road leading up past the Windsor Station into Dominion Square. A very dear friend of my father's, Frank M. Raphael, was the angel behind this kindness. Frank Raphael, a bachelor, lived with his two sisters, Mrs. Cockburn, and Doris, in a beautiful old terraced house on Seymour Street. He was one of nature's gentlemen who ran a successful business importing cashmere knitwear from several of the famous Scottish Border mills distributing it to upmarket stores across Canada and the U.S.A.

Within days I found accommodation in a flat on Drummond Street. It was in fact the maid's room off the kitchen with its own small bathroom. Late September in Montreal in 1954 was a beautiful sunny spell – not too warm. Doris owned a country cottage in a small orchard at Mont St. Hélène south-east of Montreal. I have happy memories of more than one day-long visit. Canadian McIntosh apples are not everyone's favourite, but I can tell you that a brilliant red McIntosh plucked from a branch when within an ace of being ripe was a great treat.

However I had not come to Canada to pick apples and abuse the friendship of these very kind souls. Mr. Raphael gave me 50 dollars per week until I found a job. But where to begin?

With several relatives around Chicago and an introduction to the senior administrator at the huge Chicago show-grounds and stockyards, Bill Ogilvie, I contacted an uncle and aunt living in Oakridge just west of the windy city, purchased a train ticket and set off. It is a long haul from Montreal to Chicago by train and we arrived around 10 o'clock at night in a cloud-burst.

Details of my uncle and aunt's invitation to stay with them are vague but as we drew into the station I espied a large neon sign on the end of a building only yards away, Y.M.C.A. With my small bag I hot-footed it in the rain to this God-sent haven, checked in, and was given a clean comfortable room more like a ship's cabin than a hotel room but adequate for my needs.

After breakfast I telephoned Uncle Norman, married to my mother's older sister Chrissie. Half an hour later he duly arrived and his first words were "Hello, James, <u>you</u>

<u>are living dangerously."</u> For a moment I was puzzled by his comment until I realised that it was a Y.M.C.A. for black men. Having served for three years during and immediately after the Second World War with askaris from Nyasaland (Malawi) in Africa, India and Burma it never crossed my mind that I was at risk. What is being at risk? Without an iota of bombast, since quite young, rich or poor, black or white, have always been human beings to me – a blessing inherited from my parents – and so these days in my eighties I sign my letters "world citizen and child of God".

My stay in Chicago must have extended to a week or ten days during which time I made several trips to the Chicago show-ground and stockyards to the south of the city.

Unfortunately (but to be realistic in hind-sight my trip for employment in the U.S.A. was a non-starter) my arrival coincided with the autumn dairy show and understandably Bill Ogilvie the chief administrator had other things to do than spend time with a wandering peasant from Scotland, even if I possessed a degree in agriculture from Edinburgh University.

However I did spend the odd happy spell in the huge club bar even chatting to the president of one of America's great breweries and standing my hand for one of his products although my total wealth in dollars was minimal in the extreme.

Back to Montreal, a trek out to some agricultural supply business in a sort of abandoned desert area south-west of the city, and then a transfer to Toronto with a trip out to the large Massey Ferguson works just west of downtown only to find a huge sign outside the office "ON STRIKE". From memory I was given coffee and wished well.

Memory fails me but at some point in my searches I had made contact with the Quaker Oats Company of Canada with their large factory and office in Peterborough, Ontario. This led to an interview in their Toronto office with Ross Hay, the Ontario sales manager. Ross took me out for lunch in the dining-room in Union Station across from the Royal York Hotel. The waitress made out separate bills and as I had spent my last cent on breakfast at the Y.M.C.A. on College Street that morning I pushed my bill over towards Ross as we chatted. More than likely he was programmed to pay for both lunches – but when life's piggy-bank runs empty on one's 31st birthday the heart starts to miss a beat.

Back to the third floor office – would you like to work in the credit department in the office at Peterborough or venture out on the road as a feed salesman around the farmers of Ontario? I chose the job as assistant credit manager.

In the 1950s banks in Toronto closed at 3 p.m. and as we sat chatting my eye was on the office clock. In my hand I had a cheque for $100 advance expenses. Doing my best not to look mildly agitated the time on the clock came to 2.50 p.m. As we shook hands I left the office down two flights of stairs three steps at a time and ran about 300 yards to a branch of the Toronto Dominion bank on a corner. The side door was being closed as I barged in. The balances for the day were nearly completed but after a panting explanation of my predicament the cashier cashed the cheque.

19

PETERBOROUGH AND OTTAWA AND TORONTO

FOR EIGHTEEN MONTHS I was assistant credit manager in the head office of Quaker Oats Canada, the overall head office being in Chicago. In addition to the wide range of porridge and breakfast cereals animal feeding stuffs were produced. In the 1950s raising and feeding broiler chickens was the great rage, supplying the expanding supermarket chains. It was a quick turn round business in farming terms, beef cattle being two to three years from birth to market. Most of the broilers were marketed at three months. Even quite small family farms of 100 acres were keen to start feeding broiler chickens often in batches of 10,000. Many of them did not have ready cash to pay for the feed and this is where I entered the "fray". Quaker had an "application for credit" form which the individual farmers would fill in giving details of their bank accounts. We had applications from Ontario, Quebec and the Maritimes. In a few cases I would contact their banks who, for the most part, were helpful. A reply from a bank in Quebec could have a footnote "Le Canada est un pays de deux langues – écrivez en français s'il vous plait".

Occasionally I would spend the best part of a week with George Gray, the salesman based on Guelph. He was a super guy and these visits to farms around Mount Forest, Orangeville, Fergus and down into the Niagara Peninsula were most interesting and enjoyable. Quite a few farms were being farmed by Dutch families who had come to Canada immediately after the Second World War. One of them was elated on the day of our visit having just paid off the mortgage on their farm. The source of the final payment had been a bumper crop of small gherkin cucumbers sold to a pickling factory.

One trip ended late on a Friday afternoon near Niagara Falls. It was too far to return to Peterborough that night and so I checked into the General Brock hotel. After a meal I walked across to the U.S. customs and immigration – after a friendly chat with a couple of guys in "boy scout hats" I went into the States for an hour. I didn't drive a car at that time so I didn't have a driving licence; in fact I had no identification of any sort, not even a bus ticket.

One evening after supper I was seated on the veranda outside my "digs" when a tall man wearing a clerical collar came bouncing up the path. It was Charles Boyd, minister of St. Paul's Presbyterian Church, Peterborough, who will feature again later in this tale. I began attending St. Paul's where at a congregational meeting I had the temerity and cheek to propose that the stipend be increased from $3,500 per annum to $5,000. The financial board had had in mind to propose an increase to $4,500 plus a back bonus of $500. I felt the back bonus had a slight odour of guilt about it in the sense that the stipend should have been increased sooner. My proposal was accepted.

St. Paul's was a large congregation of over 1,000. Among the members was a talented good soul, a musician and dramatist (sadly I do not remember his name) who, when he heard my voice – I exaggerate – nearly fell on his face. He paused and said to me "You should have been in Hollywood." I don't know about Hollywood but during twenty-five years in the parish ministry I never had to resort to a microphone.

One Easter my gifted new friend produced a play in which I had the role of Caiaphas.

Peterborough was a prosperous city, one of the gateways to the Kwartha and Muskoka lakes, beautiful lakes with their shores lined with summer cottages. For anyone who enjoyed swimming as much as I did it was a kind of paradise. Of course the lakes froze over in the winter not with ice a few inches thick but two or three feet. In the 1950s many of the thousands of cottages did not have electric power and so to cut huge blocks of ice long saws were used and the blocks were slid up a ramp on to a lorry and stored in ice-houses ready for sale in the summer.

During the time that I was an employee of the Quaker Oats Company a minibus would arrive twice a year to transport company blood donors to Peterborough Civic Hospital. I joined them, which was the beginning of thirty years of donating over sixty times. My flow was super fast and I used to tease the doctor and nurses by suggesting that a sweep should be run on the shortest time taken to fill the bag with the winner getting an extra biscuit from their tin.

Ontario has no real spring. My first winter in Canada, 1954/1955, seemed as if it would never end and then almost by magic it changed to the first of the summer days, days which were hot and sunny with occasional fierce thunderstorms.

Readers will begin to get the idea that I am a restless soul when I say that in the spring of 1956 I left Quaker Oats to become manager of a large farm and garden seed business in Ottawa, Kenneth MacDonald and Sons, which occupied a four storey building in the downtown farmers' market area, five minutes' walk from the Chateau Laurier hotel.

The number of employees varied with the seasons, but in the spring and summer there were over fifty on the staff. Ottawa being the capital of Canada the diplomats and ambassadors were good customers, some of them easier to deal with than others. I could write a small book of reminiscences. Here is one – an item on the large order for the Indian High Commissioner's garden was six dozen mixed canna lilies. Now cannas grow from rhizome tubers not unlike dahlia tubers but much firmer. They are almost indestructible and so after several telephone calls to say that there was no sign of growth I drove up to India's Canadian base. A most gracious sari-clad young woman whom I took to be a member of the family ushered me into a large room with a more than life-size portrait of Gandhi above the mantelpiece. Identifying the lady as a member of the family by her graciousness is not a class or caste assessment but the fruit of raking around the world exercising sympathetic imagination. My experience of Indian servants was their amazing gift of being gracious without being servile. The gardener was summoned and the three of us set out to inspect the site of the cannas.

The tubers had been planted in small groups around the perimeter of the large garden rather than as features in a flower bed. Be that as it may the sites of the plantings were still easily seen. The gardener had a spade and on my instruction he began to excavate. Now I have no desire to exaggerate but the cannas were planted in holes at least a foot deep. Reaching the first of the tubers it had large healthy sprouts. At that point I began to wonder whether the "gardener" was really a member of the domestic staff who had been detailed off for outdoor duties. He was a smiling gracious soul who did not demur when told that all that was needed was to dig up the six dozen cannas and replant them covered by two or three inches of soil.

We sold a large number of rose bushes supplied by a German who budded them on his farm near Toronto. Once a year we had a stand for a week or ten days at the Exhibition ground on the lakeside at Toronto on which we displayed over two thousand blooms of about one hundred varieties. Sadly I do not remember the grower's name. He was a big hard-working friendly soul a few years older than me.

While at the Exhibition ground I stayed with the family on the farm. Transporting two thousand fresh blooms to Toronto meant an early start – a cooked breakfast and then off to Toronto. After preparing the stand for another day the two of us repaired to a lunch counter for another breakfast, and while I forget my friend's name one thing I will always remember – with a plate of bacon and egg (sunny side up) in front of him he would surgically remove the white leaving the yolk intact, then he would slide his fork under the unburst yoke and pop it into his mouth whole.

Toronto's Exhibition ground is a huge affair. The only time I saw Field-Marshal Montgomery was at the Winter Fair. He was in his dress blues with a huge "fruit salad" of medal ribbons on his left breast and his head was covered with his famous two badge beret.

At all seasons the ground was a great mix of the serious and the frivolous. Not far from our stand there was a guy with a wee table in front of him loaded with little wind-up dogs. The story is told – he wound one up and it pranced around his feet with a terrific excited bark. Sales were brisk at $1 per time. Further down the broad walks parents and kids were struggling to produce barks when it began to dawn on them that the seller was a dog-barking ventriloquist. Not far from our stand there was a public telephone with the chute and tray for returned money. A group of youths realized that a few pages torn from a Bell's telephone directory stuffed up the chute prevented money from being returned when calls didn't get through, so when the pages were removed coins came tumbling into the tray. Keeping an eye on their new found source of wealth they would visit the booth maybe twice an hour and most times there were quite a number of dimes and quarters. We remonstrated with these entrepreneurs but received the 1950s equivalent of "up your...".

One day late in May I ventured out of my office on to the sales floor. Nearby were two ladies, the older of the two bearing a striking resemblance to my mother. A saleswoman approached them and I heard them say "Thank you but we would like to speak to the gentleman with the Scottish voice." "Good morning ladies. What can I do for you?" "We would like to buy twelve or fifteen rose bushes", spoken with a broad Irish accent. We selected the bushes from a catalogue and I promised delivery before the end of the week. While signing her cheque the older soul with a huge smile asked innocently "Do MacDonald's have gardeners to plant the bushes?" knowing fine that they didn't. Not to make too long a story of my meeting with these souls who became good friends to me I said "I will plant the roses for you." No sooner said than done. A day and a time were fixed. They were cousins, the younger one, Olive, was a civil servant. "Olive will collect you on Thursday at 5 p.m., a meal will be ready and then the planting can be done." Sure enough Olive turned up and drove us to 14 Renfrew Avenue where fillet steak with trimmings followed by strawberries and cream were much enjoyed. A grand start to a great friendship.

Mrs. Stinson, who was a widow with an adult son, had lived in Ottawa for over fifty years, retaining her Irish accent. Olive, her younger cousin, caught the bus to work rather than drive. Most mornings at the bus stop was another civil servant, Gladys McRae. Mrs. McRae, a widow, mentioned that she would like to have a lodger. Again the story is told. "I think we have the very one for you, a young Scotsman, James Blyth." I was not the only young Scotsman in 1956 looking for good digs but I certainly landed on my feet. My special friend was Douglas Mitchell, a government vet, son of Professor Mitchell the Principal of the Dick Veterinary College in Edinburgh. Mrs. McRae had an older friend, Mrs. Chown whose husband had been a Canadian senator. Before long Douglas and I were installed, Douglas with Mrs. Chown and myself with Mrs. McRae. These good souls were not looking for "toy boys" but for the peace of mind of having a male in their homes overnight. I blush when I think of the modest payments we made for all the comforts of home. While in Ottawa Douglas was married to Naomi, a bonny lass from south-west England. The wedding reception was held at Mrs. Chown's home. I have never been a great one for stag nights and initiations and was less than enthusiastic when two or three pals from the rugby club grabbed Douglas in his kilt and popped him into the boot of their honeymoon taxi.

Mrs Stinson was a good friend to me, not solely as thanks for working in her garden but as one who encouraged me to consider training for the ministry. She had a younger sister not long arrived in Canada, a Mrs. O'Driscoll, a widow with a son who was training for the ministry.

One day while working in the garden at 14 Renfrew Avenue I was stung in the lobe of the ear by a wasp (hornet?, whatever). I had been weeding a small rockery and was aware of the presence of several such insects under the stones. I began to feel a wee bit strange but for a moment put it down to bending over after a more than adequate lunch on a hot day. Things got worse – I went into the house, down to the basement to dab the sting with "dolly blue" a gauze enwrapped substance for bleaching clothes which was reputed to take the sting out of a sting. By the time I returned upstairs my heart was gathering speed and a few moments later I was lying on a couch in the back porch soaked with perspiration and my heartbeat going off "the Richter scale". Needing the toilet I stumbled through the house and collapsed at the foot of the stairs. A doctor was called – he was a Scot who had been at Fettes. He gave me a jag and I soon came round. I was one of the lucky ones. Many good souls die each year from such anaphylactic shocks.

Mention was made earlier about my pleasure in swimming and I became a regular at the beautiful pool in the Chateau Laurier hotel. Late one afternoon I was in the pool, and the only other person was an elderly man swimming slowly up and down. At that moment there was not an attendant in sight – I am certain it was the Canadian Prime Minister, "Papa" St. Laurent.

I had modest savings which had been depleted by a trip home to Scotland at Christmas 1956. My ticket cost over £400 at a time when £10 was quite a good week's wage in Britain. Today one week's wages would secure a ticket for a similar trip. West of Scotland weather during that trip home was exceptionally mild. On the day of my return to Canada golfers were playing the course at Prestwick in bright sunshine. Back in Ottawa twenty-four hours later it was 40 degrees below, a difference of over 90 degrees.

You will be begin to wonder if I am mad, but in September 1957 I left Ottawa for Toronto having enrolled at Osgoode Hall to study law. By that time Charlie Boyd had left St. Paul's, Peterborough and was the minister of Parkdale Presbyterian Church in west Toronto. He expressed no surprise when I told him my plans but in the next breath asked "Where are you going to stay?" "I have no idea." "Go right up to Knox College (the College of the Presbyterian Church in Canada) on St. George Street and they will give you a room." Sure enough I was given a large bay-windowed room and Knox became my home for the next four years.

Knox College is a fine building right at the heart of the University of Toronto. There was accommodation for around one hundred students in three "houses", not separate buildings but a well designed part of the whole college built round a garden quadrant. Lectures began at Osgoode Hall, imposingly situated in its own garden grounds behind high ornate railings near the old Toronto City Hall, but today cheek by jowl with the modern curved City Hall.

Shortly after taking up residence in Knox I was invited to be a don, an older and hopefully quieter and wiser version of student, to keep watch over the flock of younger residents many of them away from home for the first time. The dons at Knox College sat at the high table with the professors at lunch time, one of whom was David Hay, a Church of Scotland parish minister who had been at St. Margaret's, Dunfermline and who was appointed to the Chair of Systematic Theology at Knox after the war. In return for this supervision, a don, of whom there were three, received free board. This was a wonderful item in helping to balance my latest adventure. Another source of income was delivering beer orders, like a milk round, for a brewery on Saturdays. After an early breakfast I went down to Hertz to collect a rented lorry, and then round to the brewery to load up with perhaps as many as one hundred orders. The bottles of beer were packed in sixes and dozens. My district was south of College Street and west of Spadina, mostly older traditional Canadian homes many of them sub-divided into flats. The range of nationalities in that section of the city ran into double figures, many of the people from war-torn Europe. The cases of beer on an open lorry were a temptation and an eye had to be kept on them while handing over an order and counting the cash payment. By the end of the day there was a considerable sum of money in my bag. The whole exercise was in cash ending with me being paid something like $30, a good pay for a day in 1957.

The range of lectures at Osgoode Hall was interesting and I attended them diligently and sat the first year exams. There must have been nearly one hundred in the class – I have a group photograph somewhere. Now I have no desire to be critical of lawyers or the legal profession but the bulk of the classmates made no secret of the fact that they had chosen to study law for the high standard of living which most Canadian lawyers enjoyed.

20

KNOX COLLEGE, TORONTO

LONG BEFORE THE year was up at law school I enrolled at Knox College for a three-year course leading to a Bachelor of Divinity degree. In the summer of 1958 a resident in Knox graduated from Osgoode. I bumped into him on the day of his graduation when he told me that he had just resigned from a part-time job in the Connaught Medical Research Laboratories. Without waiting for more details I ran round to the laboratories and got the job. Quite by coincidence the laboratories were in an earlier Knox College, a large Gothic building north of College Street and on an island caused by a division in Spadina Street, a main north-south artery in the block street plan of Toronto. The two Knoxes were in minutes' walking distance.

And so in 1958 I changed from law to theology, and beer deliveries to after-hour duties in the laboratories. Please allow me to explain the duties. Basically the telephone had to be manned for sixty hours per week. The laboratories closed at 5 p.m. and so the sixty hours was made up of 5 p.m. to 11 p.m. five week days, i.e. thirty hours and weekends 8 a.m. to 11 p.m., another thirty hours. There were three of us in the team and so long as the telephone was manned for sixty hours we could split up the hours. One of the team was an older retired man, Sunday suited him best. I chose Saturday and the third member of the team was another student whose need for cash and enthusiasm for the job was less than mine and he was quite happy to alternate with me for the weekday evenings. My weekday hours varied from week to week.

For one hundred and thirty weeks, apart from the very occasional Saturday off, I would leave Knox at 7 a.m. without breakfast, travel by tram to a main sorting office in north Toronto, collect several bags of mail, and taxi down to be in the laboratories by 8 a.m. Fifteen hours is quite a long time to sit at a desk, and we were not supposed to leave the building. However there were two watchmen in the building, a day watchman and a night watchman. Their job was to tour the building every two hours to ensure ongoing experiments had not gone awry. They were equipped with a time clock disc which had to be punched at a number of points on their route.

A hundred yards down Spadina on the west side was a typical Canadian lunch counter, open 24 hours per day. With a watchman at the desk I would nip down for something to eat. It varied slightly depending upon the time of day. Sometimes a bowl of soup, but one item, more than a favourite since I must have had at least four hundred, was a fried egg in a kaiser roll, a slightly crisp, white roll with a few poppy seeds on top. The cheery good soul behind the counter was a Chinaman and we became good friends. One of his party tricks was to take an egg from the large bowl at the side of the hot plate and, holding it in his palm, crack it and plop the egg on to the hot surface all with one hand. I never saw him break a yoke unless a customer asked for it spread out.

Most weeks for the three years I would have done twenty-seven hours, occasionally more. The bonus was that the laboratories were peacefully quiet leaving plenty of time for study and the writing of essays.

The laboratories had a wide range of products including treatment for rabies, which was not rampant but quite common in the bush country of northern Ontario. There was a rabies vaccine and also the cruel treatment of fourteen large injections into the stomach of anyone bitten by a rabid animal or one suspected to be a carrier. Most days there would be visits from pharmacies to collect products when they had run out of stock.

Many a night after leaving the building at 11 p.m. I would nip down for an egg on a kaiser plus a fine little pot of tea, and then off to bed.

One night I was coming down the steps at the front door when a large lorry swung in and parked. It had a consignment of several hundred mice for experimental work. Back in for a large trolley, load up the crates of mice, sign for them, then up to the third floor on the large goods lift (elevator). I don't suppose any of you have ever been in the confined space of a lift with several hundred mice and so I have to tell you that the pong was overwhelming. Perhaps I went home to Knox that night unrefreshed.

Not long started on the course at Knox I became student assistant to Charlie Boyd at Parkdale Church where I would be involved with a senior bible class and occasionally share in the conduct of a service. Traditionally the divinity faculties in Toronto University, certainly Knox, finished early for the summer vacations. This was to allow small mission stations across Canada who never had a full-time minister to have at least an embryo pastor among them for the summer months.

Tied to my duties at Connaught and Parkdale I was not free for any mission station appointment. However, with time on my hands, once the lectures and exams were over, I became a garden consultant in Eaton's large downtown store. There were two of us, a much older retired man and myself. I was free to come and go as I pleased so long as I punched the time-clock when arriving and leaving. The garden department was in the basement on a level with Yonge Street transit subway. There was a lawyer, a keen gardener, on the staff. He was the intermediary between the department managers and the directors. He did everything in his power to persuade me to throw in my lot with Eaton's. "You would make far more money than you will in the church – you are a natural salesman."

Again I could fill a small book with memories of my months in Eaton's. We had a large range of beautiful African violets and I used to smile as well-to-do Toronto matrons would nip off the odd leaf cutting. One day an elderly, obviously wealthy woman approached me with a large dead rose bush in a bag. "We bought this rose in Eaton's last year and it is now dead." The rootstock was thicker than my arm and must have been dead a long time. It certainly never left Eaton's less than a year before. Eaton's had a great policy of exchanging or taking back any merchandise and, without being unkind, a lot of customers abused it. I was polite but very firm and told madam that there would be no replacement rose. She went nearly "bananas", then stalked off and probably chucked the dead rose in a garbage bin. Another day I came across two very elderly ladies weighed down with purchases wandering about the department. I took them to be sisters. They were so exhausted that they had ceased to function. I greeted them and after a very short chat said "Now dear friends, you know what you ought to do – over there is the direct access to the subway, get aboard, travel home, then put on the kettle for a cup of tea." The transformation was instantaneous – they broke into broad smiles, thanked me and toddled off to carry out my suggestion.

You will have grasped by now that between college and jobs I did not have a lot of free time and so I am not boasting when I say that some afternoons I would leave Eaton's between 3.30 p.m. and 4 p.m., grab something to eat en route and be at the laboratory before 5 p.m.

Each of the three houses in the residence at Knox had a small common room with a public telephone in the corner. By now my income was only slightly less than I had had in Ottawa. From time to time I would play a childish game with any younger residents lounging about in the easy chairs with mugs of coffee – "Ah well, I'm off to the bank" and they would roar out "Withdrawing or depositing?" "Depositing, of course" I would answer as I went out the door. A few times during my three years I was asked for a loan which I was happy to provide.

The meals in Knox were good, but active youngsters, many of them playing sports (Knox had a college football team) were always ready for another bite. The shout would echo up the stairwell of our four storey building "Anyone for chicken in a basket?" Around a dozen of us would set off across the fine spacious campus of Toronto University up the side of Hart House on to Bloor Street where there was a Kentucky chicken outlet on the north side. A quarter chicken with chips and either tea, coffee or a coke set us back less than a dollar.

During my first year at Knox I resigned as don feeling it was unfair to accept free board and lodging when three nights a week I was out until nearly midnight. Knox College was a fine complex of buildings – a beautiful chapel with pipe organ, a large well-stocked library with the lecture rooms beneath, a covered walkway to the dining hall and of course the residences forming two sides of the garden quadrant.

There were twelve in our class, aged about twenty to thirty-nine, two from Scotland, one from Northern Ireland, one American and eight Canadians, one of whom had roots in Bermuda. It is difficult to put into words the special bond which grew up between us. Since graduating in 1961 we have had three reunions, the fortieth in 2001 which included a special lunch in Knox College. But all three were held at a beautiful old cottage at Shadow Lake, near Coboconk, belonging to Bona Duncan's family. Bona is the wife of John Duncan, the American. John and Bona are a super pair. John is quite a character and not only our family from Scotland but all members of the class with their wives have happy memories of our reunions at that beautiful spot and we record grateful thanks for their friendship, hospitality and many kindnesses.

The three year course in divinity was demanding – lectures, lots of reading and essay-writing, and, for those who aspired to the B.D. degree, a working knowledge of Hebrew and Greek.

Three of the class were Assembly students, that is to say those who, when they made application, did not have sufficient educational qualifications for entry. Their efforts and success in graduating is beyond all praise and now I will write a few words about the oldest member of the class, Bill Fairley (his name crops up elsewhere). Bill was born in Edinburgh nearly ninety years ago. His first job was a message boy in R.W. Forsyth's on Princes Street (sadly the store is no more). This was followed by a long apprenticeship at Bruce Peebles. War broke out in 1939 and Bill joined R.E.M.E. (Royal Electrical and Mechanical Engineers), a vital branch of the army. He served in Africa with the Eighth Army. With his wife Rita and daughter Catherine he emigrated to Canada around 1950, another daughter Heather was born in Canada. Bill and his family were settled in Fort William (now Thunder Bay). Befriended by the local minister Bill ministered to a small group while at the same time attending classes in the local high school. Sadly Rita died a few years ago but Bill is still ministering to two small rural congregations in Ontario.

All the professors at Knox were kind gifted souls and the class had a special bond with them. The Professor of Old Testament was Keith Andrews who held a Ph.D. from Edinburgh. In his Hebrew classes nine of us used to sit like a row of monkeys in the back row of a large lecture room. One day he said "What is the idea of all you guys squatting in the back row?" After a short pause I said "Well, Dr. Andrews, it's like this – both Hebrew and the bagpipes are better heard from a distance."

We were blessed in the library by having Dr. Smith as librarian. I will not expand his willingness to help and guide at all times but recall an article which he wrote and had published in *The Globe and Mail*. It was a "take-off" on the stark contrast between the glowing coloured descriptions of flowers and vegetables in a seedsman's catalogue and the actual results. It was one of the funniest things I have ever read.

Among the dining hall staff at Knox were twins, not young, quaint wee characters. Breakfast was served from 7.30 a.m. to 8.30 a.m. and as 8.30 a.m. approached the twins would start glancing at their watches and the moment 8.30 was reached one of them would dash across and lock the doors. Some mornings it was quite a pantomime! – those who had finished breakfast had to get out and as they opened the doors to exit the most extraordinary gang of half awake, half dressed guys would burst their way in.

This tale would be incomplete without mention of Willard and Enid Pottinger, a very kind and gifted pair. Willard had been a French teacher before coming to Knox. To record all their kindnesses to us and the happy times we have had together would take a small book. Their hospitality cannot be surpassed. When our family stayed with them in their home in Ottawa in 1981 we were all up before 5 a.m. to join neighbours who had a larger TV set to watch the marriage of Charles and Diana. We toasted them with champagne – a memory saddened by the tragic end to their marriage. On another visit, this time to their home on Sherman Avenue in Hamilton, our hosts gave performances of classical and jazz played with a magical spontaneous touch on their fine piano, and again in 2007 in their smaller but beautiful home up the mountain in Hamilton. Apart from the hospitality of their homes Willard and Enid chauffeured us to the class reunions at Shadow Lake. One year en route we camped overnight in the Algonquin Park. This was a very happy but hilarious stopover. A few years ago we had the pleasure of their being with us in Ayr for a couple of nights on their way home from a visit to daughter Claire and her husband Walter in Vienna. Although long retired they have exercised their kindness in striving to help others. Willard and Enid spent several months in China teaching at a college, and at home they reach out a helping hand in particular to students from Korea and China. One student thanked Willard for the gift of making him understand his worth as a human being, entitled to dignity and respect – which sums up the broad-minded big-hearted lives of our dear friends Willard and Enid.

Leslie and I have many happy memories of times with other members of the class and I would be saddened if any of them who might read this book had any idea that we thought less of them.

I don't want to be too melodramatic but every day I give thanks for the circumstances which caused me to enrol at Knox College, Toronto.

Out of our gang of twelve I was the only unmarried guy when we graduated in 1961. Sister Elizabeth came over for the graduation. We hired a Morris 1000 car and drove around visiting and saying goodbye. My return to Scotland prompted the question "What is wrong with Canada?" There was certainly nothing wrong with Canada. I can well understand that vast and beautiful land being regarded as one of the very best countries in the world to dwell in.

Elizabeth and I sailed from Montreal to Glasgow (in fact to Liverpool as it turned out) on the *Empress of Britain*. We were booked on a Cunard ship but there had been a strike of some kind in Liverpool and the vessel was not available. By 1961 transatlantic flights were emptying the cabins on the liners and there was room for the Cunard bookings to be transferred to the *Empress of Britain*.

We went aboard early and I went down to my cabin to find three cheery lads with a case of beer half empty on the floor. I am not easily put off my stride when travelling but I did not fancy a week with three celebrating strangers. The shore superintendents in Montreal for both Cunard and the Empresses were both former pupils of Dollar Academy. Their offices were nearby and I went round to see them. From memory Captain Jimmy Locke was Cunard while Captain Derry Parsons was the Empresses. No matter, Elizabeth and I went for a walk up Mount Royal to admire the splendid view over the city, amused both on the way up and the way down by the antics of the large grey squirrels. Hardly back on board - "Would Mr. Blyth please report to the purser." The purser led me down and unlocked an empty cabin with three bunks. "How about that!!" "Marvellous – a thousand thanks" and we exchanged a firm handshake.

It would have been before the end of May and so our route was south of Newfoundland. The dining saloon was lower than the public lounges and while dining there was quite a racket as the liner ploughed through pack ice.

Memories of arriving home are hazy. My old bedroom at 20 Belgrave Crescent was awaiting me. It was good to be back with my parents from whom I had been separated for twenty-five years, apart from school holidays and short leaves from the army.

Application for Entry
to the Church of Scotland

I LOST NO time in applying to the Committee for the Admission of Ministers from other Churches for entry into the Church of Scotland. This required my appearance before the General Assembly. The Assembly meets in May and so I was too late for the Assembly of 1961. The year until the next Assembly was spent in pulpit supply all over the Borders and even over into Fife. I also attended lectures at New College, Edinburgh, under Professors Tom Torrance, John McIntyre and Alec Cheyne.

My father was in his 76th year and still busy with his consultancy work. However I was free to chauffeur my parents up north for two holidays. Both of these were based at the Fife Arms hotel, Banff where my father, a keen salmon fisherman, rented a small beat on the Deveron. His ghillie was James Geddes, a great character who arrived on his small motorbike from Macduff each morning after breakfast. Although the wee bike had sported an 'L' plate for several years James was no learner in the ways of the world. In his younger days he had been a footman in Buckingham Palace.

During the year I had an interview with Professor John Burleigh, Principal of New College and Convenor of the Committee for the Admission of Ministers from other Churches. It was rather formal and he ended by saying "I hope you have documents to support your application."

In 1961, as a licentiate of the Presbyterian Church in Canada I petitioned the General Assembly for admission to the ministry of the Church of Scotland with the result that I was called to appear before the Bar of the Assembly in 1962. I was in my 39th year. Entering the Assembly Hall from the east I walked down the aisle with a pronounced limp. After my name was recorded with the crave of my petition the Moderator called for any questions. The first questioner was Professor Pitt-Watson, Moderator of the Assembly in 1953 whose son Ian had been in my class at Dollar Academy. "Had I any war service?" My reply that I had nearly five years' service, being commissioned in the Black Watch, seconded to the King's African Rifles with service in Africa, Ceylon and Burma was greeted with applause by the Fathers and Brethren, who were speedily admonished by the Moderator, applause not being appropriate when petitioners are at the

Bar of the Assembly. Presumably the commissioners assumed that my limp was due to a war wound whereas in fact it had happened the previous evening when I twisted my ankle on the deep verge of the lawn at Aberlady manse where David MacFarlane and his wife Penny had very kindly entertained me to dinner.

The next questioner was John R. Gray, later to be minister of Dunblane Cathedral and Moderator of the Assembly in 1977. "Did I feel no obligation to the Presbyterian Church in Canada in whose Knox College, University of Toronto I had studied for three years?" Certainly I had given prayerful thought to this question but recalling the contribution of Scottish people to the spiritual, political and economic development of Canada and the fact that several Church of Scotland ministers were serving parishes in the Presbyterian Church in Canada, and that there were others such as Professor Manson and Professor David Hay who had given years of service on the staff of Knox College, my return to Scotland did not overburden me with guilt.

Not to be dismissed lightly Mr. Gray asked several more questions in a rather aggressive way and ended by making a motion "that the Assembly do not accept the crave of my petition under any circumstances whatsoever for reasons which must be obvious to the Assembly". There was no seconder.

Without further ado the Moderator asked the Assembly their wishes in the matter and the crave of my petition was granted.

The animosity of John Gray – there is no other word for his behaviour – calls for a word of explanation. At an early session of the 1962 Assembly there had been a long, rather gloomy discussion concerning the shortage of ministers and the shortage of candidates in training. This coupled with the rather unwelcoming question of Professor Burleigh's at the end of our short formal interview "I hope you have documents to support your application" prompted me, wisely or unwisely, to pen a letter to *The Scotsman*, politely but justifiably critical of the whole process for considering applications from ministers from other Churches seeking entry to the ministry of the Church of Scotland. Without being facetious I had not expected a pipe band reception at the dockside as my feet touched Scotland once again! During the twelve months from May 1961 to May 1962 no member of the Committee or any living soul enquired after my welfare – this from the kirk with WELCOME signs at the door. At the time I got the impression that John Gray was a self-appointed guardian of the Kirk of our Fathers and boat-rockers need not apply.

As this tale unfolds I hope readers, if there are any, will gather that I have no animus to any fellow human being, and so I not only forgive Professor Burleigh for his rather chilly welcome but record with grateful thanks the happy evening which a small bunch of us spent later in his home at 4 Braid Avenue with special gratitude for the magnificent supper provided by Mrs. Burleigh.

22

MASTRICK, ABERDEEN

BESIDE ME AT the bar of the Assembly was another seeking entry to the ministry of the Church of Scotland. David Hogg had been Baptist minister in Grantown-on-Spey. The crave of his petition was granted. By great good fortune the Committee sent us to Aberdeen for our probationary year, David to Stockethill and myself to Mastrick. We became good friends. Many a happy evening was spent in his home with Effie his wife and their family of three, David, Una and Norman. David Hogg was a great hero of the faith who died in 1992. Effie has endorsed my belief that David killed himself with overwork. David was minister of St. Andrew's East in Glasgow for over twenty years.

Neither Effie nor I are seeking to make "greeting in our tea" capital out of David's departure, but emphasize the fact that the parish ministry is not a soft touch in life's struggle to earn a crust of bread.

From time to time stress tables appear assigning stress levels to a whole range of occupations with the clergy well down the list. Ministers exercise their calling in their own individual ways – and that was one of the glories of the parish ministry for me. Ostensibly under the "heel" of Presbytery, Synod and Assembly I was a kind of "heretical loose cannon". Having said this it was a dear, dear privilege to be a parish minister in the Church of Scotland, and what spurs me to be critical is the sad way in which the "good tidings of great joy" have been trivialized with earnest debate as to whether counting sweeties in jars is less sinful than buying raffle tickets. A colleague on Deeside used to sit outside the village hall taking the names of members who were going in for a flutter on the bingo, while here we are, six or seven billion of us on our planet home orbiting through space at 66,600 m.p.h. and God has given us in Christ a new life and eternal hope. I quote Kierkegaard again "Dear Father in heaven, must this go on for ever?"

Mastrick was a housing estate west of North Anderson Drive and north of the Lang Stracht. The minister James Tyrell was a friendly soul who had entered the Church of Scotland from ministry in the Baptist Church. Still unmarried I had good digs at 80 Osborne Place, the home of three sisters who were daughters of a minister. Transport was by bicycle, a beautiful dark green, encased chain, locking at the forks, Raleigh purchased for £28 from a cycle shop near Holburn Junction. While at home in Edinburgh during 1962 I had a low-key role with the youth fellowship at St. George's West and on my departure for Aberdeen I was presented with a cheque which more than covered the cost of the bike. Twenty-eight pounds was quite an investment in 1962 and so I took the precaution of insuring the bicycle. Events went something like this – purchased the bicycle one day, insured it the next, into the back of a stationary car while cycling with head down on a gusty day at a stretch of road where parked cars were seldom seen, buckled the front wheel and spokes. In full view of a terrace of houses where there was usually an old buddy keeking out to see how the world was getting on I was determined to remount. A wobble round the corner out of sight was all I could manage. I wheeled it down to the cycle shop for repair then walked along Union Street to the insurance company offices for a claim form. The insurance clerk made some remark that mine was the shortest time between taking out an insurance and a claim which he had ever handled.

We shared the services on Sunday, with a sermon from me perhaps once a month. Conducting funerals occasionally and visiting the hospitals and homes engaged a lot of my time, also weekly visits to two schools. Home visits were always a pleasure to me not just for a warm cup of tea on a winter's day but for the friendly crack. Two special ports of call come to mind, Dick Dargie, the beadle, and his wife, and Harry and Marie Robertson with son Ian. Many of the homes in Mastrick were designed for retired souls and there was a flourishing Old People's Club. One evening well after 8 p.m. I was in a pensioner's home when the good lady said "You'll tak a cup o' tea Mr. Blyth?" "Thank you, that sounds like a good idea." Husband and I kept on newsing away then there was a cry "Tea's ready". Turning round to the dining alcove in the small flat there was a plate with a large finnan haddock and a poached egg on top. I managed (easily) to do it justice.

The wife of one old pensioner, both of them well into their eighties, died. They had no family and the old soul was bereft. We sat quietly opposite one another in front of a big open fire. Eventually he retired to bed. I popped down to the digs to tell the "girls" the reason for my absence over that night and I went back up the road to sit quietly at the fireside until morning. I made tea and we had breakfast together, by which time a young relative and his wife, I think a nephew, arrived from England.

An early funeral, perhaps my first, was the second of a pair of twins. Mr. Tyrell had buried the first twin and told me of the likelihood that the other twin would die also. He had another appointment which could not be cancelled. Sure enough the tiny soul died and I met the parents at the cemetery near the Duthie Park. The wee white coffin was the size of a shoe box.

On another occasion I was conducting the funeral for the companion of an elderly woman in her eighties. There was some delay in the arrival of the principal mourn- ers. The fire in the grate in the small room was blazing with half a bag of coal. About thirty mourners were packed into the room. I was wearing a fine Crombie overcoat. By the time the service began, which was one of my first funerals, my knees were shak- ing uncontrollably and I was in quite a state to put it mildly. Embarking on a prayer my knees were trembling so badly that I put out my hand to steady myself on the end of the mantelpiece. Now the elderly lady should not have been keeking during a prayer but her eagle eye had spotted my wandering hand. The next day I paid her a visit and after help- ing to fold the newly washed and dried bed linen of her departed friend we sat down before a much reduced fire to enjoy a cup of tea and a crack. It was not long before she asked me "Was the budgie bothering you?" The budgie had been making quite a racket in its cage during the service, not surprising with the temperature of the room and the invasion of about thirty mourners. For a moment I was puzzled by her question. Then the penny dropped for I had been quite unaware of any budgie unease and I was able to tell her that I was so emotionally overcharged in conducting the funeral that I needed support to conclude the words of comfort in Jesus' name. We had a good laugh and perhaps a wee dram – but certainly another cup of tea.

This section seems to be about funerals and here is another one. One September afternoon my father returned to 20 Belgrave Crescent from his office at 22 Walker Street, had his usual cup of tea, turned to have a snooze before the evening meal and suffered a massive stroke. He was in his seventy-seventh year. There is a fine photograph of my parents taken at a Norton wedding only days before his death. He lay in a hospital bed for a week but never gained consciousness. As you know from earlier pages he was a great old hero whom we loved and admired and he was greatly missed by my mother and by my brother, sister and myself. My father's funeral was conducted in St. George's West Church by Murdo Ewen McDonald, and his burial service in the Western Cemetery in Dundee by Gillies MacNab, minister of St Luke's Church in Broughty Ferry.

One of my recreations while in Aberdeen was visits to the Justice Mill Lane swimming baths. At the deep end the water was fifteen feet deep and I used to amuse myself diving off the edge and down to the bottom. Fifteen feet is a long way down, and after turning to re-surface there was a second of not panic but wondering when one was going to break the surface.

It was a happy year, and identifying only two homes where I received much kindness does not mean that I am less grateful for the kindness of so many others. Now nearly fifty years on we still exchange Christmas cards with a good number of the old friends in Mastrick and the only sadness is that hopes of calling to recall memories have mostly been unfulfilled.

A visit from a minister and a cup of tea traditionally go together. Early in my parish ministry Leslie and I with baby James had a short holiday at Crieff Hydro where Church of Scotland ministers could stay at greatly reduced rates under the William Meikle and Paton funds. The Hydro is hardly recognisable today from the teetotal, sixpence in the mission box if late for breakfast regime (the latter before my stays there), but as far as I know ministers and their wives still have holidays at reduced rates. On that visit to the Hydro we shared a table in the dining-room with the late Bill Whalley and his wife. Bill was for many years minister of Newton-on-Ayr church. Conversation turned to ministers and cups of tea. I mentioned that one day I drank seventeen cups – Bill smiled and said "I can beat you. I once had twenty-three." Now all you good souls who put on the kettle for the boys and girls who shake their heads in our pulpits please do not jump to the conclusion that "brewing up" is a waste of time. The number of cups drunk is largely irrelevant. There is something about a shared cup of tea which tightens the bond which binds us together in Christian love. You may know the story of the minister who called on the elderly lady who had just had her afternoon "fly" cup when the minister knocked at the door. Her cup and saucer were still before her. She was not only elderly but very slow on the legs. "You'll take a cup of tea, minister?" "That would be very nice." Whereupon the old soul poured the tea into her own empty cup. As they chatted the minister was seen to be drinking out of the reverse side of the cup as it were, and the old lady said "Oh, I see you are caurry-fisted tae." (i.e. left-handed).

Every Friday while at Mastrick I would join the Tyrell family for high tea, and a good high tea it was. One Friday, well through the meal, the bread plate was offered in my direction. As I raised my hand slowly to decline, Jean, who must have been aged ten or eleven, piped up "Mr. Blyth has had thirteen slices already."

Before pulling down the curtain on Mastrick I have to record the sad fact that James Tyrell never enjoyed years of retirement – he died suddenly on the day the family were due to leave the manse at 13 Beechgrove Terrace. The Tyrrells were good souls who were kind to me. Young Jean had a brother, Graham, and I hope life has been kind to them.

PARISH OF MONIMAIL

LONG BEFORE MY year's probation was up I began to give thought to looking for a parish of my own. Details of this search are vague but the time came when I was invited to be sole nominee for Monimail parish in Fife. I was given a "call" and ordained and inducted before the end of September, 1963, weeks before my fortieth birthday.

At that time there were two churches in the parish – the old parish church built in 1792 just west of Letham village, and the other church at the Bow of Fife on the south side of the main road from Cupar to Auchtermuchty, a former Free church with a red-tiled spire but now no longer a place of worship. Still unmarried I rattled around in the large manse which was built in 1843 and was of course a Free church manse until the union of 1929. Services were held in the two churches on alternate Sundays. The former Free church building was sold many years ago and has had a chequered career since.

Fifteen months after my induction, on 5th December, 1964, I was married in St. Leonard's Church, Ayr, to Leslie Smith, the eldest daughter of Dr. James and Mrs. Smith, Dr. Smith being the Director of the Hannah Dairy Research Institute. We had a week's honeymoon at Peebles Hydro. Leslie was the eldest of four sisters, followed by Sheila, Alison and Brenda, and here I pause to insert with great sadness the death of Alison two years after we were married. Alison graduated B.Sc. from Edinburgh University and was a Queen's Guide. She was a dear good soul full of imaginative loving-kindness who spent a year with V.S.O. (Voluntary Service Overseas) in Nairobi hospital. She volunteered to extend her time in Africa for a few months and during that time she was murdered shortly before she was due to come home.

The fifteen months of bachelorhood in the manse were supported by various domestic helps, including even a resident housekeeper for a short period, but the best of them all were my dear neighbours, Jimmy and Agnes Bryce, then in their seventies.

The afternoon that we returned from Peebles in our wee Austin A40 Jimmy must have been watching through his cottage windows because by the time we got out at the door of the manse he was there with a large cake of shortbread in his hand. I was instructed to carry Leslie over the threshold and as I did so the cake of shortbread was broken over her head.

Monimail parish was not an easy hirsel to shepherd in the sense that is was rural apart from the small village of Letham. There are hundreds of similar parishes in Scotland but the spread of the members here was compounded by their membership of the former Free Church. There were members in Falkland, Cupar, St. Andrews, Auchtermuchty, Ladybank, in fact all over the East of Fife, who did not want to sever their ties with the wee kirk at the Bow of Fife.

Our son James was born nine and a half months after we were married, and not long afterwards Cupar Presbytery had a week's visit from the Moderator of the General Assembly, Dr. R. Leonard Small of St. Cuthbert's Church in Edinburgh. At a reception in Cupar Mrs. Small chatted to Leslie being interested to meet a new manse wife who had been in the parish for such a short time, and was delighted to hear that a baby had arrived in the manse.

Mention of Dr. Small reminds me of the year I was a commissioner to the General Assembly. On entering the Assembly Halls from the High Street in Edinburgh there was a small suitcase leaning against the wall with the letters R.L.S. inscribed below the handle - for a second I wondered whether the author of *Treasure Island* had dropped in for a visit.

The elders and their wives were keen to meet the lady of the manse in a more personal way than standing in a crowded hall balancing a cup of tea and so Leslie and I set off on the rounds. One afternoon we visited a delightful elderly farmer and his wife who were by nature reserved. We must have been in the farmhouse for an hour when the good lady slipped away without saying anything – an hour later she returned to say tea was ready. The four of us went through to the large dining-room where the table was spread for a traditional farmhouse tea – which began with beautiful fried sole. The reason for the quick departure from the wee sitting-room without inviting us for a cup of tea was that the farmer's wife had caught sight of the fish van in the farmyard and felt that if she had paused to extend an invitation the van would have been off. The only complication was that we had been invited down to the manse at Ladybank for supper by Sandy and Vera Philip. Sandy had been interim moderator during the vacancy at Monimail. Sandy and Vera were a very kind pair but we did not know them well enough to suggest that a cup of tea and a biscuit would be fine. Fortunately it was some time before we went through to the dining-room by which time we were able to do modest justice to a fine display of eats.

One fine feature of the years at the Bow of Fife was the monthly fraternal. Cupar was a relatively compact presbytery and around a dozen of us took turns to host the monthly fraternal. An interesting fact was the presence of wives and under-school-age children (in another room). In the 1960s few manse wives (I was going to say "worked") had careers or jobs. Apart from being elected president of Monimail Woman's Guild while we were on our honeymoon (not having ever attended a Guild meeting!) Leslie was on a steep learning curve having come into the manse new to all spheres in this change in her life. Willie Martin, the gardener at Barham with Robert and Joanna Spencer-Nairn, sometimes cut the large lawns and Mrs. Martin gave a hand in the manse. Mary their daughter, with two daughters of her own, Ruth and Jill, later on followed her mother at the manse. The whole garden was well over an acre including a fine walled garden. My bedtime reading at the moment is *Rose: my life in service* by Rosina Harrison, Lady Astor's personal maid, and if I tell you that Andrew Inglis, a retired farm grieve, worked in the walled garden on occasion you will begin to think that I am trying to impress you with the size of our staff. In fact they were never staff, but friends.

The walled garden was a wild-looking scene and while I love gardening this had to be well down my list of priorities. I grew potatoes, onions and sweet peas, and we inherited from my predecessor Willie McCraw an old strawberry bed. Despite being old it was so large that one beautiful summer morning Andrew Inglis and I picked 45 lbs of super fruit. On another occasion we picked a large amount of strawberries and blackcurrants. Mrs. Inglis was a great jam maker and so we made a deal, we supplied the berries and sugar and she made the jam. By nightfall the following day there must have been approaching one hundred jars of beautiful jam on her kitchen table and we split them half each.

Strawberries bring to mind a tale when the McCraws were in the manse. They had two sons and a daughter. One morning one of the sons was awakened very early by the squeaking of the garden gate, and by the time he stirred himself and got to the open window an elderly widow from a nearby cottage was in the middle of the garden helping herself to the strawberries. Kenneth had an air gun – he fired a couple of shots over the head of the intruder who promptly fled, leaving her bowl behind her! In the early evening of that day the son of the manse knocked at the cottage door and handed over her bowl full of lovely berries. Any embarrassment soon dissolved into laughter.

Large acreages of potatoes were grown in the fertile fields in the Howe of Fife, many of them by potato merchants. One firm based on Glasgow was called Witherspoon, Donald & Graham. By coincidence one of the directors, Graham Donald, was a fellow pupil at Dollar Academy. Graham served in the navy during the second world war. One day in the 1950s I bumped into Graham in Glasgow and he very kindly took me for lunch in the club, the R.N.V.R. vessel the "Carrick" berthed on the Clyde.

One of the tattie squads belonging to the company annually began lifting earlies down the Ayrshire coast near Girvan and then as the year progressed they moved east and took up their abode in an old cottage at Letham Toll on the main road from Kirkcaldy to Dundee. One of this squad became my special friend – he was Irish, Hughie O'Donnell. We used to receive wee notes and postcards from Ayrshire from Hughie telling us how much he was looking forward to seeing us again.

One year Hughie fell out with the priest in Cupar over Hughie's indulgence with the drink. Like most friendships ours developed slowly. Social events were held in Letham Hall, yards from the wee "tattie squad hotel" and not surprisingly some of them would turn up – even if only for the hot tea and sandwiches. This is where our friendship began. One evening Hughie was eating a bag of crisps, our faces fairly close together so that we could hear above the hubbub of the Hall. Believe me when I say that being bombarded with half-chewed crisps from a mouth speaking in the most delightful Irish brogue was one of life's great experiences. Not to spin out the tale of this special friendship but Hughie started to attend services in the two churches in Monimail parish. He would spruce himself up, put on his best gear and wind a home-knitted Celtic scarf around his neck – it must have been twelve feet long if it was an inch. Hughie was a perfect gentleman during the services, his only small eccentricity was if a hymn had a catchy tune Hughie would leave the pew and march up and down keeping time to the music. One final memory of him. On a cold October day I had reason to track down Hughie in a large tattie field near Ladybank. Perhaps with a message for him – I do not remember. I found the squad and there he was dressed in an oversized overcoat and wearing a <u>bowler hat</u>. Laugh if you like, but Hughie was a total master and could lift tatties faster than anyone I had ever seen at that back-breaking task.

The church at the Bow of Fife had a super pipe organ, a gift from the Nairn family. The organist was Willie Couston, the former head of the primary school in Auchtermuchty, who played that organ for over fifty years. The time came for him to retire, the organist at Monimail church, Ritchie Miles, helped out and we advertised for a successor. There was only one reply, from a man not in the first blush of youth. On the Sunday of his audition I was absent on Presbytery business so did not hear him. It was summer time and in the evening I went up to Letham to ask Tommy Malone, an elder, how they had all got on. Tommy smiled and said "Well, it's like this. He was like the Hill Town Mountain Band – we don't play too good but we sure make plenty of noise."

Other characters frequently in the parish were a family of Stewarts, father, mother and adult son. One very hot day Leslie, our young son aged two and a half, and I returned home from a short holiday in Arisaig, a long drive. We drove in the manse drive to the back door to be welcomed by the skirl of the pipes. Moments later father Stewart with the bagpipes under his arm arrived at the back door – this must have been the first real occasion of our meeting. "Hello there, how are you?" The answer was a request for bagpipe reeds. One of my regrets in life is that I never pursued the learning of the bagpipes. I still have a chanter. However that afternoon I popped through to the study where I had in a desk drawer a Benson & Hedges red tin box with several reeds (do chanters have different reeds to bagpipes? - no matter). I went out to the back door and the look of surprise on the piper's face was marvellous to behold. Without being unkind I think money would have been behind the request for reeds. I have always been a good touch for a pound but Leslie and I thought it better not to start with them. From that amusing encounter we had a long friendship with these hardy nomads and many a time we have filled their smoky tea cans and given them food.

Switching back to before I was married, six weeks after my induction I was lying on my back in the Adamson Cottage Hospital, Cupar, with a leg under traction – the diagnosis was a slipped disc. It had nothing to do with a slipped disc, it was the traumatic outcome of my brazenness in believing myself called to the holy ministry. This theme is developed in a paper I wrote bearing the title "The Good Tidings of the Gospel – The Global and Economic Embrace of Jesus Christ" which will appear later in the book.

Six weeks is a long time to be on one's back – here is a little light relief. I was in a single room and one evening a nursing auxiliary looked round the door on her rounds for nightcap orders, tea, cocoa, etc., and she let out a mighty shriek – on the floor there was a mouse which dashed behind the small wardrobe. At my prompting she returned with a small sweeping brush. The mouse was still behind the wardrobe. "Please move the wardrobe an inch", the mouse ran out along the skirting board, I was ready with the brush, and with a quick well-timed lunge killed the wee mouse. Smiles all round. Cocoa was served.

As a break from Presbytery and Session meetings, Sunday services and their preparation, parish and hospital visiting, funerals and weddings, from time to time I would join the worthies in the wee pub at Freuchie where mine host was George. A great character but much overweight George died during our time at the Bow and I conducted his funeral at Mortonhall Crematorium in Edinburgh. One of the worthies was Dave Scott, a lorry driver, I think with the county council, father of Mrs. Petrie whose husband had the garage in Springfield. Dave was a great Burns man who inveigled me into taking part in the annual suppers. Over the years I gave the Immortal Memory several times in local halls, but once in Fernie Castle Hotel with the Alexander Brothers in full flow.

Mention of Fernie Castle turns my mind back to the years with F.K. Balfour in Strathardle. The castle was owned by an uncle, William Balfour, whose wife was a Nairn. They had no family and on their deaths F.K. inherited not only the castle but two farms, Fernie Mill and Lindifferon. During the later part of my time in Strathardle Arthur Walker and I made several trips down to Fife with fencing posts and other sawmill products for farm and estate repairs.

Geordie Keiller, a retired gamekeeper on the estate who lived in a cottage near the castle, was caretaker until the castle was eventually sold to Crawford, the biscuit folk, and turned into a hotel. Geordie was a great old character who, well on in years, had occasion to visit the doctor's surgery in Cupar. After an examination the doctor disappeared and returned after a longish interval. "Mr. Keiller we cannot find your records – when were you last here?" Geordie's reply was "It must have been 1928."

Several branches of the Nairn family lived in the parish. Suppose I confine these words to the nearest branch, Robert Spencer-Nairn at Barham. They had three of a family, roughly the same ages as ours, and we used to share the chauffering back and forwards to the school at the top of Letham village where, interestingly enough, the schoolmaster lived in the schoolhouse which was attached to the school. Robert is now Sir Robert and he and his wife were always very kind to us.

Over the ten years that we were in the manse at the Bow of Fife we received many kindnesses from lots of people. One particular friend was Mary Grossert, the district nurse, and then of course George and Leila Storrar, farmers at Rossie near Auchtermuchty. They hosted Leslie on her first overnight visit to Fife and always included us in their special New Year's Eve party at the farmhouse. Speaking of Leslie's first visit to Fife – the two of us went into the old parish church where close to the communion table was the manse pew. As it so happened I had a tape measure in my pocket and so I slipped into the pew, measured it, and told her there was room for her and six kids!

In large letters inside one of my folders there is written NOLO EPISCOPARI – I do not want to be a bishop (I don't know where I transcribed this from). Translated in my case this would become I do not want to be a moderator. Although invited I knew in my heart and mind that I would be useless as a moderator. In case anyone should think that my decision was shirking presbytery duties here is a factual account of three years as an interim moderator. This was when Cupar was a separate presbytery before uniting with St. Andrews.

In 1969 Jack Scroggie left Flisk and Kilmany for Mains, Dundee. I was appointed interim moderator. After about eighteen months the vacancy committee invited Mr. Logan Ayre to be sole nominee. Almost on the same day the minister of Creich and Monzie announced that he would like to retire. Enter the Presbytery Unions and Readjustment Committee who wanted to join up the four vacant parishes. Mr. Logan Ayre went off to a charge in the south-west of Scotland where sadly, from memory, he died not long after being inducted. The manse was at Creich, the manse at Monzie was occupied, and probably owned, by a great presbytery stalwart Adamson Fyffe. After the usual "argy bargy" Monzie was closed with the proviso of services two or three times a year. A new vacancy committee was formed which dragged on and on, and at that point my memory starts to get hazy. I think a new interim moderator was appointed to cope with the final details leading up to the induction of the new minister of Flisk, Kilmany and Creich (Monzie). I am not "greeting in anyone's tea" – all the parishes under my care in the east of Fife were on rich arable land and with my experience in farm and estate management we had a special bond. It was a lot of motoring and hard work on top of my own parish work but I have many happy memories of those three years.

For several years I was a member of Cupar Rotary and one day I was part of a small group of leading lights in the small Royal Burgh discussing the vacancy at the parish church, Cupar Old and St. Michael of Tarvit with a roll of well over a thousand members. As they chattered away striving to draw up their idea of the ideal minister for such a charge I reached the point where I could not believe my ears. I will not embarrass anyone with details of their expectations. The fact of the matter is that the expectations of most congregations far exceed those which can be fulfilled.

24

Parish of Glenmuick, Ballater

IN THE SPRING of 1973 the vacancy committee of Glenmuick Parish Church, Ballater, which included the little church in Glengairn, invited me to be a candidate. The interim moderator was Tom Nicol of Crathie, and so one beautiful sunny morning I conducted a service in Crathie church. The beadle gave me a cheery and encouraging welcome. His name was Mr. Fairweather, which helps me to remember that it was a beautiful sunny day.

Along with my application I enclosed a small photograph of a fine family group taken sitting on the lawn in front of the manse at the Bow of Fife. James, Helen and Anne were seven, four and two respectively, and I am sure the photograph of Leslie and the family was a factor in my being called to Ballater. I was in my fiftieth year. In June we said good-bye to the good folks at Monimail after ten years and set off in company with two furniture vans. Driving north we were caught in a terrific thunder and lightning storm. The Ballater manse was a fine large family house (with twelve rooms and a floored attic!) in over an acre of grounds.

It had not been built as the manse. The manse of Glenmuick had been a building out of the village on the south bank of the river Dee across the road from the old kirk and burial ground at the point where the river Muick joins the Dee. Many years ago the manse had been cut in half by flood waters, a fact which was quite obvious from the vertical windowless wall built to retain what was left after the flood.

Our manse had been built as a home for the daughters of Robert Neil who had been minister of Glengairn church as a charge on its own for many years. The Misses Neil in their will offered Fasnadarroch to the parish for £1,250, giving the session and congregation a few months to decide. At that time the manse was the fine house on the green directly opposite the church. The congregation agreed to accept the Misses Neil's offer and sold the manse in the centre of the village for £1,750. How house prices have risen, this change of manses took place not long after the Second World War. (A few years ago the manse which we occupied was sold to private buyers, and a new manse was built in part of the back garden.)

Mention of the wee Glengairn kirk has been made already. It was built around 1800 and is on the east side of the hill road to Strathdon. Adjacent was the wee glen school.

Even today winters in Glengairn can be severe but in the school logbook of over a century ago there is a very amusing entry "This day the ink departed the liquid state".

Nearby is the old humpback bridge over the river Gairn where the large modern tourist buses have had a few anxious times. Quite a common sight in the summer was to come across a bus "rocking on its belly" while all the passengers got out. Alongside the bridge were several heavy wooden battens. Like small railway sleepers, and with these under the wheels, sufficient clearance was achieved to continue the journey.

The kirk session held a beautifully written document from the 1860s granting Glengairn kirk the full status of a parish church. This document recorded that there were 660 souls living in the glen at that time. In the 1970s there would have been about thirty souls resident plus a few holiday homes, among them one owned by Amy Stewart Fraser, the author of two fine books on Glengairn, *The Hills of Home* and *Roses in December*. Mrs. Fraser's father, Rev. James Lowe, was minister in the glen for many years.

Hundreds of thousands of words have been written on the cruelty of the highland clearances, but without making any excuses for the landed proprietors and their factors many souls must have left the glens at their own volition to seek a better life away from the monotonous round of porridge, potatoes, homespun clothes, rabbit stew and the occasional treat from a sheep which had drowned in the spate of the burn.

Catherine Neil wrote a fine short account of life in her native glen, *Glengairn Calling*, and during our time in the parish we had several repeat issues printed by P. Scrogie, Ltd., Peterhead.

The installation of electric power to the glen was taking place when we arrived in Ballater in 1973.

Back to my interview with the vacancy committee in the session house of Crathie kirk after the service. The only question I remember them asking was "What is your stand on raffles, Mr. Blyth?" I answered with a question "Why do you ask?"

Like many parishes and congregations Ballater had a fund-raising effort every August when the village was full of visitors who were a major source of income not only for the kirk but for the whole community. For many years the Queen Mother, her residence of Birkhall being in the parish, gave two or three handsome gifts which rightly or wrongly were raffled. (We have posted a tea-set overseas.) Understandably the raffle raised a considerable sum and the congregation were reluctant to be denied this windfall to the kirk income – hence the vacancy committee's question.

Whether it was the same elder who sincerely sought to honour the guidance of the General Assembly and preserve the purity of the kirk of our fathers or not I do not know, but during our time in Ballater an elder in Bieldside, between Banchory and Aberdeen, wrote letters to the session, pursued the matter through Presbytery and would not let the matter rest.

From memory a compromise was reached. Traditionally a lady's age is not a matter for common knowledge, but in the case of the Queen Mother her age was public knowledge, and so the Presbytery compromise was that Glenmuick continue to raffle the royal gifts until the Queen Mother departed this earthly coil.

Harry and Nan Rae, who feature elsewhere in this tale, were custodians of the wee kirk in Glengairn which called for a couple of visits per week to clean the building and refresh the flowers. The church was open to visitors from Easter to the end of September, and then for the services at 3 p.m. on Sunday afternoons from the beginning of June to the end of September Nan would play the organ (harmonium) and Harry would welcome the folk and ring the bell. Welcoming the folk had a special touch insofar as Nan used to buy 7 lbs. of pandrops every spring and these were offered with a hymn book. The last service in September was the Harvest Thanksgiving and in July a communion service was celebrated.

Miss Neil in Glengairn Calling writes:

'The Sacrament of the Lord's Supper was celebrated in the church once a year on the third Sunday in July. All through there was a spirit of reverence and solemnity. Nature at that season was at its greatest beauty, and there was a pause in the work of the farms before the hay was cut or the peats ready to be driven home to keep the winter fires burning. A suggestion was at some time made to change the date to one in the month of May, but this proposal was turned down. One of the congregation voiced his opinion in the following words – "The very flowers at the roadside tell us this is the time for gathering ourselves together, to keep in remembrance the dying love of the Saviour." '

Certainly there was a special atmosphere in and about the wee kirk on a beautiful summer day. A minibus ran from the square in Ballater up the glen to the kirk, and in addition quite a number of folk from Aberdeen and all the way up Deeside came to worship, complete with picnic for after the service. Many a summer Sunday if the weather was good the kirk could be nearly full. During our time quite a few weddings were held in the Gairn church and then of course there were funerals. In fact one of the last funerals I ever conducted was a very sad one in the wee kirk – a young lad had taken his own life. The church inside was full but there was a greater number of mourners outside.

Somewhere among my papers there is a letter from Prince Charles. When Charles and Diana were engaged we sent a letter of congratulations from the session and people of Ballater – with a note that if there should be any hitch with their wedding in St. Paul's Cathedral then the Gairn kirk was free on that date. Unless I can lay my hands on his letter his amusing reply must rest in peace.

Between the kirk and the bridge over the river Gairn was a property belonging to the Royal Family called the Teapot Cottage, a favourite picnic spot when the Queen and Princess Margaret were young. In fact the only time I ever saw King George VI was one summer day when I was with my parents driving south from a holiday on Speyside. The King was leaning on the gate while footmen were unloading picnic baskets from an old Rolls Royce shooting brake.

During the season the Queen Mother, the Queen and various members of the Royal Family would visit the wee kirk on a weekday and sign the visitors' book. Harry Rae, who was a great old character, was in the church one day when a lady-in-waiting looked in to say that the Queen was on her way. When Her Majesty went to sign the visitors' book she fumbled unsuccessfully for her spectacles. Harry offered his specs, the Queen graciously put them on (whether she could see better with them on or not no one will ever know), but Harry, who lived in the heart of Ballater village and liked to toddle up and down Bridge Street chatting to visitors and locals alike, was almost in orbit. History does not record how many times he recalled the tale of the Queen borrowing his specs.

The manse was a superb family home. Seventeen miles further up the valley of the Dee lies Braemar which holds one of the coldest temperatures ever recorded in Britain in a community. The temperature on top of Ben Nevis or Ben Macdhui is another matter. Ballater was never far behind. We once had a very long spell of several weeks when the temperature seldom rose above zero. The water supply to many houses was frozen. We were fortunate in the manse and I remember supplying our friends Hugh and Isobel Craigie next door in Glenbardie with a long garden hose from our taps. Despite having secondary double glazing installed on the ground floor of the manse a year or so after our arrival, heating the manse knocked a big hole in the stipend. Electricity demands in the very cold spells were huge, and oil was required for the Rayburn and coal for an open fire. Soon after this particular exceptionally cold spell the roads were dug up and the pipes carrying water lowered a few feet.

During one of these very cold spells Helen's duvet was frozen to the wall in her bedroom! Her bed was lengthwise against the thick outside wall and the frost had penetrated. Lying on her side with face to the wall her breathing had "iced up".

Glenmuick church has a beautiful sanctuary with a pulpit at one end with the entire congregation in full view. I have preached in churches with galleries on three sides, with some worshippers hidden from the minister, causing one to wonder whether they were keeking down to see whether the minister was reading the prayers. The sanctuary was blessed with a fine pipe organ and the parish with gifted organists, Mrs. Clarke, Mrs. Helen Milne and then Marshall Smith, Mrs. Clarke's nephew. Marshall is still playing and not to make comparisons but Marshall would be the most gifted of the three. Then there was Baillie Taylor from Aberdeen who had a holiday home in the village. Baillie played during holiday times both in Glenmuick church and in Glengairn.

We were also blessed with readers for pulpit supply, Dr. Sheila Sedgwick, the wife of the pharmacist in Braemar, and James Innes who had retired from being headmaster of the school in Kincardine O'Neil. Weeks before the end of the Second World War James stepped on a mine and lost both legs well above the knees. This did not prevent him from getting around and mounting the steps into the pulpit and driving his car, not just in Upper Deeside, but down south into England for James was a very active and senior executive in BLESMA (British Limbless Ex-Servicemen's Association). James died some years ago and the last time our paths crossed was in the Little Chef on the road between Auchterarder and Dunblane.

During our time in Ballater there were many funerals, more than half of them burials either in the old ground at the foot of the river Gairn or at the Tullich cemetery. Personally I am going to be buried, which is no adverse reflection on the modern fashion for more services at crematoria. There was something extra specially moving standing at the edge of an open grave and committing a loved one to the peace and rest of eternity. More than once the grave diggers had to dig not only the grave but clear paths through nearly two feet of snow for the burial to take place.

Once only we were at the wrong site – the burial was at the old burial ground at the junction of the river Muick and the Dee which had been closed for many years. As soon as we entered one relative said "that is not the right place", a hasty consultation confirmed that he was right. The mourners returned to Ballater to wait while the grave was dug in the correct site.

While on the subject of the old burial ground here is a further tale. One day there was a ring at the front door of the manse. The unknown callers were Donald and Marty Pyper from Toronto whose forebears hailed from Aberdeenshire in the Buchan area near Fraserburgh. An ancestor's stone inscribed Pyper in the Glenmuick burial ground had fallen off its base without being damaged. They were seeking help to have it restored. We exchanged addresses and assured them that we would look after their request. At the time we were thinking of a family holiday in Canada where I had lived for seven years and for the family, none of whom had been to Canada before, to meet my colleagues and their families. A most pressing invitation was extended by Mr. and Mrs. Pyper to stay in their Toronto home if and when we made the trip. Donald was a little older than I was; he had served as a major in the Canadian army in Europe and was the owner of a successful contracting and engineering business. In 1981 we had a wonderful five-week trip to Canada which included a Knox College class reunion at Shadow Lake at the cottage belonging to John and Bona Duncan, and two or three days at Donald and Marty Pyper's huge summer cottage (built by Donald and his sons) at the Muskoka lakes. Our son James was nearly sixteen and so it turned out to be the last of our summer holidays when all five of the family were together. It is hard to find words to express gratitude for such a superb trip.

Otherwise family holidays were spent in the early years in rented cottages, and then we bought a caravan and tent and spent many happy holidays at Hopeman on the Moray Firth. We also spent a few days each year with Leslie's parents in their lovely home and beautiful garden in Ayr (my dear mother died a few months after our arrival in Ballater).

The request of the Pypers brings to mind that we had many calls at the manse and letters from overseas from people keen to trace their ancestors. Often we were able to help, for at that time the old parish records were kept at the manse, and it was rewarding to be able to provide the right information for the ancestor-seekers, and direct them or show them where the ancestral dwellings would be.

As a manse family we were very fortunate to live in such a friendly community as Ballater midst the peace and beauty of the eternal hills. The annual Ballater Highland Games, held two or three weeks before the world famous Braemar Gathering, were quite an occasion in themselves. A dozen of the top heavyweights (including Bill Anderson) competed. There was piping, Highland dancing, and I was convenor of the light events, (high jump, long jump, pole vault, etc.). The occasion was compèred of course by Robbie Shepherd at the microphone. Early on in our time in Ballater, when as usual the whole family were at the Games, there was near tragedy because the dolly which Helen was clutching lost one of its arms. Robbie Shepherd to the rescue at the mike – "There's a wee quine here who's lost the arm of her dolly, she's no greetin' yet but she's gey near it." In less than five minutes Helen's doll was four-limbed again.

Committee members of the Deeside Highland Games circuit, Aboyne, Ballater and Braemar, took turns in being guests at one another's annual dinners. One evening in the Fife Arms in Braemar there was a great gathering of worthies, and when it came to the meal I was squeezed between two of the really big heavyweights. I had quite a job to get my soup spoon up to my mouth!

For nearly all our years in Ballater I was President of the Ballater Flower Show, nowadays a two-day event. President sounds rather an exalted title for chairing the meetings, but that was my task. One couthy member of the committee was George Bissett from Crathie, a keen exhibitor. Many a laugh we had classifying carrots etc. when revising the schedule – were they long, stumpy, medium? Donald Coutts was a great character, not only on the Flower Show Committee but in the life of the village. Assisted by others we played a major part in preparing the hall for the show. Over the years the manse family put in quite a few entries (aye, and came home with prizes) – Leslie with jams and baking, and James, Helen and Anne with posters, pressed leaves and flowers, baking and so on. One year I did not read the schedule carefully and went down to the hall with four globe beetroot as a single entry. Lo and behold the schedule called for two beets per entry. Four beets, two entries, which won first and second prizes. However my greatest achievement was to beat Jim Kerr, the Queen Mother's gardener from Birkhall to the first prize for the box of tatties – twelve tatties of four varieties, one of the varieties to be coloured.

During the years in Ballater I was twice interim moderator. Not long after we had settled into Ballater a vacancy arose at Braemar and I was appointed to care for the parish until the new minister was appointed and installed. This allowed me to deepen friendships which I already had through Ballater folk with relatives in Braemar. The task of the interim moderator was to chair session meetings, vacancy committee meetings, conduct communion services and baptismal services, and usually funerals and weddings.

The second interim moderatorship was for Lumphanan when Sylvester Skinner retired. We were not far into the vacancy when Dr. Urie of Kincardine O'Neil indicated that he wished to retire. This became a long drawn-out affair for the Presbytery Union and Readjustments Committee became involved and it was decided to link the two parishes of Lumphanan and Kincardine O'Neil, and eventually James Seath was appointed to be the first minister of the linked charge. One of the services I conducted was the closing of the old parish church in Lumphanan – not easy when most of the congregation that day had long years of happy and sad memories of services in the old kirk. Later that day an elder said to me "You did a good job this morning."

The manse of the old parish church had been sold some years before and was occupied at that time by Andy Stewart and his family. As interim moderator I visited Andy one afternoon lying on a hospital bed in Aberdeen. He was not well (of course he was not well, after all he was in hospital) but he was still the cheery chap loved by so many for his songs in the White Heather Club.

When conducting services at Lumphanan I would call on the organist, Mrs. Grant, to arrange the hymns. Mrs. Grant lived in the old station house. For a hobby, and am sure income, she bred Yorkshire terriers and Shetland sheep dogs. One day I visited and hardly was I seated on an old couch with a few bones and canine toys when at least eight friendly Yorkies were using me as a climbing frame. One extra friendly one had a wee nibble at my ear. You can't beat the parish ministry for variety!

Back to Ballater. One Sunday afternoon I went to visit an elder and his wife. They had retired to Ballater from Aberdeen and Peter was already an elder in the Church of Scotland having been ordained during army service in India during the war. This was my first visit to their bungalow home which had an in-and-out drive. I drove in, parked the car just past the front door, rang the bell, when lo and behold a large hand with a large dram appeared round the edge of the curtain at the corner of the bay window. Peter's wife had spotted the minister's car and issued the warning "psst Peter, here's the minister." Once they knew me better we shared a dram together.

In most Highland communities and glens and certainly on Upper Deeside, among the estate keepers, ghillies, shepherds, and so on, a dram was the lubricant of life. No one respects those who are teetotallers more than I do. Great distress and havoc are caused in many lives and families by the demon drink.

During spells away from the pulpit I used to tramp the hills with many local folk but principally with Derek Petrie, the factor of Invercauld, and George Smith, who I am going to call the uncrowned provost of Ballater, for George's services to his native village were legion – Chairman of the Highland Games Committee, organiser of the summer Sunday afternoon Highland dancing displays on the village green, organiser of the Christmas meal and entertainment for Ballater's senior citizens, and so on. The renowned Bobby Watson, the first-class teacher of Highland dancing conducted classes up the length of Deeside and round Aberdeen. Helen and Anne attended his classes in Ballater and in due course performed with their class-mates on the stage on the green for the pleasure of visitors and locals. Collections were passed round at the interval for the Braemar Mountain Rescue Team. A piper played for the dancing and for many years the piper was Bob Nicol, retired from being Queen's piper at Balmoral. George was compère and as well as introducing and describing the dances he invariably would mention how even though the weather in Ballater would seem pleasant up on the mountains it would be a different story.

One day, on a long "hoof" as we liked to call the walks, a large body of us walked from the Spittal of Muick up to Broad Cairn, Cairn Taggart and down to Loch Callater, and then on to the golf club in Braemar for high tea. At the third or fourth halt on the shores of the loch we were sharing a dram together when George announced "I think we are doing about four miles to the dram." On these walks we would see a variety of wild life, a capercaillie on the Invercauld estate, a golden eagle, and grouse. In the manse garden the red squirrels active among the pine trees were a source of much interest. In the woods of Craigendarroch hill behind the manse garden the woodpeckers could be heard at certain times of year.

Sadly our time in Ballater came to an end for I was suffering from "burn-out" and I could not regain full health.

Retirement

WRITING AN AUTOBIOGRAPHY is not achieved without a lot of crossing out and dupli-cate scribbling leaving my desk and immediate surrounds snowed under rejected ruled and blank pages. With the end in sight I started to "redd up" and came across a sheet headed "Parish and Congregational Life".

I cannot repeat too often my wonder and gratitude for the circumstances of life which led me to study divinity at Knox College, Toronto University, beginning in my thirty-sixth year.

Looking back it is no surprise to me that a big hearted, emotional ape like myself should fall from the branches with "burn out". Long before retiring I knew that I was "cruising for a bruising".

Traditionally Monday was thought to be the minister's day off – but what do you do in any parish or congregation, but more particularly in a beautiful, peaceful Highland village such as Ballater, when the telephone rings at 7 a.m. on Monday to say that a good soul died an hour ago? I am not going to spoil treasured memories of our years in the manse by comparing different styles of ministry but take it from me when I say that it is not a calling for the faint-hearted.

Our departure from Ballater was a sad time. For almost five years, since the first signs of exhaustion showed at the age of 58, I had struggled to keep on top of all my parish duties. I was a bit of a puzzle to the medical profession because I had been en-dowed with excellent physical health. I was signed up with Dr. David Weeks in the Royal Edinburgh Hospital and I attended his clinics for a short period. But the basic fact of the matter was that I was worn out. In the parish ministry one is either fit for the seven-day-a-week job or one is not.

It is better to be eighty than to be seventy according to an article in our O.I.R. news-letter. Here it is:

'I have good news. The first 80 years are the hardest. What comes next is a succes-sion of birthday parties. Once you reach 80, everybody wants to carry your luggage and help you up steps. If you forget your name or someone else's name or an appointment or your own phone number or promise to be in three places at the same time, you need only explain that you are 80.

Being 80 is a lot better than being 70. At 70, people are angry at you for almost every mistake you make. Actually, being 70 is no fun at all. At that age, they expect you to retire to Florida and complain about your arthritis and ask everyone to stop mumbling because you can't understand them.

But if you survive until you are 80, everybody is surprised that you are still alive. They treat you with respect just for having lived so long. At 80, you have a perfect excuse no matter what you do. Try to make it to 80. In some ways, it's the best time of your life.'

Discovery of this article on the benefits of living to be over eighty allows me to repeat again my profound gratitude for a pain-free, medication-free carcase in my 85th year. However I have not escaped the trauma of lying in a hospital bed.

I have already mentioned that I spent six weeks in the Adamson Hospital, Cupar, soon after my ordination and induction to my first charge, the diagnosis being a slipped disc. However in fact it was the body's rebellion against my brazenness in allowing myself to be ordained.

Many males suffer from prostate trouble and I was no exception. Whether I should have been in hospital sooner is now academic. The fact is that I reached the stage when urine would not flow and one night at 1 a.m. our good neighbour Allan Forbes and his wife Lorna drove me into Foresterhill Hospital in Aberdeen, with several very painful halts without result on the way. Soon after my arrival a very gracious lady doctor with a catheter withdrew a flagon of urine and the resulting relief is beyond description. I then had an operation for this complaint.

My second stay in Foresterhill was because of defects in the same department of the anatomy. One morning I woke with a testicle the size of a grapefruit. Ballater doctors, Peter and Margaret Crawford, were on holiday and I was visited by a young lady doctor from Aboyne. Understandably she did not want to handle the minister's privates but she made a valiant attempt to disguise her diagnosis and to give me the impression that the swelling would subside. In fact both she and I knew that the swollen testicle would have to be excised. The result was that my right testicle was removed and perhaps that goes some way to explaining why I walk with a slight lean to the left!

Having lived in a tied house we had no home of our own, and having no means with which to buy one, (our savings consisted of three yet-to-mature life assurances) we were most grateful to be granted a loan from the Church of Scotland Housing and Loan Fund and together with a very kind gift from Leslie's parents we were able to purchase a small bungalow in Ayr. Anne was still at school, about to enter the fifth year. Our dear neighbour, elder and friend, Allan Forbes, flitted us in his scrubbed and hosed out float. It was a two-day trip with an overnight stop in Blairgowrie. It was a traumatic experience for each member of the family to leave the friendly family-like community of Ballater where the children had spent a major part of their lives. In one of my journals I recorded with gratitude and wonder the uncomplaining way Leslie, James, Helen and Anne accepted the drastic change in our accommodation.

Once in Ayr there were many visits to the Social Security Offices to sort out pension details and at 63 (nearly 64) I was granted Invalidity Benefit (at that time tax free) until I qualified for the State Pension at 65, and the Church of Scotland had my retirement pension already in place. I took a small job as gardener/handyman and also as a chauffeur (in her car) to an elderly widow, and Leslie had a Saturday job in a local store. The financial situation gradually straightened out and we both joined a new organisation for the over-50s and retired called "Opportunities in Retirement". It was the best thing I could have done. This organisation, then in its infancy, run by the retired for the retired, now has over 1700 members and about 60 groups of activities. I became the Treasurer, and apart from a break of four years in Perthshire, I still am. Leslie and I each helped with some charities, my main involvement being with the W.R.V.S. as a driver and distributor of Meals on Wheels, and also for the W.R.V.S. Leslie and I did the newspaper round in the Ayr hospital once a week. We greatly enjoyed the walks with the O.I.R. walking group and with the Ayr and District Rambling Club and did three long distance walks, the West Highland Way with the S.Y.H.A., followed by the St. Cuthbert's Way and the Dales' Way.

On innumerable occasions in my lifetime I was Father Christmas. One occasion which stands out was one of the Christmas parties held at a Mother and Toddler Group in Ayr where Leslie was a helper. She had not long been in the job, and the mothers decided to raffle a large hamper for Group funds. One of the mothers had made a superb outfit and very kindly I was presented with a bottle of whisky for playing my part. I was just about to "go off with my reindeer" when I was asked to draw the raffle – Leslie and I were so embarrassed when the winning ticket drawn was Leslie's! We wanted to decline and let one of the mums win the beautiful hamper, but we were not allowed – Santa came away with two bottles of whisky that day! (The following year there were three prizes.)

As I began to recover from the burn-out (though I was not able to resume any ministerial duties at all) the idea grew in my mind that I would like to run a newsagent's shop. After eight years in Ayr we rose to the challenge, sold our bungalow in Ayr and bought the newsagent's business in Muthill, a conservation village south of Crieff in Perthshire. I have always loved Perthshire and it is difficult to record my reasons for taking this plunge but I must have felt sufficiently well to consider tackling it. We owned the shop for exactly one year. The experience was enriching (up at 5 a.m. every day of the year) but we didn't have the energy or the resources to develop the business. After another three most enjoyable years in Muthill (in a house with the most marvellous views over the fields to the hills) we came back to Ayr. For family reasons we thought it better to be in a community with good public transport, and also Leslie's parents were now well into their nineties.

In 1986 several ministers left their manses with burn-out, a nightmare which was not always viewed with sympathy. Harry Reid in his book *Outside Verdict* leaves no doubt about the fact that the parish ministry is not an easy way to earn a crust of bread. George MacLeod of Iona declares that a major factor in the sad tragedy of kirk decline and ministerial burn-out is the atomisation of the faith into an individual thing. For all the talk of fellowship in congregations we live as individuals – not only in our congregations but in our families – separated from one another. Hence so many divorces and family "dust-ups" which beggar all description.

The conduct of a funeral is not a ministration solely to the bereaved family – it is to the whole congregation, the whole community. A house visit with or without a cup of tea is not a ministration solely to the folk in the home - it is a ministration to the whole community. The sad thing is that folk take umbrage and spread discord in the community by chatting in the supermarkets and on street corners saying "the minister was in visiting my neighbour but never looked near me". Mercifully Ballater was largely an exception to that sad state of affairs – the whole village and beautiful surrounding heather-clad hills vibrated with a bond which was almost tangible.

As I have already said having to leave the good souls in Ballater because of "burn-out" was a sad traumatic experience not only for our family downsizing from the beautiful large manse and garden to a small bungalow in Ayr but for the parish themselves. Hindsight suggests that it would have been wiser to call it a day "when no longer able to conduct services and funerals". Saying this should not diminish the encouragement and loving-kindness of colleagues in the ministry, not least my nearest neighbour Keith Angus of Crathie, and the sessions with Dr. David Weeks in the Royal Edinburgh Hospital to get me back on the rails.

On one occasion return to parish duties coincided with major repairs to the inside wall of the beautiful sanctuary of Glenmuick Church and services were held in the different but equally fine sanctuary of St. Kentigern's, the Episcopal Church in Ballater. I think the session and congregation expressed more than gratitude to our Episcopal friends at the time but if not I say now how grateful we were.

Believe me when I say that standing up and "shaking one's head in a pulpit" is a very nerve-racking business. Sir William Arrol of Forth Bridge building fame and a resident in Ayr for part of his life (his large home being the core part of the former Seafield Children's Hospital) said "I would rather build several Forth Bridges than stand up and make a speech". Then Harold MacMillan, when prime minister, used to say that he was physically sick each time he had to make a major speech in the House of Commons.

My genuine love and concern for the disadvantaged in society might lead people to believe that I am a socialist which is not the case. Socialism is too heavily seasoned with envy. Instead I am a Conservative-Communist, which on first encounter looks like a contradiction in terms. I will try to explain.

Stalin's reign of terror was not communism but bare-faced state thuggery. Communism is a biblical concept "and they had all things in common".

Conservatism allows enterprise to flourish and while global capitalism as I write steamrollers its unchecked way minds and hearts are being engaged increasingly with the simple wisdom that money-making without ethical seasoning is a crime against the global family.

Here are two quotations used by that wise gifted Australian, John Pilger, in his superb book *Hidden Agendas* as chapter introductions. The first is from, I was going to write, the heart and mind of Napoleon Bonaparte, however on reading it for the umpteenth time suppose we just say, from the head of Napoleon:

'There is only one thing in this world and that is to keep acquiring money and more money, power and more power. All the rest is meaningless.'

The second quotation Pilger gives comes from a book of George Kennan, American Ambassador to Russia for a few months in 1952/3 and later Professor of the Institute for Advanced Study in Princeton, New Jersey. I have two of his books. He is obviously a highly intelligent soul who can write, and so I am puzzled by this quotation of his taken from another book *US Cold War Planner 1948*:

'We have 50% of the world's wealth, but only 6.3% of its population. In this situation, our real job in the coming period is to devise a pattern of relationships which permit us to maintain this position of disparity. To do so, we have to dispense with all sentimentality... We should cease thinking about human rights, the raising of living standards and democratisation.'

No one <u>admired</u> – past tense – America more than I did, with many branches of my family spread widely across the United States, descendants of those who emigrated before the First World War, and there is a small library of books on American history in our home from early schooldays. I think one factor in the production of such sentiments as in the above quotation is the all too common notion that if every lazy bum got off his bum he or she would prosper and grow rich. Free enterprise and ingenuity have been a great boon to mankind but this has to be very heavily seasoned with the basic fact that there never can be gainful employment for great masses of the global family.

For nearly forty years we have been members of the National Trust during which time we have visited many castles and stately homes in beautiful surroundings and enjoyed particularly the small beach and open acres of Culzean Country Park. However any enjoyment of these visits is tempered by a feeling that these places are obscene. Dumfries House near Auchinleck featured prominently in the national and local press of recent months – my contribution was a short letter published in *The Herald* dated 8th June, 2007, which reads "Bearing in mind the chief source of the Bute loot, the coal-fields of South Wales, I invite Johnny Dumfries to gift Dumfries House, well endowed, to the nation."

The time was when I had quite a large collection of estate agents' advertisements for old Church of England rectories. Depending on their location, and other factors, many changed hands (now) for several millions of pounds. This coupled with visits to Church of England sanctuaries full of memorials to dukes, earls, baronets, generals, majors and even lowly ensigns of suitable families made me wonder what all this glorification of the titled and upper class dead was about. In the obituary tribute to a senior lay member of Archbishop Michael Ramsay's staff there is recorded the lay member overhearing the Archbishop while relaxing in Lambeth Palace muttering "I hate the Church of England."

Then Bishop Holloway, emeritus Bishop of Edinburgh while attending a memorial service to Archbishop Runcie, coped, mitred and croziered said to himself "What am I doing here?"

For many years the Church of England has been thought of as the Tory party at prayer – it is hard not to think of it as an ecclesiastical pantomime. And yet without it there would have been no material for the well-loved Victorian novels such as those of Anthony Trollope and his *Barchester Towers*.

One autumn walking the Dales' Way from Ilkley to Lake Windermere we trod a path along the edge of a large rectory garden and it required little imagination to hear the carriage wheels on the gravel as the coach from the big house came to collect the parson's daughters for their next chaperoned ball.

A few thoughts on the Baptists and adult baptism. There are millions of good saintly souls in the Baptist fold but unfortunately, even sadly, they are looking through the wrong end of the telescope as it were – focussing too much on themselves and their salvation. John 15:16 "You did not choose me, but I chose you."

Leaving individuals to make decisions for Christ appears to be very devout, but as Dietrich Bonhoeffer says "Decision for Christ is not a biblical concept." When a saintly soul Professor David Hay, whose parents were the senior Salvation Army Officers in

South Africa and himself a Church of Scotland minister, army chaplain during the Second World War and minister of St. Margaret's, Dunfermline before his appointment to the chair of Systematic Theology in Knox College, Toronto, began to, if not choke over his porridge, have difficulty swallowing when on the subject of Baptists then it was wise to pay attention.

Then what about that gifted saintly Christian autocratic Russian Nicolas Berdyaev who wrote in his autobiography *Dream and Reality* "Least of all I liked the Baptists; I could not stand their harping on salvation and their stubborn self-sufficiency."

The time was in Europe when Baptists and their co-religionists were so narrow and piously officious that they were proscribed.

That wise Orcadian from Cowdenbeath, Ron Ferguson, frequently refers to the Church of Scotland as a broad church and it is good that it should be so – broad in the sense of not patronisingly, but compassionately and imaginatively, able to appreciate the wide spectrum of gospel interpretations, never forgetting the wise words of Martin Luther King "the paralysis of analysis" – for the good tidings of the gospel are simplicity itself, God yearning to embrace every soul on the planet with the arms of His Son, Jesus of Nazareth.

Many of the "Taliban clerics" in the Church of Scotland are not unduly worried by the drop in the Church of Scotland's membership believing that with prayer the time will come when the false shepherds will die away and their proclamation of the "true faith" will usher in a new age of peace and blessedness for our beautiful native land – which of course is nonsense.

These gospel "turn or burn" souls have definite views about baptism. I think some of them would like the Church of Scotland to establish adult baptism for all who would be members, while others would like to have the option within the fellowship of their own parish or congregation to practise adult baptism. I hope my attempt to set down this distinction is understandable.

I could not resist the temptation to label them "turn or burn" merchants. While at Knox College in Toronto there was a great character Dr. William Fitch, a scion of an evangelical family in Scotland, who I think hailed from Falkirk. He was not the only one from his family in the ministry. He was minister of Knox Church on Spadina, one block west of the college. He had quite a following among Knox students. Frequently Dr. Fitch was on the radio in a programme "Faith for Today" announcing "This is Dr. William Fitch speaking – Faith for Today" in his deep gravelly Scottish voice. Without being too unkind I could raise a good laugh in our class of twelve by, in an equally gravelly Scottish voice, bawling out "This is Dr. William Fitch – Faith for Today. Turn or Burn."

Before leaving the Fitch family I would just mention that during our stay in the conservation village of Muthill near Crieff we became good friends with the retired doctor, Dr. Martin, whose charming wife was a sister of William Fitch.

"Turn or Burn" leads me on to further thoughts on the "doctrine of election" expansively recorded in the *Westminster Confession of Faith*. The President of the Westminster Assembly was a Dr. Twisse, the author of an 800-page thesis on Supralapsarianism, a fancy title for the doctrine of pre-destination, or election – i.e. that some are saved and the rest are damned. As sure as death he would have regarded himself as one of the saved, but how any one could produce such a huge book on the "doctrine" is beyond comprehension.

In the appendices you will find my consigning of the *Westminster Confession of Faith* to the archives of history, and a copy of the *Robsland Avenue, Ayr, Confession of Faith,* dated 10th August, 2007.

26

Further Thoughts

RECENTLY I HAVE been enjoying Terry Wogan's anecdotes about his youth in Ireland. I came across these words "This small, black leather-bound diary is not a Life of Johnson. There is no comment or reflection here, no indication of any real feelings about anything or anyone."

Terry's comments set me thinking that now in my 85th year (how many times have I revealed my age hoping for the proper response "Oh, you don't look it") if my book is ever to see the light of day and be more than a string of anecdotes then the time is here to begin revealing some of my inner thoughts on the great pantomime of life.

Please allow me one more tale from university days in Edinburgh in the late 1940s. One day Jimmy Black, younger brother of Gus Black who played scrum half for Scotland a few times, and I decided to go to the circus situated in a field near the Maybury roundabout beyond Corstorphine. We were waiting at the tram stop in Nicholson Square for a No.1 car Liberton to Corstorphine. There was no other vehicle in sight as the tram approached when suddenly a large Austin taxi heading south did a U-turn and approached us at a fair speed. The tram was virtually stopped as we made to step off the pavement. Quite rightly we had assumed that the taxi would stop. Not on your life – we leapt back and to show our displeasure I gave the window of the back door a thump with the back of my fist (please note not a boxing punch but a good bang with the back of the hand). Surprise, surprise, the thick glass of the taxi window shattered and disappeared into the back seat.

The taxi made no sign of stopping. Jimmy and I boarded the tram car going upstairs. When we turned the corner on to Princes Street at the North British Hotel (now the Balmoral Hotel) here was an agitated guy with the points policeman in his white coat. They came up the stairs beside the tram driver and as they approached the constable said "Show me your hands." "No need to see any hands – this is the taxi driver who failed to stop." Not to spin out this tale any further I will report that we finished up in the old police court off the High Street near St. Giles' Cathedral. While waiting our turn in the witness box the court proceedings with a variety of cases were a mixture of sad and funny. One old dear was fined a couple of shillings for putting out her bin before the permitted hour. Two or three "bookies" were on the carpet for taking street bets. In those days there were no betting shops. One "bookie" was a regular offender and he was fined the huge sum for those days of £30. He left the box, walked over to the clerk of the court while taking a wad of notes from a pocket. He peeled off thirty notes and promptly left the court in time to take bets on that day's favourites from clients either on the street corner or gathered in the pubs.

The time came for the case of the broken taxi window. The driver had been charged with failing to stop. I felt sorry for him – he kept referring to me as the "accused". My turn came – "Keeping in mind section 32, clause D of the Highway Code we looked right, looked left, looked right again and started to board the tram. The taxi did not stop and we had to jump back for our lives. Displeasure was expressed by a tap on the window." Of course the Highway Code details were fictional but impressive. The poor guy was fined ten shillings. Believe me if I say that I would pay the fine if anything similar were to occur now. Many people are not happy with the "cut in" jump-the-queue tactics of so many taxi drivers. Personally I wonder how a lot of them make a living. The odd one may be a "dodgy dealer" but many of them have families to provide for. Some own their own cabs, possibly in partnership with a friend, allowing them to work most of the hours in a day. We are not taxi-user regulars but when we do I always give the guy a handsome tip.

I am not blowing my tooter – my sole aim in writing in this way is to encourage mind and heart expansion, to escape from the prison of self, and with sympathetic imagination embrace and enter into the lives of others. Somebody said "without compassion it is impossible to be human."

Once I was parked in the large car park behind one of the banks in Ayr making one of my regular visits as treasurer of our superb organisation Opportunities in Retirement. The car park was nearly full and as I emerged from the bank a lady was parking a large Mercedes which was blocking me in. "Is my car in your way?" I know that I am an old retired guy with some time on my hands but I said to her "You are in luck; you have just met one of the most patient guys on the planet." She replied "I will be only a couple of minutes." Fifteen minutes later my new friend came out and we had a pleasant chat. Ladies' ages are taboo, she must have been sixty, but I made her day by telling her that on reaching fifty she could join O.I.R.

Harry Reid in his fine review of the ails of the Church of Scotland *Outside Verdict* lists twenty-one proposals as recommendations for new life in the auld kirk. The second proposal is, and I quote "The office of Lord High Commissioner should be abolished forthwith. It is anachronistic, serves no useful practical purpose, and sends out all the wrong signals."

Monimail parish in the 1960s was largely feudal; the top branches of the tree were branches of the Nairn family of linoleum fame. Head of the clan was the Dowager Lady Spencer-Nairn who lived at Over Rankeillour, a large house, with staff headed by Germaine the butler. From time to time I would deliberately omit the Royal Family from the prayers and I was not surprised to receive a polite letter from Lady Spencer-Nairn pointing out this omission. Now I have no desire to be rude, particularly as I treasure the kindness of her grandson Sir Robert Spencer-Nairn and his wife Joanna and of Sir Robert's mother, Mrs. Spencer-Nairn who lived in the old manse of Monimail, but down the centuries the dukes, the earls, the barons, the knights, those near the apex of the social pyramid have had varied degrees of unease in case the lower orders should pull the carpet from under the edifice and the whole hierarchical system collapse like a pack of cards.

Down the centuries the Church of Scotland has kept at bay the monarchy and one has to question the Queen's title as Defender of the Faith when in fact she is really the defender of the status quo. Her Majesty the Queen has fulfilled the role which life placed upon her with an amazing devotion, beyond words to express gratitude and admiration. The Monarchy has served Britain well over the centuries and I for one would not vote for its abolition.

Allow me to be flippant for a moment. In the days when I was minister of the beautiful parish of Ballater people had freedom to walk almost anywhere on the Balmoral estate, and one of our favourite walks was through Scots pine woods on to the banks of the Dee and back past the Scandinavian chalet beside the Queen Mother's favourite salmon fishing pool. (The chalet was a present from the Royal Family to the Queen Mother on her eightieth birthday.) Walking past the edge of the pool one day there was a wading stick half hidden in the grass. "Aha" I said to myself, "I know whose stick that is." Of course it was the Queen Mother's. Later in the day I knocked at James Pearl's (the ghillie's) door, he answered and I produced the lost stick. His face lit up with a great smile. "Her Majesty has been missing her old friend." "You tell her the minister found it." I was profusely thanked but was always hopeful of a more concrete recognition, perhaps a knighthood or a C.B.E. (knighthoods have been awarded for less meritorious service).

Many years ago there was an outbreak of typhoid in Aberdeen which was traced to a large tin of corned beef. The wags used to say that it was the only city in the world where four hundred people could contract the disease from one tin (thin economical slices). Continuing on a flippant note Dr. McQueen, Aberdeen's Medical Officer of Health, was awarded a C.B.E. which the wags translated into Corned Beef Expert.

About to embark on criticisms, some of them harsh, of the Kirk I declare again that it was a dear dear privilege to be a parish minister in the Church of Scotland.

Where to start? Communion Rolls and Supplementary Rolls should be phased out. Consider for a moment a group of worthy citizens, men and women elders of the church, gathered in a rather dingy cold session house discussing whether to allow the local butcher back on the Communion Roll. He has attended the last two communions but it was nearly five years since he communicated before – "let's wait and see if he attends the next communion." The role of the church is to invite folks to embrace, or be embraced by, Jesus – Saviour, Redeemer and Friend – and is not a struggle to construct a fellowship of "squeaky clean" respectable citizens.

Another one to be phased out is the award of Long Service Certificates, the awarding of which stokes the fires of belief in the church being a sort of religious club.

It is only now, twenty years into retirement, that one feels free to express inner thoughts. Visiting an elder in Ballater, not long home from major heart surgery in Edinburgh, there in the hall was his long service certificate beautifully framed and proudly displayed. He was an excellent elder, a dear genuine friendly soul which prevented me, another dear genuine friendly soul, advocating from the pulpit a halt to the award of long service certificates.

Some years ago Mr. Jones, the minister of Kirkmichael and Straiton (near Ayr) thought the time was ripe for the Church of Scotland to prepare a doctrine of dedication, a proposal which prompted me to write a letter to *The Herald* in reply to his letter in *The Herald*. Here it is:- May 4th, 1991.

'Sir, I was interested by the letter from the minister of Kirkmichael and Straiton on surplus kirks and the quandaries that arise, particularly since these buildings were "dedicated to the glory of God".

Mr. Jones feels that the time has come for the Church of Scotland to elucidate a "theology of dedication" and suggests that the Panel on Doctrine is probably the body to deal with the matter.

During my 25 years in the parish ministry we received many handsome memorial gifts, not least a magnificent royal blue carpet to enhance the beautiful sanctuary of Glenmuick Church, Ballater. Not one of these gifts was dedicated.

If we dedicate pulpit falls, stacking chairs, hymn books, choir gowns, electronic organs, etc., why do we not dedicate the hospital drinking vessels that give sips of water to seriously ill and dying persons?

The dedication of buildings and other material things creates an unnecessary barrier between the rough and tumble of the world and the community of the Church, adding to the still prevalent view that the Kirk is a closed and dying sanctuary for the "unco guid" rather than a fellowship of heralds bearing the good news of God's grace to all in the gift of His Son.'

By all means dedicate the bread and wine of the sacrament which is a special sign and a seal of our ingrafting into Christ – so long as we do not overlook the fact that the whole of life should be communion. A cup of tea with a friend, with the minister (who hopefully should be a friend and not a "put the fear of death into you" ghoul from the past) is communion. Some years ago Leslie and I spent nearly four years in the conservation village of Muthill near Crieff where we owned the paper shop for a year. In a well written local history book there is noted that the parish minister in Victorian times was renowned as a preacher – his sermons were described as "bountiful unto terror".

We move on to the subject of baptism. Professing myself to be an apocatistasian – a universalist – who believes that all will enter into the blessed peace of eternity, the question quite naturally arises "What then is the use of the <u>sacrament of baptism</u>?" One of the great characters on the stage of life was Martin Luther who was a leading player in triggering off the Reformation. Luther was a strange mixture of saint and thug. Like Churchill he used to find the "black dog" on his back from time to time. Luther would pause and admonish his darkness by shouting out "Martin, <u>you</u> are baptised" and the cloud of darkness would disperse like the dawn of a beautiful spring day.

Calling Luther a thug calls for a word of explanation. During his role as leader of the Reformation in Europe there was a peasants' revolt in the summer of 1525, one of many throughout history. The revolt in Germany was put down without mercy by the killing of about 130,000 peasants and the mutilation of many more. Luther's comment was "better the death of all the peasants than of the princes".

During the two thousand years since Jesus walked the earth the poor have been trodden underfoot. We do not forget the self-sacrifices, the courage and compassion of good Samaritans, in groups and individually, but the institutional churches have fawned and danced attendance on the princes and potentates of this world.

In August 1773 Boswell and Johnson en route to their tour of the Hebrides called at the manse of Laurencekirk where a Mr. Forbes was the minister. When summoned to the door the minister at first refused to meet with a stranger. When he eventually arrived at the door Boswell remonstrated with him for not coming to a stranger. The minister defended himself by saying that he had once come to a stranger who sent for him and he found him "a little worth person".

Elsewhere I recorded the sad tale of the minister of St. Cuthbert's Church in Edinburgh, the Rev. Dr. Norman Maclean, enraged when daughter Margaret married a seaman. In Margaret's words "My father cut me off and never spoke to me again for marrying beneath myself. I saw him on his deathbed but he did not know me then."

Over a hundred years ago there was much talk in church circles of "plum charges" and "princes of the pulpit". One prince of the pulpit in a plumb charge was Dr. James MacGregor of St. Cuthbert's, Edinburgh.

A century before my ordination and induction to the parish of Monimail in Fife Dr. MacGregor was inducted there as the minister. His stay in the parish was short but during that time he was able to spoil the old Georgian manse by adding bay windows to the rooms on the west side of the front door - not only bay windows but a raising of the drawing room (sitting room) ceiling which meant two steps up into the bedroom above. Now Dr. MacGregor baptised my mother in St. Cuthbert's Church during his Moderatorial year and after administering the sacrament called out "Come back, I have not kissed the bairn."

Mention of the old manse of Monimail brings to mind the evening when Mrs. Spencer-Nairn held a cocktail and supper party. Arriving with Leslie and wearing a Black Watch tie instead of a clerical collar I entered the large hallway. Just ahead of us was a tall man with his wife. Taking off my jacket I said "Good evening". There was no reply but even in the dimly lit hall it was possible to sense the unspoken "Who do these peasants think they are speaking to". The silent gent was chairman of a large Scottish public company and his identity shall remain unrevealed.

Another encounter with a mute was at the foot of the Mound near the Floral Clock and abreast of the entrance to the subterranean gents' toilets. He and I had been two of a foursome of lieutenants who shared a four-berth cabin on a troopship from Mombasa to Ceylon. My former colleague in arms was wearing a "British warm" overcoat and a bowler hat. A quiet "Good morning – I think we shared a cabin during the war" spawned a silent look as if I was a pile of the offending stuff on the pavements. At the time he was a judge, later to become a Senator of the College of Justice. No doubt he was deep in thought with a complex case.

Among my books is the large *Memoir of Dr. MacGregor* by Frances Balfour. He was inducted to Monimail in August 1862, taking up residence in the farmhouse at Lindifferon. The following year, 1863, he was much involved with the vacancy at Dunbog, a neighbouring parish – and here we come across a supreme example of the old adage that "there is no business like kirk business". The heritors of Dunbog presented to the congregation their nominee, a Mr. Edgar. The parishioners did not fall in love with him and objected to his appointment. Early in January Dr. MacGregor records in his diary "The church crowded. Afterwards violent excitement and disorder. Call signed by twelve members and six concurrents amid hissing and yelling". After prolonged meetings the nomination of Mr. Edgar was upheld and he duly arrived for his induction despite the continuing and growing objection to him being their minister. On the day the hills all around flew large black flags and the avenue of trees up to the church and manse were draped in black. Quite a welcome!!! It did not end there since a few days later a few of those most opposed packed the hub of a farm cart with explosives, lit them and rolled the wheel towards the manse. During our years in Fife we were friends of Johnstone and Sigrid Titterington who pointed out to us the scars of the assault on the manse. Mr. Edgar must have been a stout-hearted hero of the faith because history records that he ministered on, and the time came when most of the folk were fond of their shepherd.

Down the years the stipend paid to ministers has been a minefield. Invariably housed in large manses the general feeling would be that they were doing rather well for themselves. The time was when many parish stipends were tied to market prices. A fall in the price of oats and barley could rock, if not sink, the manse family budget. Many of these stipends based on market prices were paid quarterly – and there were many cases of ministers being inducted into a charge and having to wait three months for their first portion of stipend On the other hand there were many ministers who were more than handsomely paid – and this did not always equate with the wealth of the parish being a plum charge.

Dr. James MacGregor by any standard of measurement was "wee", in fact he was affectionately known as "Wee MacGregor" – "Wee Mac" would have been going too far in the days when Christian names were rarely used even among close friends. Now I am going to insert a long quotation from Dr. MacGregor's diary regarding his response to a delegation from the Tron church in Glasgow seeking a new minister. The entry is dated June 15th, 1863.

'The four men came here on Saturday with the most exorbitant preconceived opinions of your humble servant. Somebody had been putting it into their heads that I am about as near perfection in the ministerial point of view as is permitted in this sublunary scene.

They moreover believe that if I was in the Tron everything would go on in the most swimming way. Well. With these views they were authorised to offer me the full stipend of £425 in the meantime, with the assurance that when I come to the full charge I should have £500. I showed them to their own satisfaction that to accept of such an offer would be a dead loss, and that I would never entertain the idea at all unless on these terms – a guarantee of £500 in the meantime, and an assurance of £600 on the death of Dr. Boyd: on which terms I would be inclined to entertain their proposal favourably, giving them however no promise.'

"On the death of Dr. Boyd". Many larger parishes in those days had two ministers - minister of the parish with a colleague and successor. Some of these shared ministries were harmonious – not surprisingly many were not. Kirk records are full of accounts of, if not fisticuffs, then copies of letters back and forth between the two of the most vitriolic content. I am not well enough versed in the historical minefield of stipends but some very old parish ministers continued to receive their full stipend "until death do us part" and consequently there was less in the kitty for the colleague and successor. I am interested that a parish minister should dismiss £425 as being a dead loss, asking for at least £500 when a shepherd or head keeper on an estate would receive £25 per year. Twenty times as much. Small wonder that Dr. MacGregor could jaunt about the continent on holiday. There are copies of quite a few letters in his Memoir from Italy and other European resorts, some addressed to no less a person than the Duchess of Argyll.

Even today in some travel agents there are faded replicas of Thomas Cook posters offering all-in ten-day packages in Europe for £10. I am not in the business of "roughing up" the wee guy who baptised my mother but have included all the above as a contribution to an understanding of the extraordinary elevation of ordained friends of Jesus who were held by their parishioners with a mixture of affection and fear and trembling.

From time to time I would throw into the ring of our coffee fraternal discussions the question of "how appropriate it was for disciples to live in the ten and twelve room houses?" To be fair to the guys – all guys in those days – the normal response was a few smiles and deaf ears. I do not suggest that I was the only one uneasy with our large abodes (perhaps my colleagues privately shared my views), for I have to say that during all my adventures in the journey of life colleagues in the ministry were a special breed – totally genuine human beings – a view endorsed by Harry Reid in his *Outside Verdict* where he wrote:-

'The Church of Scotland is so infuriatingly elusive; it is not a meaningful target at all. It has much wrong with it, yet the paradox is that its component parts and its servants are for the most part overwhelmingly good. If I compare it to some other component parts of the Scottish anatomy – the law, the media, education, the finance sector, even the worlds of medicine and science – it is in a different class.'

In one chapter of his most interesting review book *Outside Verdict* on the ails of the Church of Scotland Harry Reid mentions the kirk session where one elder always turned up clutching a copy of *Cox's Practice and Procedure*. This is one of the saddest things I have ever read.

There are dicta, dicta, dicta, but one of the truest is "it is the letter of the law which killeth and the spirit which giveth life".

One elder at Monimail (kind host to Leslie on her first visit to the parish before we were married) successful farmer, Second World War veteran, awarded the Military Cross, with a seat on the local magisterial bench, was once heard to say "Oh, but Mr. Blyth has no idea how to conduct a session meeting."

To be fair Monimail had twelve elders and Glenmuick less than twenty, but from memory we never once had a vote. Not a hundred percent agreement in every decision but as brothers and sisters in Christ (yes sisters – before retiring I ordained at least one lady to the eldership) harmony had to reign before I pronounced the benediction.

I have recently received a gift from Sheila Gould, Leslie's sister, a copy of *Scottish Piety* compiled by Professor Alec Cheyne, a superb wee book. One of the gems is the tribute by David Cairns to his father who was minister of the rural parish of Stitchel in the Borders. Here is a quotation "My father never once in his long ministry of forty-five years in Stitchel had even a vote in his session."

There must have been many clerical families throughout Britain in straitened financial circumstances, and we were one of them. In 1973 the stipend for Glenmuick Church, Ballater, was about £1,500. However we were hardly in the door, Leslie and I with the family, James, Helen and Anne, rising eight, five and three respectively, when inflation took off and soon was well up into double figures. The manse was a magnificent family home but Ballater being one of the coldest parts of Britain (I recall the period of several weeks when the temperature very rarely rose above zero) much of the stipend went "up in smoke" as it were. To say that Leslie never worked would be a scurrilous blasphemy. She had been a librarian at the Royal College of Physicians in Edinburgh before our marriage. Ministers' wives entered into the life of the parish and Leslie was no exception being involved with the Woman's Guild, the church ladies' Work Party, the running of the twice-yearly church sales to raise funds for congregational purposes, and for a time taught in the Sunday school. During our years in the ministry offices for the parishes were almost unknown and so all the telephone calls came to the manse. I must record our thanks, for which there are not adequate words to express, to Mrs. Lorna Forbes, Mrs. Rona Sturrock and Mrs. Rita Simpson who so kindly and willingly "baby-sat" in the manse when occasions demanded. In our two parishes the opportunities for library work that would fit in with the family were virtually nil, and in any case I have never ceased to wonder how wives run a home, look after a family and work full time without break-downs. For the last two years of my ministry in Ballater Leslie obtained part-time work in the village library and the income from this was a boost to our vastly overdrawn account and eased the strain somewhat.

In closing the family left the manse in June 1986, "old Uncle Fred" as they called me, having suffered "burn out". A word of explanation for that sobriquet. When the family was young one of the children's papers which they read from time to time was *The Teddy Bear* comic. The main feature on the front and back pages was based upon the goings-on of a family of teddy bears – the usual father, mother and junior members – plus a rather scruffy uncle, who was dressed in jerseys with holes in the sleeves and loved pottering about in old cars. He of course was called Uncle Fred – just my type of guy! I have never liked getting dressed up in uniforms and even the clerical robes gave me a little unease.

On the Hoof

SCOTLAND IS BLESSED with a great range of mountainous scenic country where for the most part we are free to wander at will. In October 1973, our first autumn in Ballater, I was invited to join a party of around twenty on a walk through the Lairig Ghru, which can be as long as twenty miles depending upon the starting and finishing points.

We drove round to Aviemore and began walking from the northern end. One photograph taken at the midday midway lunch halt is of Donald Coutts holding a golf umbrella, Derek Livingstone with a long hairy sporran as part of his outfit, and myself well happed up alongside Ian Murray, the pharmacist. Donald had a whole chicken for his "piece" and it was quite a sight seeing him devour it.

At the end near the Linn of Dee we were greeted by a bunch of good souls from Ballater with a van belonging, I think, to Davidson's the butchers. It had a sliding door which when opened revealed a Calor gas stove on which there was a meal ready to be heated again before serving it.

Walking is enjoyable but thirst creating, and the sight of a case of McEwan's red tins was welcome. Ian Cordiner was another member of the walking party. Next day he was seen hirpling around Ballater and the assumption was that his feet had been badly blistered on the long hoof. In fact what had happened was that Ian, in party mood, had been jumping up and down on the empty beer tins to flatten them in the box and went over on his ankle and sprained it.

This was not my first long walk but it was before I owned walking boots, and I had on my feet a pair of Lotus Veldskoen boots, old friends, purchased several years before for £5 or 5 guineas.

Another parish expedition occurred on the night of 6th/7th June 1978, the time of the Silver Jubilee of the Queen's coronation. The plan had been for a bonfire to be lit at Windsor Castle, the signal for a second bonfire to be lit on a hill twenty or thirty miles north, and so on, bonfire after bonfire, finishing with one on Ben Hope, the most northerly Munro (hill over 3,000 ft) on mainland Britain. The whole progression of bonfires with commentary was on BBC TV.

Fourteen of us left Ballater late on that June evening but by the time we were struggling up the steep boulder field called The Ladder, above the loch in Lochnagar's huge corrie, we were in deep snow.

Eventually we reached the site of the bonfire, not on the summit, but built on a prominent peak nearby. By then the short darkness of a June night had fallen. A bunch of hardy souls had constructed a snow shelter for themselves, giving an idea of the depth of the fall. It was quite obvious that any bonfire on Lochnagar that night would not be visible for more than a few yards. The technicalities of overcoming this hitch in the TV programme were left to those involved – we were concerned about our next move.

Among our party was a great hero, Bob Todd, the oldest by far, attired in his knickerbockers lovat suit. Bob declared that he was descending while some wished to stay and see what would transpire. Well of course nothing was going to happen in connection with the lighting of the bonfire. It was cold and blowing a gale with limited visibility. I suggested "No splitting up. Either we all stay for daylight in an hour or so or we all descend." We agreed to descend and went down by the path to the Glas-allt Shiel at the head of Loch Muick. Halfway down the falls we paused and one good soul's tomato sandwiches were half frozen, which gives some idea of the cold wildness of even a June night on a Scottish mountain.

Over the years at Ballater, with various companions, the summits of Cairn Toul, Cairngorm and Derry Cairngorm, Ben A'an, Beinn a' Bhuird, Glas Maol and many more were reached. The happy memories of those trips are recorded with great pleasure and gratitude for the stamina and health which allowed me to do them.

Since retiring to Ayr Leslie and I have done many walks, some on our own, but many with Ayr Rambling Club and the long-walk groups of Opportunities in Retirement. A few years ago we were members of an O.I.R. week's walking holiday based on Newton Stewart.

While living in Muthill we enjoyed many walks in beautiful Perthshire, and climbed Ben Vorlich on the south side of Loch Earn and Ben Lawers, but probably the biggest single day challenge was Stobinion and Ben More starting from Inverlochlarig at the west end of Loch Voil (the site of Rob Roy's house according to my superb four miles to the inch Newnes Motorists' Touring Map published in 1965. Apart from all the old railway lines being shown the detail on such a relatively small scale is amazing – Kindrogan, Enochdhu, Balvarran, Finegand in Glenshee where we failed to rescue the lady vet in the snowstorm).

Our biggest challenge of all was born one day while sailing up Loch Etive to see the seals and possibly a golden eagle. The day was a pause during a fifteen day Caledonian McBrayne rover ticket trip round the western isles – the ferry for Barra did not sail from Oban until 5 p.m. Leaning over the side admiring the view on the east side of the loch Leslie said "That would make a super walk."

Here it is – bus from Ayr to Glasgow, Glasgow to Oban, getting off at Taynuilt. The first night we camped at the head of the loch in a small pea pod tent belonging to our son James. We woke to find frost on the tent and on the grass although it was early June. On the second day we climbed over the pass into Glencoe with a night at the Youth Hostel. The third day we took the bus to Fort William, Inverness, and Aviemore, and then walked to the Youth Hostel at Loch Morlich where we burnt the toast in the morning, setting off the fire alarm, much to the excitement of a school party from Dundee, though no evacuation was necessary.

On the fourth day we accepted a lift to the top car park for Cairngorm and walked (on frozen snow) to the summit of Ben Macdhui and back along the ridge above the Lairig Ghru. On the fifth day we entered Lairig Ghru by the Chalamain gap and with an early supper at the famous Corrour Bothy we camped beside the infant Dee, near the White Bridge due west of the Linn of Dee. On the sixth day (a showery day, we had been fortunate with the weather otherwise) we walked through Glen Tilt to Blair Atholl, and on the seventh day we took the bus and train home to Ayr where I weighed my pack at the railway station, it was 45 lbs.

After all this hoofing I cannot resist the temptation to recall a four day march in India, before I was mule officer. We covered eighty miles, quite a bit at night. The colonel had issued an order "No officers' beds to be transported." With no thought of bucking the colonel's order but simply for a bit of daft devilment I thought no one can object if I carry my bed. Now an officer's canvas folding bed with wooden frame weighed 24 lbs.

Off we set, myself complete with full equipment – big pack, small pack, water bottle, tommy gun and two pouches each with four filled magazines, and the bed across the top of my pack. The askaris were tough little guys but short of stature and so from time to time I would swap my tommy gun for a bren gun which would have been twice as heavy. Once or twice during the eighty miles I had a spell carrying an anti-tank rifle, a long weapon which weighed 38 lbs. At one of the halts my orderly was busy erecting my bed and brewing up a mug of tea. He had a broad grin on his face and I asked what was going on. A couple of fellow officers had thought if that daft b... can hump all that gear a little more won't hurt. As a little light relief (heavy relief) to season the rather long hot monotonous march my "friends" had put five or six apple-sized rocks into my big pack among the vests and socks.

With training like that it is small wonder that I was able to tramp the hills well through my seventies with pleasure and profound gratitude.

THE CHRISTIAN FAITH

GOD IS LOVE.

Today love has been devalued and trivialised into a sentimental pop song embrace when true love is a cosmic power beside which the largest man-made atomic explosion is a damp squib.

Jesus calls us to grow in grace unto the measure of the stature of Himself. In other words to be <u>Christlike – to be human</u> – to be compassionate – for without compassion it is impossible to be human.

To a large extent the institutional churches have replaced the idol of the golden calf with Jesus. Jesus has become an idol endlessly sought in prayers, and anxious institutional activity, <u>when in fact He may well be the person sitting next to us on the local bus</u>.

Most folk think of faith, belief, as a diminishment of life – a burden added to the already heavy load of the daily round – when in fact it is a liberation from the agonising pettiness of selfish concerns and anxieties to join the global family.

Sadly this liberation has been confused and lost by too much ecclesiastical tinkering with the domestic fabric of life's adventure.

And so I draw this rambling life's tale to a close with the first verse of one of my favourite readings from the Bible, 1 John 4:7

'Beloved let us love one another for love is of God and he who loves is born of God and knows God.'

END OF JOURNEY

WHEN I WAS a wee chap my prime possession was a beautiful green Hornby engine – the Flying Scotsman – long since passed into the mists of memory.

By nature I have been a kind of flying Scotsman who feels it is time to bring this long tale to a close. My tender is still half full with the fuel of ideas and anecdotes – the problem is getting these into the fire box to create heat for more steam. And so I will lay down my pen, if not for ever, at least for a good pause.

Among the gifts I received at Christmas was a beautiful album with eight DVDs, each disc having two or three great railway journeys of the world. The other evening I travelled from Singapore to Bangkok and then to the Bridge on the River Kwai on the Orient Express. These discs are a wonderful way of travelling through other countries from the comfort of a favourite armchair.

I close with thanks to those readers who have read this far, hoping that my ramblings have been of some challenging interest. Try and visualise me travelling the world with the feet up and a wee dram ready to hand. Although not too wee – "How do you tak yer dram, minister?" "Oh about half and half, and see that there is plenty of water."

And there's more! Here I am again seated at my desk with pen in hand much, much sooner than I ever imagined. The arm chair journeys on great train trips, even the dram, will have to wait for what is a "train driver" tale teller to do when suddenly five tons of top grade stoking coal are dumped in the "tender" of the mind.

The fuel comes from Sally Magnusson's very moving, beautiful but hilarious interview with Bishop Desmond Tutu on Songs of Praise, BBC1 TV, Sunday 17th February, 2008. Desmond, Sally and I would not have been the only ones with tears in their eyes. An added bonus was the glimpses of Father Trevor Huddleston in his cassock among his black friends in the slums of Johannesburg. On frequent train journeys back and forward between Huddersfield and Leeds I would not have been very old when my parents were asked "What is that large red brick building?" From the tenor of their reply "That is the Community of the Resurrection" I sensed that it was a very special place. And of course it is, and Trevor Huddleston was one of the most famous members of that community.

Apart from the moving pleasure of reading his classic gem *Naught for your Comfort* he has been a lifetime hero of mine who was distinguished by a passionate belief that the doctrine of the universal brotherhood of men in Christ should be universally applied.

Mother Teresa of Calcutta was another great champion of the faith who some would have us believe was on an ego trip. Such a judgement is blasphemous. Calcutta in 1944 was bursting at the seams with hundreds of thousands of extra destitute souls, resulting from a catastrophic famine in Bengal in 1943.

Without a divine embrace, the embrace of Jesus, care of the destitute dying from the filthy streets would never have begun, never mind begun and grown. Her "House of the Dying" was opened in 1952 and today there are over 650 charity houses in 124 countries including a leper colony called Shanti Nagar (Town of Peace) near Asansol in West Bengal.

Aligning myself with the great heroes of the faith causes me acute embarrassment, however if the raising of the lid on the stew pot of my rambling life's tale should cause any reader to imagine that I have been on an ego trip my heart would break because, like St. Paul, "I have been determined to know nothing among you save Jesus Christ and Him crucified." And so I close with the Aaronic Blessing:-

> 'The Lord bless you and keep you:
> The Lord make His face to shine upon you and be gracious unto you:
> The Lord lift up His countenance upon you and give you peace.'

AMEN

Appendices

Appendix 1

THE GOOD TIDINGS OF THE GOSPEL

The Global and Cosmic Embrace of Jesus Christ

THE LATE ARCHIE Craig, Moderator of the General Assembly of the Church of Scotland in 1961, introduces his Warrack Lectures on Preaching with the following paragraph –

"A year or so after I was ordained to the ministry I happened one day to meet Principal Alexander Martin on Princes Street in Edinburgh, and he greeted me with the question 'Well, how's the preaching going?' When I replied that I was finding it very difficult he exclaimed 'Preaching's not difficult, man, it's impossible!!'"

Further on in his first lecture Professor Craig introduces a long quote from a book written by the great Swiss theologian, the late Karl Barth (The Word of God and the Word of Man).

"What are you doing, you man, with the Word of God on your lips? Upon what grounds do you assume the role of mediator between heaven and earth? And, to crown all, to do so with results, with success? Did one ever hear of such overweening presumption, such Titanism, or – to speak less classically but more clearly – such brazenness? One does not with impunity cross the boundaries of mortality. One does not with impunity usurp the prerogatives of God! But does not the profession of the ministry inevitably involve both? Is not the whole situation in the Church an illustration of man's chronic presumption, which is really worse here than in any other field?"

<u>Can a minister be saved?</u>

Five weeks before my fortieth birthday I was ordained a minister in the Church of Scotland. The same evening I was inducted to the parish of Monimail in Fife. In 1963 there were two churches in the parish – the service was held in the former Free Church with its small red tiled spire at the Bow of Fife. My fortieth birthday was on All Saints Day, 1st November, 1963. Before the month was out I was lying on my back with a leg under traction in the Adamson Cottage Hospital, Cupar – the diagnosis a slipped disc. Unmarried and rattling around in a half-furnished twelve-roomed manse, and having conducted my first communion service, periods of wakefulness in the middle of the night gave me time to ponder the enormity of what I had done. The excruciating pain prompted good neighbours (and they were good neighbours, Jimmy and Agnes Bryce) to summon an ambulance – six weeks on traction had nothing to do with a slipped disc, it was the body and mind rebelling against my brazenness in believing myself called to the holy ministry.

This is no place for arguments, or even discussion, as to what constitutes a call to the ministry. A fellow student at Knox College, Toronto, used to say that he had only to shake hands with a person to know whether he or she was a true believer, regarding many of us as false shepherds.

Please allow me to introduce another small spiritual classic – "Letters of Direction. Thoughts on the Spiritual Life from the Letters of Abbé de Tourville." The Abbé Henri de Tourville was born in Paris on March 19th, 1842, and died at the Castle of Tourville near Pont-Andemer on March 5th, 1903. The translator gives an explanation of this little book "It is set forth in the hope that it may be of use to many perplexed and anxious souls. <u>May it help us to understand better that in spite of all our weaknesses and suffer-ings human life yet remains a masterpiece of Divine Love.</u>"

As these quotes and thoughts are an introduction to a dissertation questioning the way the church has exercised its role as a servant of the gospel I hesitate to endorse some of the Abbé's beliefs.

Chapter 4 in the Letters of Direction is entitled Forerunners and it is with a mixture of sadness and joy that I feel that I belong to them. As you read the following quote you cannot escape the conviction that here is an old mortal in his dotage desperate to make some mark on the world's stage. Believe me when I write that it is impossible for me to distance myself far enough from such a conviction – so far as I know in my own heart and mind the chief inducement for endorsing the Abbé's thoughts is love for the Lord Jesus Christ.

"We belong to the Church universal, universal in time. And is it not interesting to see how in the nineteenth and twentieth centuries, God sends into the world souls like our own, which in some aspects belong already to the twenty-first century and in others to the twenty-fifth? We are as it were the first proofs of an edition printed only for connoisseurs but destined later on to be given to the world at large. It is good to be among God's experiments for the future, only we must realize that we do belong to the future.

There is nothing presumptuous in thinking or feeling that we are right. It is in fact necessary to get used to this kind of spiritual vigour. Otherwise we lose all clearness of thought and are bound to go wrong."

The Gospel sheds light on the adventure of life as we orbit through the vastnesses of space on our planet home at 66,600 m.p.h.

From 1958 to 1961, in my mid-thirties, I was a divinity student at Knox College in the University of Toronto. Once or twice a term I would lunch downtown with a friend from Edinburgh who was an investment banker on Bay Street. Access to the large office on the fourth or fifth floor was by elevator. The operator was a charming ex-service man from Northern Ireland. In student garb I sensed that he was curious as to what I did for a living visiting the striped suits and polished shoes of the stockbroker investment world. One day after many visits I let drop that I was studying for the ministry of the Presbyterian Church at Knox College – in a flash he blurted out in his delightful Irish brogue – <u>"Oh! The wife's been saved."</u>

Frequently there are letters in the national press from intelligent people – judges, lawyers, statesmen, M.P.s, doctors, poets, and others, telling the clergy in no uncertain terms to stick to their last – <u>the saving of souls</u>. The extent to which society is saturated with the notion that the role of the church and its clergy is to save souls is staggering. And furthermore not only to stick to the saving of souls but refrain from interfering with the daily life of business and politics. I think it was Lord Melbourne, Queen Victoria's Prime Minister, who once said "Things are coming to a pretty pass when the church starts to meddle in politics". Quite simply the role of the church and its clergy is not to save souls but to proclaim in all its incredible and mind-boggling glory that our souls are safe. This is not a hair-splitting distinction but a basic fact in any attempt to understand the unsearchable riches of the Gospel.

Zeal for saving souls created a belief in the church as a task force to build the Kingdom, which prompts a quotation from Werner Pelz's "Irreligious Reflections on the Christian Church", S.C.M. Press, Religious Book Club Edition 128, published 1959 –

"We are not here to build the Kingdom. To think we are is pretentious and silly. We are here to point – in thought, word and deed – to him who has established his rule in the world quite apart from us, and who in this world rules from a Cross."

Having been a Church of Scotland parish minister for a quarter of a century acknowledging that there is truth in the saying <u>"the nearer to the church the further from God"</u> makes my heart ache.

The saintly German theologian, pastor Dietrich Bonhoeffer executed by the Nazis in April 1945, wrote a letter from Barcelona dated 7th August 1928 from which I extract a quote –

"I'm getting to know new people every day; here one meets people as they are, away from the masquerade of the "Christian world", people with passions, criminal types, little people with little ambitions, little desires, and little sins, all in all people who feel homeless in both senses of the word, who loosen up if one talks to them in a friendly way, <u>real people</u>; I can only say that I have gained the impression that it is just these people who are much more under grace than under wrath, and it is the Christian world which is more under wrath than under grace."

Please allow me to introduce to you a theological gem. A small Fontana book "The Divine Pity". The author was the late Gerald Vann, a Dominican father. The subject is a study in the Beatitudes. Great emphasis is laid on the fact that all of us are members of a global family who are called to live on our planet home in wonder, awe and gratitude regarding the common everyday things – eating a meal, talking with friends, even I suppose cleaning one's teeth – as simple acts of worship.

"Worship is not part of the Christian life, it is the Christian life."

"We are right to have a special place in our hearts for our own family and our own friends; but if we are to live as Christians then the whole world has to be our family, and all men friends."

In one chapter he refers to another theological gem "A Serious Call to a Devout and Holy Life" by William Law 1686-1761 in which Law speaks of those who try to escape from the terrifying reality of God by seeking refuge in the externals of religion. Despite the millions of souls during the past 2,000 years who have martyred themselves in forgiveness and practical loving kindness, despite the hauntingly beautiful music and chants of the church, the awesome beauty of the abbeys, cathedrals, parish churches and all things ecclesiastic, the question remains, to what extent has this busyness saved the generations from an encounter with the living God? Some weeks ago I ordered a book from the United States entitled "Why the Jews Rejected Jesus?" Before I had a chance to read it I loaned it to a brother-in-law, a retired lecturer in chemistry at Edinburgh University who is a fully ordained non-stipendiary Episcopal clergyman. The title of this unread book prompts the question whether anyone has ever really accepted Jesus on his terms not ours.

The late Professor William Barclay of Glasgow University felt it very strange that the modern church confines the celebration of Easter to one day in the year – when every day, every moment is Easter. Which prompts us to ask the question to what extent the church's calendar based upon the events in the life of the carpenter's son from Nazareth – his birth, life, death and resurrection – is a subtle avoidance of the challenge of the Gospel to fall on our knees seeking mercy?

The life, death and resurrection of Jesus brought in a NEW AGE for the whole global family; for the whole of creation. A basic axiom for the presentation of the unsearchable riches of the Gospel is to acknowledge the fact that the challenge of Jesus is global and cosmic. Banish forever any thought that the church is a task force to win the world for Christ. Stop thinking of the church as the people of God. The global family is the people of God. The title of our supplementary hymn book "Songs of God's People" should have been called quite simply "Songs of Praise".

Thomas Bilney (1495-1531), Protestant martyr, a member of Trinity Hall, Cambridge, used to proclaim from the pulpit "The Jews and Saracens (Arabs) would long ago have become believers had it not been for the idolatry of Christian men in offering candles, wax and money to stocks and stones".

Some months ago there was an article in the Guardian Weekly bearing the title "Religion is a Bloody Disgrace". In actual fact it can be far worse than that. The wise and saintly theologian the late Karl Barth used to declare with great vehemence "Christianity is not a religion – it is the very antithesis of all religion". The great challenge not only for believers and church members but for the global family is to unscramble the institutional church. This calls for a totally different mind-set from our earth-bound materialism and anxieties about tomorrow. The question is not whether we are being good parents or good grandparents, but are we being good ancestors? What will the dwellers on our planet home think of us 1,000, aye even 3,000 years from now?

The late J.B. Phillips, translator of the gospels into modern English, wrote a book entitled "Your God is Too Small". In fact He is not too small, He is too wee.

Stating again the fact that our planet home is orbiting through space at 66,600 m.p.h. in a universe vast beyond our understanding what has happened is that the Cross has been dismembered.

Jesus said "I am the light of the world". The conflict between light and darkness is a conflict between God and man; between heaven and earth. Dismember the Cross – set the vertical timber aside – leaving the horizontal member to be broken in two, one part for the goodies the other for the baddies, and the scene is set for Crusades, Inquisitions, heresy trials and all sorts of bloodshed and mayhem in the name of Jesus.

Mention of heresy trials reminds me of a solemn promise to myself to visit a grave in Roseneath cemetery in Dunbartonshire.

In 1872 the Rev. John McLeod Campbell was laid to rest. In the 1820's he had been minister of Rhu where his "sin" was to preach "the doctrine of universal atonement and pardon through the death of Christ". In 1830 he was libelled for heresy before the Presbytery of Dumbarton. The case went by appeal to the Synod and finally to the Assembly which, in spite of a petition in his favour signed by nearly all his parishioners and a moving appeal from his own father, resolved by 119 votes to 6 to depose him from the ministry.

It is true to say that McLeod Campbell was the victim of the ecclesiastical climate of the Victorian era but that is no reason for crucifying him. Before the Church Council of Constantinople in A.D. 543 many great champions of the faith, Clement of Alexandria, Origen, and Gregory of Nyassa, preached the doctrine that ultimately all will share in the grace of salvation.

We mention again the saintly German theologian and martyr Dietrich Bonhoeffer murdered by the Nazis in April 1945 who warns ministers and colleagues against feeding their flocks on "cheap grace", dispensing with the agonies of Christ on the Cross while offering an "anything goes" palatable porridge.

Apocatistasis, there's a good word for Scrabble, the doctrine that all will enter into the grace of salvation is the antithesis of "cheap grace". It is the gift of God given to many over the centuries who have knelt in adoration before the Cross, yearning for the Saviour to be free in the turmoil of the life of the world.

I believe that Jesus of Nazareth is the long promised Messiah, and the rejection of Him by the ancient people of Israel, to whom the global family owe gratitude beyond measure, has been and is an unspeakable tragedy. If the early believers instead of putting the boot in with loud shrieks of "Christ killers" had embraced the Jews as children of God how different history might have been.

If our great-great-great-grandchildren are to have a planet home, hopefully to enjoy its beauty and abundant fruits the time is here now for global currency to be loving kindness and, despite the mind-boggling diversity of languages and cultures, to have as its foundation stone the basic fact that we are all worthy of dignity as human beings; children of a Father who is in Heaven.

Two or three times a year in sermons I would declare that if I thought that God looked upon me as an ordained minister with more favour than upon a wee infant dying in its mother's arms in the slums of Calcutta I would never mount the steps of a pulpit again.

As we gaze into the unknown future the crying need is for Jesus to be released from the shackles of the institutional churches to roam freely in every land, to roam freely in the person of believers. Recently we watched Richard Attenborough's magnificent film "Gandhi" which led to a second reading of Louis Fischer's "The Life of Mahatma Gandhi". From Viceroys to untouchables the opinion was lovingly expressed that Gandhi was the most Christ-like human being any of them had ever met. Speaking of Scotland I do not suggest that we start going about our daily tasks dressed in tartan dhotis and flip-flop sandals but we have to raise our eyes and thoughts from our dearly loved churches and favourite pews quite simply to see the world and the whole of creation through the eyes of Jesus – for the world and the universe is a holy place and life is a sacred gift.

A final quote, from *Jésus-Christ, cet inconnu* by Pierre Maury, Editions Oberlin, Strasbourg, 1948 – and in using so many quotes I recall the words of Boswell and Johnson at Auchinleck House "Thank God we do not speak from books" for each of the quotes has been passed through the crucible of my mind and heart and are beliefs of my own –

"Mon dessein n'était pas d'exposer ou de défendre une doctrine, mais simplement d'annoncer Jésus-Christ; comme on annonce une nouvelle à quelqu'un qui l'ignore et qui éprouve grand'peine à la croire tant elle est bonne: trop bonne, trop belle, disent certains, pour être vraie.

Les objections à cette nouvelle, je ne les ai pas évoquées pour les démontrer fausses, mais uniquement pour souligner l'incommensurable splendeur de l'Evangile."

"My intention was neither to expound nor to defend any doctrine, but simply to announce Jesus Christ; as one announces a piece of news to somebody who has not yet heard it and who has great difficulty in believing it because it is so good: too good, too beautiful, some say, to be true.

I have not mentioned the objections to this news in order to prove them wrong, but solely to emphasise the immeasurable splendour of the Gospel."

Please allow me to append a poem which I encountered while thumbing through a pile of old Dollar Academy magazines. The author was James Hayter, the gifted character actor who appeared in several films. He was a pupil at the Academy leaving in 1923, the year of my birth.

Here it is:-

The Spirit is Willing

The Holy Ghost is not concerned with how much money we have earned
Or that we own a Cadillac, or whether we are white or black.
He lives within us everyone, a link with God, and Christ his Son
(Or if not Christ, Mohammed or the Buddha, or a dozen more,
whatever intermediary we choose
For Hindus, Muslims, Christians, Jews,
Which, to the others may seem odd, all send our prayers
through them to God).
Why is it then so many fear to be alone with no one near,
Why is it, when we are alone, we just must use the telephone,
Watch television, chat, or read – why should we feel this urgent need?
It's fear, I think, that leaves no choice – we fear to hear our inner voice
Our "conscience" as some people say, that tries to show us all the way.
We scoff at it, we will not hear; the more we scoff, the more we fear
But when our time draws near to die, and we must say our last goodbye
What have we then to help us face our journey to – who knows what place?
Yet, from birth until life's end, we have within us all a Friend,
A Comforter, a piece of God, to love us, so it does seem odd

If all our lives we should deny our sole Companion when we die.

The day after locating this gem I bussed from Ayr to Dollar on my free pass. On the return journey waiting for the Glasgow bus at Stirling two Sikh gentlemen joined me on the bench. As they sat down the younger of the two greeted me with the most beatific smile. Instant rapport. A casual observer would have thought us to be lifelong friends.

Brought to Britain as a child about sixty years ago he lives with his family in London where he had worked in a factory, and also as a roofer and on the high tension pylons (I hope his beard was not singed!). Accompanied by an older friend the two Sikhs were spending a few days' holiday in Scotland and were delighted with their visit to Stirling Castle.

A genuine smile is a gift from God to dispel the walls which needlessly isolate us from one another.

APPENDIX 2

THE CONFLICT OF WILLS

OUR FATHER WHO art in Heaven hallowed be Thy Name; Thy Kingdom come; Thy Will be done on earth as it is in Heaven.

What is the Will of God?

President Abraham Lincoln penned these wise words in a letter from the Executive Mansion dated March 15th, 1865 – "Men are not flattered by being shown that there has been a difference of purpose between the Almighty and them."

Ignoring the words of the prophet Isaiah "For my thoughts are not your thoughts, neither are your ways my ways saith the Lord" (chapter 55, vv. 8 & 9) the global family was determined to exercise its own will – hence two thousand years of religious mayhem.

Faced with the futility of settling differences by armed conflict and the prospect of global atomic meltdown time is running out for a prayerful seeking of the Will of the Heavenly Father.

What is the Will of God?

His Will is that all dwellers upon our planet home come to know themselves as His children.

His Will is that we become world citizens seeing Jesus in every man and woman and child – for in Him there is neither Jew nor Greek, there is neither bond nor free, for we are all one in Christ Jesus.

Rabbi Albert Friedlander of Westminster Synagogue declares in the final chapter of his book of enlightenment "Riders Towards the Dawn" –

"I often meet Christians who shine like incandescent candles and light up the world for me with their faith."

APPENDIX 3A

THE WESTMINSTER CONFESSION OF FAITH

Ratified by the General Assembly of the Church of Scotland
27th August, 1647

A DOCUMENT PRODUCED by an assembly of divines at Westminster in 1643 to SET IN CONCRETE the beliefs of the Reformed Churches as a subordinate standard, to the ultimate standard the Bible.

"By calling the Confession of Faith a subordinate standard we must not suppose that we give ourselves liberty to set its exposition of doctrine aside in favour of any other interpretation of Scripture passages bearing on that doctrine."

The Westminster Confession of Faith was ratified by the General Assembly of the Church of Scotland on the 27th August 1647 and its acceptance still features in the Ordination Service of men and women to the ministry of the Church of Scotland.

The President of the Westminster Assembly was a Dr. Twisse the author of an 800-page thesis on SUPRALAPSARIANISM – quite a word (too many letters for SCRABBLE but a marvellous clue for a large general knowledge crossword). Supralapsarianism is the fancy title for the doctrine of predestination, or election – i.e. that some are saved and the rest are damned.

While the Assembly did not endorse his "masterpiece" the whole confession is saturated with belief in the preordained election of some and the damnation of the rest.

In chapter III of the Confession, entitled "Of God's Eternal Decree" section III reads –

> "By the decree of God, for the manifestation of his glory, some men and angels are predestinated unto everlasting life, and others foreordained to everlasting death."

Section IV reads –

> "These angels and men, thus predestinated and foreordained, are particularly and unchangeably designed; and their number is so certain and definite, that it cannot be either increased or diminished."

Martin Luther King, the saintly black activist, had a marvellous insight into the destruction of the good tidings by endless discussion about the nature of God's love for man in Jesus Christ – he called it "the paralysis of analysis".

The Westminster Confession of Faith with its demonic separation of the global family into the saved and the damned is a supreme example of the paralysis of analysis with its tortuous dissection of church doctrine enshrined in twenty-three chapters – a document which laid the ground for the awful soul-destroying moralizing humbug of the Victorian Church and should be consigned to the archives of history.

APPENDIX 3B

THE ROBSLAND AVENUE, AYR, CONFESSION OF FAITH

10th August, 2007

FEAR OF THE Lord is the beginning of WISDOM.

Fear which the institutional churches have preached as a way of putting the "frighteners on people" so that the sheep are humbly obedient when in fact fear of the Lord is a divine spiritual liberation which generates awesome wonder and gratitude.

Stand fast in the liberty wherewith Christ hath set us free and become not entangled again with the yoke of bondage – the bondage of religion.

The unsearchable riches of the gospel of Christ which passeth knowledge.

The New Life in Jesus – not just for individuals, but for the global family, the whole of creation.

Jesus the bearer of this gift declared "It is finished." – God's New Age has been established in Him for ever. And so our true lives are hid with Christ in God.

True lives which are not a pious orbiting into space leaving behind the bloodshed and turmoils of this earthly coil but ones enshrined in the words of the hymn "Firmly bound, forever free."

Not split personalities with separate earthly and heavenly existences but those who are <u>made whole</u>.

The riches of our inheritance in Christ Jesus.

There are no words in all the languages of the peoples of the earth to convey fully the massive magnanimity of God's forgiving grace to all mankind in the gift of Jesus Christ.

Glory be to the Father, and to the Son, and to the Holy Spirit – as it was in the beginning, is now and ever shall be, world without end. AMEN.

APPENDIX 4

OUR BETRAYAL OF THE POOR
SCOTLAND'S DISGRACE

DAILY WE ARE bombarded in the press and on television with the growing disparity between the rich and the poor. The plight of the poor in Scotland is more than a national disgrace, it is a blasphemous betrayal of our common humanity, for the poor are not some sort of alien self-destruct sub species but brothers and sisters in Christ.

We have a daughter and son-in-law in Strathclyde police who are dedicated public servants beyond the call of duty but my heart aches that so much of their shifts are involved with "domestics" the details of which stagger belief.

As the old soul was overheard to remark "there has to be a heaven because it's hell here."

Sadly the kirk has to bear blame for its role in the destruction of community life by its almost paranoid obsession with individual salvation. The late George MacLeod of Iona fame in his small book on the ails of the church "Only One Way Left" writes – Part of our sickness is that Christianity has become an individual affair."

Some years ago, with thoughts of rekindling the fires of community spirit, a plan for the creation of a "super church" with 700,000 members, composed of Church of Scotland members, Episcopalians, Methodists, United Reformed and Scottish Congregationalists, was launched. Published in The Herald on Tuesday 11th April, 2000, there was a comprehensive review of the hoped-for union written by Rosemary Free. This report was presented to the General Assembly of that year, i.e. in May, 2000.

At the time my comment was that the last thing on the planet needed by our beloved land was a kirk cobbled together from different communions. The late Professor James Whyte of St. Andrews University thought it was ill advised and a waste of time.

The earth is the Lord's and the fullness thereof, the world and all that dwell therein.

The kirk became not only an individual affair but a very snobbish affair. Before me is a Herald obituary of 24th October, 2001. The obituary is a glowing tribute to Margaret MacPherson who died in her 95th year. It bears the title "The First Lady of Crofting who represented the people of Skye". Margaret was the daughter of the Rev. Dr. Norman Maclean, minister of the prestigious charge of St. Cuthbert's at the west end of Princes Street, Edinburgh.

The Macleans hailed from Skye where as neighbours there was a family of MacPhersons. The second son Duncan was a seaman – Margaret and Duncan struck up a friendship. Her parents were atomised with anger. Margaret was sent to school in Switzerland and forbidden to visit Skye again. To no avail. Margaret and Duncan were married on the day Margaret graduated from Edinburgh University.

The obituary states that parental reaction was swift. In Margaret's words "My father cut me off and never spoke to me again <u>for marrying beneath myself</u>. I saw him on his death bed but he did not know me then."

One evening in Spring 2007 on Panorama there was a question and answer debate chaired by David Dimbleby. The panel consisted of two men and two women, among them William Hague, former leader of the Conservative Party. All five intelligent socially concerned human beings were bombarded with questions about teenage delinquency, drugs, crime, antisocial behaviour, youth unemployment, the carrying of knives, and so on.

Like so many of these panels the discussion and arguments are about problems and not about flesh and blood fellow citizens. For all the genuine concern where is the recognition by the better off <u>of our guilt</u> in the plight of the poor.

A few years ago The Herald granted me a couple of inches in its correspondence columns to précis an article by The Herald wise man Alf Young on how Scotland ticks. The essence of my précis was that a basic axiom for any real understanding of how Scotland ticks is the need to recognize that there are as many dodgy dealers in the New Club as there are in Saughton Jail.

At the end of April in The Herald we were confronted with a table of the assets of Scotland's richest. Being crudely critical of our fellow citizens in Scotland is light years away from the thoughts which are buzzing around in my aged brain and heart.

Million pound gifts for a great range of worthy causes are commendable but all of us, from whatever step we occupy on the social ladder, have to start to break down the awful walls which divide us from one another. The huge walls in Israel between the Jews and the Arabs are a monstrous obscenity but so is forelock touching of too much of the relationships between the rich and the poor in Scotland.

The laird of Beaufort Castle and Kinfauns Castle was involved in a dispute at Beaufort with one of her tenants about a grass verge. During the negotiations her lawyer asked the sad question "Are you asking my client to knock on the door of her tenant's dwelling and enter to discuss the matter over a cup of tea?"

To my mind this is exactly how this peccadillo should have been resolved.

Since the theme of this article is the great disparity between the rich and poor in Scotland here is an interesting quote from "The Old Régime and the French Revolution" by Alexis de Tocqueville published in 1856 and translated the same year. de Toqueville is also the author of the famous work "Democracy in America" published in 1836.

"Of all the various ways of making men conscious of their differences and of stressing class distinctions unequal taxation is the most pernicious, since it creates a permanent estrangement between those who benefit and those who suffer by it. Once the principle is established that noblemen and commoners are not to be taxed at the same rate, the public is reminded of the distinction drawn between them year by year when the imposts are assessed and levied. Thus on these occasions each member of the privileged class takes notice of the practical interest he has in differentiating himself from the masses and in stiffening the barriers between himself and them."

One of the great figures in the ecclesiastical life of Scotland was Dr. Thomas Chalmers, leader of the Disruption in 1843 and first Moderator of the Free Church.

The Gospel being a call to proclaim God's salvation in Jesus Christ and not a social welfare programme led the Victorian Church to become almost paranoid about salvation and the saving of souls. Dr. Chalmers and the Free Church as a body had a huge social conscience but it was a conscience fired with a desire to alleviate the plight of the poor without any fundamental change in the awful class structure of Scottish society.

Should anyone seek to dismiss me as a radical boat-rocker perhaps a quote from Dr. Chalmers' address at the laying of the foundation stone of the Free Church College at the top of the Mound in 1846 will stretch minds, aye and open hearts.

As late as 1846 the lairds and the comfortably off still had in their nostrils the "reek" from the turmoil and bloodshed of the French Revolution and in some of Dr. Chalmers' speeches we can detect a real fear of radicalism.

Here are Dr. Chalmers' words from chapter eight of David Paton's book "The Clergy and the Clearances".

"We leave to others the passions and politics of this world; and nothing will ever be taught, I trust in our halls, which shall have the remotest tendency to disturb the existing order of things, or to confound the ranks and distinctions which obtain in society."

When a Moderator can deliver such unchristian sentiments it is not surprising that Edinburgh has been and is one of the most class conscious and snobby cities on the planet – I write as an insider, born in Edinburgh and baptised in St. Cuthbert's on 1st December, 1923 and with a parental home at 20 Belgrave Crescent for a quarter of a century.

Money alone from whatever source will not consign the plight of the poor in Scotland to the mists of history. What is needed is a huge national change of heart for rich and poor and all the middle class sandwich fillers between those extremes to embrace one another with sympathetic imagination and humble loving-kindness.

No one in our beautiful land is more proud of being a Scot than I am, but now in my 84th year as we orbit through space on our planet home at 66,600 m.p.h. I think of myself as a cosmic and global citizen, overwhelmingly aware of the almost insurmountable difficulty for the seed of equal human worth to germinate and bear fruit.

As James Baldwin, the black American activist declared "It is easy to proclaim all souls equal in the sight of God; it is hard to make men equal on earth, in the sight of men".

On my shelves I have many biographies. Lord Boyd Orr's "As I Recall" is one of my treasures.

Lord Boyd Orr was the son of a house painter from Kilmaurs and West Kilbride who became a Member of Parliament, Rector and Chancellor of Glasgow University, winner of the Nobel Peace Prize – but best remembered for his work in building up the Rowett Research Institute outside Aberdeen – as Director-General of the United Nations Food and Agricultural Organization and ceaseless worker for the abolition of poverty and malnutrition and for understanding among the nations.

With great vehemence he declared "What Scotland needs is more houses and not prisons". Politicians instead of rabbiting on about being tough on crime should devote more thought and effort to the causes of crime.

Please allow me to insert a letter which The Herald thought fit to publish on 17th December, 1998 –

"With the prospect of a Scottish Parliament it is imperative that top of the agenda is the provision of a reasonably spacious, warm dwelling for every citizen. Looking straight in the eye the fact that many do not have the income for the full financing of a home, the shortfall must be a priority charge on the common purse.

Those of us, often through no real merit or effort of our own, who have fading trades-men's entrance signs and memories of bottled milk deliveries paid by the month, should abandon any thought that the disadvantaged in our society are the result of their own sloth and not the victims of the tough turmoil which is the unpredictable, even scary, life of the industrial world."

The creation of jobs, higher rates of pay coupled with better working conditions are wholly commendable. However these targets have to be seasoned with a wise grasp of the facts of life.

One fact which must govern plans and hopes for better living conditions for the poor is the simple truth that in our technologically productive world there is no way that everyone seeking a pay packet can be usefully employed – which brings us to the basic need to bin the Victorian work ethic which encouraged the better-off to believe that anyone who was not toiling forty, fifty and more hours per week was an idle layabout.

Roy Hattersley's collection of essays "Between Ourselves" has one entitled "Bringing Home the Truth About the Very Poor" from which I quote "God knows, I have no moral judgement to make about such families. The concept of the undeserving poor – a pecu-liar English heresy – is one of the most repulsive notions known to man".

Let's not get swamped with details but begin with, at first glance, the mad idea of a basic state income for all over eighteen whether people work or not, with an opt out "no thank you" clause for those who are content with their earned incomes.

Sing the praises of leisure time with the inevitable reduction of stress and a saving drop in the demands upon the National Health Service.

Free housing for the good souls at the bottom of the social heap.

Free transport.

Scotland is rolling in wealth – the trouble is too much of it is mothproofed in the wrong sporrans. OK, there will always be chancers at the public trough and those who can trash a new home before the first week of their residence is out, but these should not be excuses for turning off the tap of imaginative practical loving-kindness.

Volunteers would be needed to ease the burden of care for the growing numbers of elderly, volunteers who get "brownie points" for their commitment which can be traded in for care for themselves if and when the need arises.

For centuries Scotland has been well seasoned with open-minded and big-hearted souls. To name but two. Alice Scrimgeour, honoured in Ron Ferguson's Herald trib-ute on Monday 7th May, 2007, was commissioned as a "church sister" in the Church of Scotland 69 years ago. Among her many labours of love for the disadvantaged was Stroove, a large house in Skelmorlie, a haven of peace and reconciliation for poor Glasgow families. Sheriff Principal John Maguire, whose obituary is in The Herald of 7th May, 2007, found great satisfaction in his career on the bench. His sense of duty and obligation to society moved him to give much of his free time to those less fortunate than himself. He spent many hours in voluntary work, particularly with the disabled.

Then there are tens of thousands of parents and volunteers coaching teams and indi-vidual young people in a great range of sports while encouraging good citizenship. The Herald of 7th May, 2007, reports the imaginative plan to transport a group of teenage potential school drop-outs to a poverty-stricken community in Ecuador. Some might think of the plan as an expensive skive. I would like to endorse it.

Come on Scotland! We live in one of the most beautiful and peaceful countries in the world. It is time for us to bucket our Scottish "kent yer faither" syndrome, "nice people don't do that" and the awful "what will the neighbours think?", life-destroying fruits of much of the kirk's moralising humbug, and launch out onto the often stormy seas of life with smiles on our faces, minds overflowing with gratitude and hearts filled with hope and loving kindness.

APPENDIX 5

OLD SCOT OF THE YEAR

LAST EVENING (FRIDAY 11th January, 2008) my wife and I were delighted to be among the fellows and guests of the Institute of Contemporary Scotland at the presentation of the Arnold Kemp Young Scot of the Year awards staged in the magnificent high-arched portrait gallery of the Royal College of Physicians and Surgeons in Glasgow. In large figures above the entrance to the gallery is the date 1599 and so a lot of water has flowed down the Clyde since then.

Two of the awards were presented by Harry Reid, a former editor of The Herald and author of "Outside Verdict" a searching analysis of the Church of Scotland. As a retired Church of Scotland parish minister, ordained in my fortieth year, I have a manuscript nearly ready for publication bearing the title "One Man's Pilgrimage" – an inside verdict.

I write as an apocatistasian, a universalist, one who believes that the world and all the vastness of space are holy and that life is a sacred gift. Belief in universal salvation is not a modern attempt to accommodate the gospel to scientific advances in astronomy. Several church leaders as early as 200 A.D. were universalists; and then the saintly Abbot Rupert who lived in the monastery of Deutz on the Rhine in the twelfth century proclaimed "To be ignorant of scripture is to be ignorant of Jesus Christ. This is the scripture of nations. This book of God which is not pompous in words ought to be set before every people, and to proclaim aloud to the whole world the salvation of all. The key to the mystery of life is Jesus of Nazareth who said 'I am the light and hope of the world'."

During the evening at the awards ceremony many photographs were taken but one photographer, whose face was familiar, was jumping about like a paparazzi – then the penny dropped – he was David Gemmell, minister of the Auld Kirk of Ayr, whose son Jonathan was leader of the Hope for Peru Group.

At the end of August 2006 I was among the mourners in the Auld Kirk for the funeral of James Stewart Brown, who was months short of his ninetieth birthday. While waiting for the service to begin I read these words printed on the back of the service sheet:-

> God saw him getting tired,
> When a cure was not to be.
> So he wrapped His arms around him,
> And whispered "Come to me".
> He didn't deserve what he went through,
> So He gave him rest,
> God's garden must be beautiful,
> He only takes the best.

James Stewart Brown was not only one of the best he was a quiet intelligent friendly Christian gentleman whom I had the privilege and pleasure of knowing well through our membership of the superb organization for the retired in Ayr "Opportunities in Retirement".

What saddened me were the two lines – God's garden must be beautiful. He only takes the best.

Here is a quotation from the prison notes of Stefan Cardinal Wysznski "The measure of God's mercy is not so much the holiness and glory of His friends as the salvation of the greatest sinners. Only the sight of redeemed criminals whom the world has despised and whom God has still saved will open our eyes to the power and scope of God's mercy".

At a more recent funeral one of the hymns was 374 from the third edition of the Church Hymnary. Verse two runs:-

> O perfect redemption, the purchase of blood!
> To every believer the promise of God;
> The vilest offender who truly believes,
> That moment from Jesus a pardon receives.

At the funeral tea a good man of eighty came over for a chat knowing me to be a retired minister. He was concerned by the words "the vilest offender" and obviously unhappy about sharing "the sweets of God's grace" with sinners.

The church hymnary revision committee have watered these words down in the fourth edition to read "for every offender".

Revising hymnaries is all very well but the fact is that there are hundreds of verses in all hymn books which, if not anti-Christian, are unchristian.

During the evening at the awards ceremony in Glasgow we met a "charming young man", probably in his seventies, a founder member of the Institute, an engineer, an elder at Cramond Kirk, Edinburgh. Pulling his leg – a thing you can do when you are in your eighty-fifth year with anyone, even on first meeting – I said to him "You are a very intelligent-looking chap which makes me feel that you must have been educated at Dollar Academy". He smiled and said "No, I was at Loretto, but we went to Dollar to play them at rugby and beat them. However the thing which overcame us with envy coming from the monastic cloisters of Loretto was to see the defeated Dollar players walking off hand-in-hand with their girlfriends".

For seven years from 1935 -1942 I was privileged to be a boarder at Dollar Academy, and during all those years I never had a girlfriend despite being quite a "dishy-looking" young guy (photographs are available!).

Life in Britain in the 1920s and 1930s was still saturated with the "Have you been saved?" moralizing humbug of the Victorian church. Their paranoid fear of hell was matched by their astonishing sexual taboos, and despite having intelligent gracious parents I was "girl-proofed" to an extent which beggars all belief.

Taliban clerics are not confined to Afghanistan – sadly they proliferate in the Church of Scotland. They are like President Kruger of South Africa who, when he was introduced at a reception to Captain Joshua Slocum the sailor who was sailing around the world, "blew a gasket" and stormed out of the room shouting "That is impossible. The world is flat."

Call it a coincidence but it is pertinent to the theme of this discourse that we should have met in the Royal College of Physicians and Surgeons of Glasgow, because heart transplants occur without surgery. "Behold I will put a new heart within you."

Many years ago I received the gift of a new heart which set me free from the greed, envy, litigations and umbrages of this world to be Christ's freeman. I look upon myself as a spiritual millionaire, who daily gives thanks for the circumstances of life which led me to study divinity at Knox College, Toronto and become a Church of Scotland parish minister.

This dear dear privilege has been saddened by the growing conviction that the institutional churches have become the biggest stumbling blocks to the entry of the good tidings of great joy into the hearts and minds of the toiling masses with whom we share the adventure of life on our planet home as we orbit through space at 66,600 m.p.h.

The late William Barclay in his book "Through the year with William Barclay" has this to say – "It is one of the strange things in the modern Church that we think of the Easter faith only at Easter time. The Easter faith should be in our thoughts not simply at a certain season of the year, it ought to be the faith in which Christians daily live".

Here is a quotation from Harry Reid's "Outside Verdict" :-

"I wish to propose that the Church of Scotland should promote a great revival of Easter as the Christian festival. This would obviously start in Scotland, but it might take off around Britain, around Europe, even beyond. If so, the Church of Scotland could yet manage to do global Christianity a great service."

It is strange how minds can think alike, for here is my kirk draft for the future –

Phase out Christmas and the church's calendar based upon the birth, life and death of Jesus and focus on the <u>RESURRECTION</u> proclaiming each second, each minute, each hour, each day, each week, each month and each year as Easter, ushering in an endless EASTER FESTIVAL not only for church people but for the whole global family for ever.

Once or twice a year I would declare from the pulpit in Ballater parish church that "If I thought for a moment that God looked on me as an ordained minister with greater favour than upon a wee child dying in its mother's arms in the gutters of Calcutta I would never mount the steps of a pulpit again".

Now in my eighty-fifth year, as the Easter seconds tick away, my heart and mind fill with awesome wonder and gratitude – as Christ's freeman, two hundred pounds of good-humoured loving kindness, global and cosmic citizen, child of God, a human being, a little lower than the angels and crowned with glory and honour – I award myself, without blushing, "Old Scot of the Year".

APPENDIX 6

SIXTY YEARS ON

From an article in the Dollar Academy Magazine, 2005

2005 IS THE sixtieth anniversary of the cessation of hostilities in Europe (May) and in the Far East ((August), a suitable time to think of the supreme sacrifice made by the seventy-two former pupils whose names are inscribed on our beautiful war memorial.

A measure of their sacrifice is magnified and made more vivid by a study of the stunning Sixth Form photograph of Session 2003-04. The one hundred and eight of you may well smile and, we hope, give thanks for the privilege of sharing years at the Old Grey School beneath the sheltering hills.

What, though, might have been the lives and careers of those who did not return from the Second World War?

It will be seventy years in September since my older brother, David, and I came to Dollar as boarders, both of us to Dewar House, which was then next to the West Church (subsequently to be called Playfair, and ultimately Rathmore). Incidentally, it was in the West Church on the morning of Sunday 3rd September 1939 that we heard Neville Chamberlain, the Prime Minister, make the mind-boggling proclamation that, since no response had been received to the 11 o'clock ultimatum issued to Hitler by the Allies, Britain was now at war with Nazi Germany.

It is not possible to assemble seventy-two photographs, but a small snap taken with a ten-shilling box Brownie at the swimming hole on the Burn of Sorrows accompanies this article. (N.B. The photograph cannot be shown in this Appendix.) The pool is no longer there nowadays, having been filled up by boulders carried down in a spate.

The boy on the left is James Rae Martin Chassells, 'Mousie', who could play the mouth organ nearly as well as Larry Adler. He was killed in NW Europe. On the right is William Duncan Gulloch, 'Dunc' who, shortly after the snap was taken, won a scholarship to King's School in Canterbury, where his name is also on their war memorial. Duncan was killed in Burma in 1945.

Both Mousie and Dunc were boarders whose parents worked abroad. From memory, Mr. Chassells was an accountant in China with Butterfield and Swires, while Mr. Gulloch was Chief of Police in Gibraltar, then in Cyprus. As for my family, my brother David and I were both commissioned in the Black Watch, to be seconded to the King's African Rifles. David served in Africa, while I served in Africa, India and Burma. Serving with the 14th Army in Burma, I celebrated my twenty-first birthday on 1st November 1944 by sharing a seven-pound tin of peaches with a few pals in a slit trench.

The late Enoch Powell used to say that, from time to time, he felt twinges of guilt for having survived what had been six years of global carnage on a massive scale. And so it is, in this 60th anniversary year, that we cherish, with heavy hearts and gratitude, memories of classmates and fellow pupils, many of whom were never to reach the age of twenty-one.

A recent survey reveals the staggering fact that over fifty per cent of teenagers in Britain know nothing of Auschwitz and the other death camps where over six million Jews were tortured and murdered by the Nazis. My plea to those who read these lines is that you open your hearts and minds to the on-going turmoil in the life of the world. Read extensively in History, Politics, Economics and Sociology. If you can afford it, buy a subscription to the *Guardian Weekly* or a similar 'boat-rocking' journal. *The Long Shadows* by Erna Paris is an excellent survey of the real role of the participants in the Second World War.

Of all the pupils who ever passed through Dollar Academy, the most unlikely to become a parish minister in the Church of Scotland was me. This is not a boast, but rather a statement of fact, as Jack Hutchison (FP 1939-47) will confirm. I was ordained and inducted to the parish of Monimail west of Cupar, Fife, in my fortieth year, following a period in estate management in Scotland and then several years in Canada, also in managerial roles.

Again, my plea, as an unlikely shepherd of souls, is that you see beyond the institutional Church, that you pause amid the busy turmoil of your lives, in order to cultivate a sense of wonder and awe as we travel through space on our planet home at the speed of 66,600 mph. The claims of the Christian faith are staggering beyond all belief and imagining – but how could they be otherwise, when a planet a million light years distant from earth is really a next-door neighbour?

I close with a prayer of thanksgiving for the blessed dead, and with an expression of gratitude for the circumstances of life which granted to me the privilege of an education at Dollar Academy.

Revd James Blyth (FP 1935-42)

APPENDIX 7

DAVID REID MILL BLYTH

Born 1ˢᵗ May, 1922 - Edinburgh

Died Cullen, Banffshire, 9ᵗʰ June, 2006

AS DAVID'S YOUNGER brother I take up my pen to write a memorial tribute.

In 1924, months after my birth in Edinburgh on 1ˢᵗ November, 1923, exactly eighteen months to a day younger than David, the Blyth family moved to Huddersfield, Yorkshire, where our father, an accountant, began his service of forty years with a firm of Chartered Accountants.

Our first home was Claremont, long since demolished, a large detached house in over an acre of garden, rented from the Ramsden Trust, the feuers of a large part of Huddersfield and the owners of Ardverikie, the mansion house on the shores of Loch Laggan – the locale for the TV drama "Monarch of the Glen" and viewed by Queen Victoria before settling on Balmoral midst the peace and beauty of Deeside.

David and I arrived in Dollar at the beginning of September 1935 from Huddersfield via a holiday in Edinburgh with our grandmother. Walking up Station Road with our wee bags, our trunks had been sent on ahead by the excellent rail service, door to door, 2/- or ten pence. Opposite Dollar post office we were directed to Dewar House, next door to the West Church, by Eddie Duncan, a day boy, whose parents were a familiar sight around the town. Not only just a familiar sight but good friends to many boarders. Eddie's dad was well over 6 feet and his mother similar in stature to the Queen Mother.

For the three summers before the outbreak of war i.e. 1937, 1938, 1939, the family spent happy holidays in St. Andrews renting a large house on Golf Place – whose rent from memory was £17 for the month. The other day my eye caught an advertisement for a house to let, also on Golf Place (perhaps the same house) - £350 per week.

Understandably the young folk get tired of hearing old geezers rabbiting on about the days when £1 could purchase 500 morning rolls, 120 Mars Bars or 240 Milky Ways so I will restrict my recall to two pre-war prices. Boarding at Dollar in the 1930's was £100 per annum with the bonus of a £5 refund if there were two of you. A month's junior ticket on the Eden Golf Course at St. Andrews was 15/- or 75 pence.

Golf was David's sport and he used to squeeze 40 to 50 rounds out of his fifteen bob ticket. Invariably he played the afternoon round on his own allowing me to have the buzz of watching and even chatting to teenage mermaids entering and emerging from the freezing waters of the old Steprock pool.

The run of David's solitary afternoon rounds was broken one Saturday when around 3 p.m., driving from the 17th or 18th tee (the St. Andrews – Guardbridge road has been realigned since the 1930's) I was determined to outdrive my brother. A mighty swipe sent my ball far out to the right where it struck the windscreen of a large saloon car. On going over to investigate a rather stunned bride and bridegroom were seated in the back on the way to their wedding reception. Normally ministers have to wait until they are ordained before confronting the newly betrothed!

From early teenage years David and I were junior members of Fixby, Huddersfield, where in our time the professional was Peter McEwen, succeeded by Johnny Fallon some years after we left. Johnny Fallon had at least one son at Dollar Academy.

While still at Dollar David played junior competitive golf at Fixby, St. Andrews, Dollar, Muckhart, Alloa, etc., and invariably came home with a dozen or two good golf balls, not a trifling prize in the days when the Open Golf yielded for the winner a few hundred quid.

Although David's sport was golf he was quite a handy lad in a rugby scrum. During holidays from school and later on leave from the Army both of us were welcome players in the pack of Huddersfield Old Boys. Carefully preserved in a small brown envelope I have an inch-deep newspaper cutting headed "Shock for Sale" reporting an 18-3 win for the Old Boys on Sale's home ground. Mention is made of the Blyth brothers' leading of the pack.

David left Dollar days after his 18th birthday in 1940 without a Higher Leaving Certificate – although he was not academically inclined he had the ability to have passed that milestone.

The carnage of the II World War began nine months before David left Dollar and the prospect of service in the armed forces created a strange mixture of euphoria and, dare I say it, fear, which was not conducive to studying for exams. I feel that this is part of the explanation for David's certificateless departure from the old grey school beneath the sheltering hills.

Hard to believe that it is nearly 70 years since the outbreak of the II World War. I remember as if it were yesterday – Sunday morning, 3rd September, 1939, in the West Church next to Dewar House where the minister was Dr. Lynn and the Session Clerk John Cordiner, housemaster of Argyll House.

The British Government had given Hitler and his gang an ultimatum to withdraw from Poland by 11 a.m. on Sunday 3rd September. Dr. Lynn had a small radio on the edge of the pulpit and when the fateful hour of eleven struck the Prime Minister, Neville Chamberlain, in solemn voice announced "Since we have had no satisfactory reply from Hitler this means that we are at war with Nazi Germany."

Dr. Lynn was a gifted saintly soul who left Dollar to serve a congregation in Helensburgh. Brave man, he used to conduct a Bible class for we boys. One morning he was struggling to extract some deep theological meaning from why David killed Goliath when towards the end of the session he was seen to be fumbling behind the edge of his lectern. Moments later, before our mad rush to the exit, he said "Boys, there are fourteen of you and I have only twelve coins." Allow me to explain – opposite Waddell the butchers, and to the west of the Railway Tavern, the Gonella family ran a successful shop, selling ice-cream, sweets, cigarettes, perhaps newspapers. Now, not to make too long a story, our church collection consisted of two pennies – one for the kirk and one for the Bible class. Mrs. Gonella had a drawer of half pennies beside the till. The tale is told. One penny for sweets and a halfpenny each for the Kirk and the Bible class. Concentrating upon the thrilling tale of Goliath's slaying by David two members of the Bible class must have overlooked their obligation to drop a mite onto the collection plate.

Changing pennies into halfpennies was not Mrs. Gonella's only contribution to the welfare of boarders. The business was located in their family home in which on the ground floor there was a large room with a pool table and an open fire. In the winter, bubbling at the side of the fire was a large pot of marrowfat peas. A ladle of hot peas on a saucer, dressed or not with vinegar depending on the customers' individual taste, cost one penny.

Now this is a memorial tribute to my brother David but even at the time of a loved one's death there is a role for smiles and laughter.

Talk about peas brings to mind one of our father's ditties –

> I eat my peas with treacle,
> I've done it all my life,
> Not that I like the treacle
> But it keeps them on the knife.

Or perhaps a slightly cruder ditty, often "sung" in the dormitories after lights out –

> Beans, beans, musical fruit,
> The more you eat the more you toot,
> The more you toot the better you feel,
> So let's have beans for every meal.

David and I each served as Head Boy of McNabb House. David left in 1940, I left in 1942, both destined for five years' army service.

To begin David served in the Duke of Wellington's Regiment at Barnard Castle, myself in the Royal Artillery Signals at Redford Barracks. Both of us were then posted to 166 Infantry O.C.T.U. at Douglas, I.O.M. David was commissioned in the Black Watch in February 1943 and I was commissioned in the same regiment in April 1943. Our service in the Black Watch was rather short as we, together with a large number of young infantry officers, were seconded to the King's African Rifles, in East Africa.

Here is one anecdote from our time together with the 8th Black Watch stationed in Winchester. During the war there were many schemes for raising money. One of the favourites was "Wings for Victory" parades. A Spitfire cost five thousand pounds. Normally a parade would be made up from Naval, Army and Airforce units with their respective bands. The Black Watch unit consisted of ninety-nine Jocks, three rows of thirty-three, a couple of sergeants, and David and myself as officers, David leading, myself bringing up the rear. For a week or more before the day of the parade we practised complete with full pipe band on the square in our camp before breakfast. Although I say it myself we were quite an impressive sight, all attired in kilts. It would have been a Saturday in June 1943 that the "Wings for Victory" parade marched down the hill and into the ancient city of Winchester. The leading unit was a very smart detachment from a light infantry regiment complete with their band. Between them and the Black Watch pipe band was an equally smart contingent of A.T.S. girls. Unfortunately the poor lassies would hear both bands, the light infantry playing 180 paces per minute and the pipe band at 120 paces per minute. There had been a slip-up in the allocation of places in the parade and the girls in khaki spent a good part of the route changing step! We all felt very sorry for them. Memory plays tricks but enough money was raised that day to provide more than one Spitfire!!

During his three years in Africa David served in Ethiopia (Abyssinia) where one day several of the officers were guests at a Royal Wedding in Addis Ababa. From memory two Princes attended Dollar after the war being boarders in McNabb House. David mastered Swahili which made him a useful interpreter. Adjutant of 5th K.A.R. both in Abyssinia and in Kenya was another appointment, and then for a period David was an instructor at the Battle School at Nakuru with the rank of Major.

Exact details of the crossing of our paths during and immediately after the war are becoming hazy but before I left Kenya for Ceylon, India and Burma David entertained me to dinner in the Rift Valley Club where he was a member. Return to Britain after the war depended upon the availability of shipping. Largely by chance I sailed up the Clyde weeks before David's homecoming.

David was very ill with amoebic dysentery when he reached home in Huddersfield, but he made a good recovery and re-entered the textile industry in which he had been an apprentice when he was called up for war service. Whilst based at home in Huddersfield he met, and married in 1949, Sheena, a daughter of Rev. Tom Fraser, the minister of the Presbyterian Church in Huddersfield, and they had one son David (also a Dollar Academy F.P.) married to Deirdre with two children, Catriona and Rhona.

David's work took him and Sheena to Renfrewshire, Ceres, Broughty Ferry, on to Ilkley, and then to Black Bourton in Oxfordshire, David then being Managing Director for the blanket firm of Charles Early in Witney.

In 1977 David decided to retire, and he and Sheena settled in Kingston-on-Spey at the mouth of the Spey where he and Sheena spent many happy years before Parkinson's Disease took its toll on Sheena and on David as Sheena's devoted carer. For the last fifteen months of David's life he and Sheena were together lovingly cared for in a nursing home near Cullen.

David and Sheena greatly enjoyed exploring the countryside by car, when Sheena exercised her artistic talents, and they were especially fond of the north-west of Scotland and of France where they spent many happy motoring holidays. David was very attached to Dollar Academy and visited many of the war graves in France of Dollar boys who had fallen in the war. He retained a great interest in the Black Watch, and for a time was a member of the T.A. He was interested in politics, and when retired travelled all over the country for Oxfam, inviting people to leave money to Oxfam in their Wills. He took a great interest too in his local church and in the Presbytery, and was able to play golf well into his retirement.

The rich arable lands of Morayshire and its couthy wee towns are a favoured part of our beloved land. On Friday 16th June David's funeral service was conducted most beautifully by the Rev. Alison Mehigan, minister of Fochabers in the Red Kirk on the east side of the road down to Garmouth and Kingston-on-Spey, followed by interment in the lovingly tended cemetery at Essil on the banks of the Spey. As a retired parish minister I can tell you that the range of attire worn by the departed is, to say the least, varied. Brother David was buried fully dressed wearing the regimental tie of his beloved Black Watch.